ALLITERATIVE PROVERBS IN MEDIEVAL ENGLAND

Alliterative Proverbs in Medieval England

Language Choice and Literary Meaning

SUSAN E. DESKIS

The Ohio State University Press • Columbus

Copyright © 2016 by The Ohio State University.
All rights reserved.

Library of Congress Cataloging-in-Publication Data
Names: Deskis, Susan E., author.
Title: Alliterative proverbs in medieval England : language choice and literary meaning / Susan E. Deskis.
Description: Columbus : The Ohio State University Press, [2016] | Includes bibliographical references and index.
Identifiers: LCCN 2016022299 | ISBN 9780814213094 (cloth ; alk. paper) | ISBN 081421309X (cloth ; alk. paper)
Subjects: LCSH: Proverbs, English—History and criticism. | Alliteration. | English literature—Middle English, 1100–1500—History and criticism.
Classification: LCC PN6420 .D47 2016 | DDC 398.9/219—dc23
LC record available at https://lccn.loc.gov/2016022299

Cover design by Martyn Schmoll
Text design by Juliet Williams
Type set in Adobe Minion Pro

Cover image: A street with shops and the coat of arms of Robert Stuart, Marshall of d'Aubigny Lucrece, from "Livre de Gouvernement des Princes" by Gilles de Rome (vellum). French School (15th century), MS. 5062 fol. 149v. Bibliotheque de L'Arsenal, Paris, France / Bridgeman Images.

♾ The paper used in this publication meets the minimum requirements of the American National Standard for Information Sciences—Permanence of Paper for Printed Library Materials. ANSI Z39.48-1992.

9 8 7 6 5 4 3 2 1

FOR MY HUSBAND, MARK

CONTENTS

	Acknowledgments	ix
1	Introduction	1
2	Alliterative Proverbs in Time	19
3	Alliterative Proverbs in Didactic Texts	62
4	Alliterative Proverbs in Romance, Lyric, and Drama	98
5	Conclusion: Summary and Suggestions	133
	Bibliography	139
	Index to Proverbs	157
	General Index	159

ACKNOWLEDGMENTS

THIS STUDY has been long in the making, and the expressions of encouragement that I have received over the years have been instrumental to its continued progress. I thank the many friends and colleagues who have read or heard parts of my work (in Kalamazoo, London, Cambridge [MA], DeKalb, Saskatoon, Oxford [MS], and Urbana) and generously showed interest in it. I thank Nicole Clifton, Joseph Harris, and Richard Harris, who read early drafts of various chapters and responded helpfully. I thank the anonymous readers from The Ohio State University Press, who facilitated the clarification of my argument, along with Eugene O'Connor and Tara Cyphers, who shepherded the volume through publication. I am extremely grateful to Margot Goldsmith for her expert proofreading and to Stephanie Opfer for creating the Index to Proverbs. I retain responsibility for all errors. Most of all, I thank my husband, Mark Richards, to whom I dedicate this book with love and with gratitude for his steadfast support.

Chapter 2 is significantly expanded from "Echoes of Old English Alliterative Collocations in Middle English Alliterative Proverbs," in *Source of Wisdom: Old English and Early Medieval Latin Studies in Honour of Thomas D. Hill*, edited by Charles D. Wright, Frederick M. Biggs, and Thomas N. Hall © University of Toronto Press, 2007, pp. 311–25; reprinted with permission from the publisher.

CHAPTER 1

Introduction

THE PROVERB is one of the most reliable currencies in medieval intellectual culture. In times and places where the constructs of orality still exert a strong influence (as in Anglo-Saxon England or medieval Iceland), the proverb serves to preserve and transmit cultural wisdom in an authoritative, memorable form. As literate culture grows and becomes more complex, the role of the proverb expands along with it. For example, the Bible is the single most important text in the Middle Ages, but knowledge of its contents was acquired in numerous ways that often had nothing to do with its status as a book: laypeople could and did learn biblical narratives by hearing them recounted in sermons, or by seeing characters and scenes depicted in stained glass, painting, sculpture, or drama. The nonnarrative, wisdom books of the Bible (among which we might include the Psalms) were excerpted, more often than not, and thereafter circulated in the form of both Latin and vernacular proverbs. Besides providing both social and moral guidance, medieval proverbs (of biblical, classical, and native origin) came to be used in the process of formal, literate education, especially in the teaching of elementary Latin. Proverbs also contributed significantly to the construction of narrative literature, both oral and written. Thus, the proverb as a form is remarkably durable through the entire Middle Ages—but it is not static. The proverb adapts to its times in language, content, and function, whether that function be hermeneutic, religious, pedagogical, rhetorical, literary, or even political. Most often, the use of proverbs reflects several of these functions at once.

For this study, I have chosen to focus on the alliterative proverb and its long tenure in medieval England. Medieval England's specific cultural, political, and linguistic history encompasses a great number of cultural changes, some more easily documented than others. The conversion of the Anglo-Saxons to Christianity and the consequent introduction of literacy and Latinity must certainly have caused cultural disruption, but our knowledge of Anglo-Saxon intellectual culture preceding the conversion is so minimal that most of its effects cannot be clearly traced. The Norman Conquest effected another upheaval of great import to literary scholars, but for this later breach, we have a fuller (though not full) set of evidence from which to draw conclusions. The alliterative proverb serves as a unique verbal icon by which we may explore some of the cultural circumstances obtaining in England both before and after the Conquest. As a durable, yet flexible, form, the proverb remains just as important in the fifteenth century as it was in the sixth.

In the Old English period, poetic alliteration represents a clear continuation of ancient Germanic tradition. In Middle English, on the other hand, the appearance of alliteration becomes a literary-historical problem, raising questions of how it survived Norman cultural conquest, and why. Alliteration seems to offer a link between the Anglo-Saxon and the post-Conquest periods, but the connection does not present an unbroken documentary record and has proven difficult to reconstruct. The continuity—or not—of an alliterative tradition in medieval England has been addressed most frequently with respect to the alliterative poetry of the fourteenth century, those poems representing the so-called "Alliterative Revival." The scholarly debate regarding the origin (or even existence) of the Alliterative Revival is rather like that concerning the early versus late dating of *Beowulf*: different sides make strong arguments, but none is likely to convince those who hold opposing views; and yet, the dominant opinion does tend to shift back and forth over time, like the movement of a large, very slow pendulum. Harold Zimmerman has written an admirably reasoned and even-handed account of the debate regarding the Alliterative Revival, covering scholarship up to (and just after) the turn of the twenty-first century.[1] The early explanations of the Revival described it as a deliberate resurrection of native English forms, either as an act of cultural resistance against the French bias of the royal court or as an index of the rising status of English cultural identity. This nationalist approach is no longer

---

1. Harold C. Zimmerman, "Continuity and Innovation: Scholarship on the Middle English Alliterative Revival."

really tenable, as Randy Schiff argues quite strenuously.[2] Schiff rejects, perhaps rightly, the whole idea of an Alliterative Revival, but the question remains open as to whether or to what degree the alliterative poetry of the fourteenth century is connected to that of the pre-Conquest past. The array of options in answer to that question has included:

1. Not at all. The alliterative form was essentially reinvented in the fourteenth century.
2. Alliterative poetry in Middle English developed from Old English alliterative prose.
3. Alliterative poetry enjoyed an unbroken transmission from Old English through the Middle English period.

The debate currently includes mostly options 2 and 3 as stated above.[3] For example, Stephen Yeager argues that the alliterative poetry associated with *Piers Plowman*, including poems leading up to and following Langland's opus, follow a tradition originating in late Old English legal and homiletic prose.[4] Thomas Bredehoft favors poetic continuity, describing three distinct but connected stages of alliterative composition, each with its own metrical parameters: classical Old English, late Old English (beginning in the tenth century), and early Middle English. According to Bredehoft's analysis, the so-called "rhythmic prose" of Ælfric adheres to the rules for late Old English poetry and thus provides a versified, not prose, model for early Middle English poets.[5] Recent studies of the meter of late Middle English alliterative poetry demonstrate that its foot patterns follow an antiquated phonology and thus must have been passed down as part of a continuous poetic tradition.[6] In the summative words of Eric Weiskott, "The Revival poems can certainly lay claim to thematic and rhetorical innovation, but metrically speaking they consist of

---

2. See Randy P. Schiff, *Revivalist Fantasy: Alliterative Verse and Nationalist Literary History*. For a response to Schiff's characterization of scholarship on the Alliterative Revival, see Ian Cornelius, "Alliterative Revival: Retrospect and Prospect."

3. See, for example, Donka Minkova, *Alliteration and Sound Change in Early English*, 14–16; Geoffrey Russom, "The Evolution of Middle English Alliterative Meter," 279–304; and Robert Fulk, "Old English Poetry and the Alliterative Revival: on Geoffrey Russom's 'The Evolution of Middle English Alliterative Meter,'" 305–12 (Russom's response: 313–14). However, Christine Chism argues for deliberate archaism in Middle English alliterative romances: see her *Alliterative Revivals*.

4. Stephen M. Yeager, *From Lawmen to Plowmen*.

5. Thomas A. Bredehoft, *Early English Metre*.

6. Eric Weiskott, "Phantom Syllables in the English Alliterative Tradition." See also Thomas Cable, "Progress in Middle English Alliterative Metrics," which reviews the work of Ad Putter, Judith Jefferson, Myra Stokes, and Nicolay Yakovlev.

the same old English stuff."[7] Although the perception of how to define a level of sameness continues to vary, the weight of the evidence currently favors a continuous alliterative tradition. Of course, the nature (and hence the origin) of Middle English alliterative poetry involves not just alliteration and rhythm, but also vocabulary, subject matter, thematics, and manuscript context. Despite the level of innovation that Weiskott describes, late Old English and early Middle English poetry and prose contributed not only rhythmic and alliterative patterns but also some thematic and rhetorical models for later alliterative poetry.[8] The interest of many alliterative poets in religious topics meant that they also drew from clerical training and Latin texts of various sorts;[9] the more courtly poems show familiarity with French literature.[10] The West Midlands have often been viewed as the center of alliterative poeticizing in the fourteenth century, but wherever they were composed, Middle English alliterative poems circulated all around the country.[11] The majority of late Middle English alliterative poems are preserved in miscellanies that "show practically no tendency to group or segregate particular kinds of medieval verse on metrical grounds,"[12] indicating that "alliterative poetry never existed in a domain hermetically sealed from other Middle English literary endeavors."[13] In sum, the composition of alliterative poetry in post-Conquest England represents not an anomaly, but a choice, one that was widely enough employed that it must have assumed different meanings for different poets and audiences.[14] As Stephen Tranter points out, a "history of metrical choice and its implications" in all of medieval England would constitute "a massive

---

7. Weiskott, "Phantom Syllables," 453.

8. Elizabeth Salter, *Fourteenth-Century English Poetry: Contexts and Readings*, 97–99; Ralph Hanna, "Alliterative Poetry," 492. Yeager's argument in *From Lawmen to Plowmen* relies heavily on this point.

9. Salter, *Fourteenth-Century English Poetry*, 97; Hanna, "Alliterative Poetry," 500–501; Thorlac Turville-Petre, *The Alliterative Revival*, 13; Ian Cornelius, *Cultural Promotion: Middle English Alliterative Writing and the "Ars Dictaminis."*

10. Salter explains that the libraries of thirteenth- to fourteenth-century nobles and courts provided French and Latin source material for English poets writing in both rhymed and alliterative meters (*Fourteenth-Century English Poetry*, 44–45).

11. Supporting the Alliterative Revival as concentrated in the Northwest Midlands: Turville-Petre, *Alliterative Revival*, 14; Derek Pearsall, "The Alliterative Revival: Origins and Social Backgrounds," 37–41. Contra: Salter, *Fourteenth-Century English Poetry*, 68–77; Hanna, "Alliterative Poetry," 509–11; David A. Lawton, "The Diversity of Middle English Alliterative Poetry."

12. Salter, *Fourteenth-Century English Poetry*, 77.

13. Hanna, "Alliterative Poetry," 497.

14. Stephen N. Tranter, "Significant Choices: The Interplay of Rhyme and Alliteration in Medieval English Poetry." Yeager (*From Lawmen to Plowmen*) describes some rationales for the choice of alliteration by the Langlandian poets.

undertaking."¹⁵ What I hope to contribute with this study is a clearer picture of the cultural-linguistic environment in which alliterative poetry may have thrived as one element of an attachment to alliteration more generally.

In order to understand alliteration not just as a contribution to poetic structure, but as a feature of the broader verbal repertoire in both Old English and Middle English, I have chosen to address its use in a realm other than the strictly poetic—that is, in the proverb. As the focus of a study of alliteration in medieval England, the proverb offers several advantages. First, it is a small unit of discourse that can be found in texts of any number of genres or larger discourse types. It appears in poetry and in prose of nearly every variety. In the Middle Ages, the proverb was a feature of both oral and literate communication (though, of course, the former is not available for study) and easily adapted to any register. As mentioned earlier, the proverb (and more specifically, the alliterative proverb) occurs in texts from both the Old English and Middle English periods. This temporal persistence allows us to trace developments across the cultural divide of the Norman Conquest. Finally, the proverb combines stability with a flexibility that allows it to move back and forth among several languages and to adapt to changing linguistic circumstances. It is a surprisingly protean form, which makes it especially valuable in the study of multilingualism in medieval England.

Because the proverb is used by speakers and writers from every rank of society, it makes a strong contribution to the language ecology of medieval England. The "ecology of language" is a concept devised by the sociolinguist Einar Haugen, who defines it as "the study of interactions between any given language and its environment."¹⁶ By "environment," Haugen means "the society that uses [the language] as one of its codes."¹⁷ In a multilingual environment, languages will differ in the levels of "status" or "intimacy" with which they are associated. A high-status language "is used by the government, in the schools, by persons of high social and economic rank, or by city-dwellers, while . . . [a low-status language] is not used by one or all of these groups." "Intimacy" refers to the use of a language "through common family and group life."¹⁸ In a pronouncement that seems particularly relevant to diachronic studies, Haugen asserts that "the analysis of ecology requires not only that one describe the social and psychological situation of each language, but also the

---

15. Tranter, "Significant Choices," 94.
16. Einar Haugen, "The Ecology of Language," 325.
17. Ibid. Despite his terminology of "ecology" and "environment," Haugen's is not a biological-evolutionary model (326).
18. Ibid., 329.

effect of this situation on the language itself."[19] A few of the questions that Haugen proposes as part of such analysis of a language include: "Who are its *users*? . . . What are its *domains* of use? . . . What *concurrent languages* are employed by its users? . . . What is the nature of its *written traditions*?"[20] All of these questions are relevant to the study of English in the Middle Ages.

Mine is not the only study of medieval English to use the analytical framework established by Haugen. Tim William Machan, in his *English in the Middle Ages*, situates his examination of numerous high and late medieval English texts within the broader context of language ecology.[21] Machan draws fairly pessimistic conclusions regarding the status of English during this period, conclusions that are certainly correct using Haugen's definition of "status." Based on his study of what we might call "high-status" documents (royal letters, chronicles, etc.), Machan concludes that the use of English carries little sociolinguistic weight relative to French or Latin. It is too far removed from the halls of power to create much political or ideological meaning.

The ecology of any language, even in a linguistic context much less complicated than that of medieval England, cannot be expected to yield up all of its secrets at once, so this current study approaches the problem from a different angle than did Machan. My study is in one way more narrowly focused than his in that the alliterative proverb represents a fairly small slice of language ecology. On the other hand, I follow that single linguistic icon through a lengthy chronology and across a broad range of genres. The choice of the proverb as the object of study provides windows into less exalted areas of verbal culture and access to populations who do not figure much in Machan's material (for example, mothers using basic primers to teach their children, or spiritual advisers guiding would-be anchorites). Although my study is thus complementary to Machan's, rather than contradictory, I would argue that social meaning *can* be found in the medieval use of English as examined through its attachment to alliteration, an especially English (in contrast to Romance) verbal structure.

In the Anglo-Saxon period, the main linguistic choice that can be tracked through written documents is that of Latin versus English, though doubtless in some times and places Old English and Old Norse competed as spoken vernaculars.[22] Contrary to practice on the Continent, the Anglo-Saxons used their

---

19. Ibid., 334.
20. Ibid., 336–37 (emphasis in original).
21. Tim William Machan, *English in the Middle Ages*.
22. On multilingualism in Anglo-Saxon England, see, for example, Rolf Bremmer, "Continental Germanic Influences"; Bruce R. O'Brien, *Reversing Babel* (ch. 2); Matthew Townend, *Language and History in Viking Age England*; and Samantha Zacher, "Multilingualism at the

native tongue substantially (alongside Latin) for legal and governmental documents. By the time of the Norman Conquest, West Saxon was well established as a formal written dialect or *Schriftsprache*. However, the Normans, predictably, replaced English with Latin (and, as we shall see, French) for the records of law and government.[23] Thus, English suffered a double demotion in status: it was no longer spoken by the powerful nor used for their records. Of course, English still prevailed in the sheer number of speakers, which accounts for its very survival. Nor did English completely disappear as a written language. Elaine Treharne lists eighty-five manuscripts produced c.1050/60–1100 in which the "main texts" are in English.[24] Furthermore, over one hundred Old English manuscripts contain glosses from the twelfth century or later, proving that they were still being read.[25] Of English texts produced in the twelfth century, there are laws, chronicles, gospels, psalters, and translations of Bede, Boethius, and Augustine, as well as proverbs, but the type of codex most likely to be copied in English during that time was the homiliary.[26] As for why English manuscripts continued to be copied and glossed, Christine Franzen offers: "Presumably the lack of much original composition in English in the twelfth century forced those in need of English preaching material to go back to the old collections."[27] Mary Swan and Mark Faulkner consider utility to be the motivation for a variety of Old English texts copied (and sometimes updated) in the latter twelfth century.[28] Treharne sees the activity as more politically purposeful, "an attempt to use the most prestigious register of the language for the composition of written texts" or even a quiet statement of resistance to Norman cultural hegemony.[29] Women readers—both professional religious

---

Court of King Æthelstan." Nicholas Brooks considers the role of gender in the choice of legal language(s): "Latin and Old English in Ninth-Century Canterbury."

23. Michael T. Clanchy, *From Memory to Written Record: England 1066–1307*, 154.

24. Elaine Treharne, *Living through Conquest: The Politics of Early English, 1020–1220*, 99–101. See also Orietta DaRold, Takako Kato, Mary Swan, and Elaine Treharne, *The Production and Use of English Manuscripts, 1060–1220*.

25. Treharne, "Reading from the Margins: The Uses of Old English Homiletic Manuscripts in the Post-Conquest Period," 329. Hans Sauer describes and assesses some examples of the use of Old English texts as late as the fourteenth and fifteenth centuries: "Knowledge of Old English in the Middle English Period?."

26. Susan Irvine, "The Compilation and Use of Manuscripts Containing Old English in the Twelfth Century," 41–42.

27. Christine Franzen, *The Tremulous Hand of Worcester: A Study of Old English in the Thirteenth Century*, 104. David F. Johnson suggests that the Tremulous Hand may have marked up some manuscripts to make them easier to read aloud; see his "Who Read Gregory's *Dialogues* in Old English?." 190–202.

28. Mary Swan, "Old English Textual Activity in the Reign of Henry II"; Mark Faulkner, "Archaism, Belatedness and Modernisation."

29. Treharne, *Living through Conquest*, 148–49.

and lay vowesses—could have formed another audience for English devotional prose immediately after the Conquest.[30] So, in the language ecology following the Conquest, English did not completely lose its position as a written language, but the status and types of texts for which it was employed underwent a change. This change can be traced, in part, as we study the history of alliterative proverbs in England, examining the fates of individual proverbs, but also of broader proverbial structures, and including the genres in which alliterative proverbs appear.

The Norman Conquest brought to England an influx of French speakers of high status (and, one must assume, their French-speaking minions of lower status). Almost overnight, French replaced English as the high-status spoken language. Written poetry also became a French domain through the twelfth and thirteenth centuries. For other secular uses of writing, French competed not with English, but with Latin. Domesday Book (1086) is a Latin production, but the *Leis Willelme* of the early twelfth century "were compiled in French, with the incorporation of Anglo-Saxon material, and only later put into Latin."[31] Anglo-Norman French is used in the records of Parliament and of the courts even after the Statute of Pleading (1362), which, as William Rothwell points out, applied only to spoken uses of the language.[32] Rothwell argues that "French was used alongside—or, rather, mixed in with—Latin in administrative texts virtually from the Conquest onwards."[33] French was also used for guild regulations and borough customs.[34] However, Rothwell makes the important qualification that the use of French (and Latin) was not spread evenly across all of England:

> The penetration of these foreign languages into the English countryside must have depended upon the penetration of the officials of all ranks who brought the policies of central government out of London and applied them in the provinces.

And a little later,

> Even at the height of Anglo-Norman influence as a vernacular [in the twelfth century], the dominance of French did not extend beyond the confines of

---

30. Irvine, "Compilation and Use of Manuscripts," 53; Mary Swan, "Imagining a Readership for Post-Conquest Old English Manuscripts."
31. William Rothwell, "Language and Government in Medieval England," 262.
32. Idem, "English and French in England after 1362," 539–42.
33. Idem, "Language and Government," 261.
34. Ibid., 259–60.

what we would call today roughly the south-east of England and the Home Counties. As time went on, French would have held sway over a decreasing area around the capital.³⁵

Where French and Latin were less in use as spoken or written languages, English was more likely to appear: the southwest Midlands is famous as an area where Old English manuscripts continued to be in use through the twelfth century (especially at Worcester) and where in the thirteenth century significant English texts like Lagamon's *Brut* and *Ancrene Wisse* were composed.³⁶ The same area produced a concentration of trilingual miscellanies that, according to John Scahill, indicate "a locally higher status for written English."³⁷ Localization affected the forms of texts even after the choice of English became fairly automatic in most domains: Merja Stenroos has shown that as late as the mid-fifteenth century, some scribes in Yorkshire and the Marches deliberately favored local dialects for certain functions even when that choice required revision of a less marked, supralocal exemplar.³⁸ The ecology of English thus varies not only temporally but also geographically, a circumstance that we must keep in mind when interpreting the presence or absence of alliterative English proverbs.

The topic of English-French bilingualism in post-Conquest England has persisted as a matter of some debate. Different assessments of who used which languages and even of what level of usage constitutes "true" bilingualism have led to substantial disagreement. For example, Ian Short presents three hagiographic examples of miracles by which monoglots acquired the ability to speak French; Short infers from these instances of divine intervention that the vast majority of Englishmen—both lay and clerical—knew no French and that bilingualism was mostly restricted to the nobility and the higher clergy.³⁹ William Rothwell points out that all of the incidents cited by Short took place far from London and thus may represent only a regional state of affairs.⁴⁰ In a more recent work, Short acknowledges the higher rate of bilingualism in

---

35. Ibid., 258–59.
36. Turville-Petre, *England the Nation: Language, Literature, and National Identity, 1290–1340*, 182–83. See also Yeager, *From Lawmen to Plowmen*, ch. 3: "Ecclesiastical Anglo-Saxonism in Thirteenth-Century Worcester: *The First Worcester Fragment* and *The Proverbs of Alfred*," 99–120.
37. John Scahill, "Trilingualism in Early Middle English Miscellanies: Languages and Literature," 31; see also Turville-Petre, *England the Nation*, ch. 6 (181–221).
38. Merja Stenroos, "Identity and Intelligibility in Late Middle English Scribal Transmission: Local Dialect as an Active Choice in Fifteenth-Century Texts."
39. Ian Short, "On Bilingualism in Anglo-Norman England."
40. Rothwell, "Language and Government," 259.

towns than in rural areas and estimates the overall rate of bi- and trilingualism at twenty percent.[41] Juliette Dor makes another argument against the perception of widespread bilingualism in twelfth- to thirteenth-century England; her reasoning is more sociopolitical in nature.[42] According to Dor, Henry I secured the support of the first generation of Anglo-Norman nobles born in England by providing them with positions in his royal administration. These nobles and their satellites still needed to speak French because it was the language of the king, but it was a variety of French heavily influenced by the English that was often spoken by the nobles' mothers and/or nursemaids. For Dor, this language-mixing created a creolized or pidginized French, and thus, she argues, this group of nobles was not truly bilingual.

Here we might pause to consider exactly what we mean by the terms "bilingual" or "multilingual," particularly as they apply to medieval England. Bilingualism does *not* mean that a speaker uses two languages equally and/or randomly across the entire range of linguistic functions. As Suzanne Romaine points out regarding multilingual societies,

> the allocation of functions of the languages in society is normally imbalanced and in complementary distribution. Any society which produced functionally balanced bilinguals who used both languages equally well in all contexts would soon cease to be bilingual because no society needs two languages for the same set of functions.[43]

Thus, language use is generally distributed by domain: "a sphere of activity representing a combination of specific times, settings and role relationships."[44] In post-Conquest England, the list of domains for which language choice is at issue is lengthy, including domestic life (noble and non-noble), the courts (royal, noble, and judicial), church functions (local, episcopal, and monastic), trade, and political discourse. As we have seen, geography also plays a role, with town and city dwellers, especially those closer to London, more likely to use French than their country cousins. Romaine explains that "In each domain there may be pressures of various kinds, e.g. economic, administrative, cultural, political, religious etc., which influence the bilingual towards use of one language rather than the other."[45] She adds: "Often knowledge and use of one

---

41. Short, *Manual of Anglo-Norman*, 34.
42. Juliette Dor, "Langues française et anglaise, et multilinguisme à l'époque d'Henri II Plantagenêt."
43. Suzanne Romaine, *Bilingualism*, 19.
44. Ibid., 30.
45. Ibid., 31.

language is an economic necessity."[46] This last point is applied specifically to medieval Europe by Kurt Braunmüller and Gisella Ferraresi, who claim that in our period multilingualism "was simply a necessary precondition for mastering the various tasks in everyday life (e.g. the need for using languages other than one's own in the fields of trade, jurisdiction, the church or in bookkeeping)."[47] This multilingualism took a variety of forms: "Receptive bilingualism, functionally restricted multilingualism or the command of a foreign linguistic variety as a *lingua franca* were absolutely normal."[48] They argue that the very normality of this multilingualism meant that it elicited little contemporary comment; "A lack of such linguistic skills would, by contrast, have been worth mentioning."[49] Perhaps this explains the miracle stories cited by Short. The most recent scholarship on language choice in medieval England accepts multilingualism as the prevailing state, as an important aspect of England's linguistic ecology, and explores ways in which that ecology shapes social and literary constructions.[50]

One type of language use that sheds light on linguistic ecology is code-switching, or moving from one language (or language-variety) to another within a single item of discourse. Literary scholars are familiar with code-switching as it appears in what are commonly called "macaronic" poems and sermons, but as Herbert Schendl and Laura Wright point out,

> Code-switching is found, in different ways and different styles, in a huge variety of text types. These included the many kinds of text to do with the law...; scientific texts...; religious writing of various kinds...; literature...; business writing of all types..., and those text types which were concerned with education.[51]

Studies of code-switching—both modern and medieval—reveal that mixed-language texts do not derive from the user's incompetence in one or the other

---

46. Ibid.
47. Kurt Braunmüller and Gisella Ferraresi, eds., *Aspects of Multilingualism in European Language History*, 3.
48. Ibid.
49. Ibid. On multilingualism in the British shipping trade, see, in the same volume, David Trotter, "*Oceano vox*: You Never Know Where a Ship Comes From; On Multilingualism and Language-Mixing in Medieval Britain," 15–33.
50. See, for example, Mary Catherine Davidson, *Medievalism, Multilingualism, and Chaucer*; and Jonathan Hsy, *Trading Tongues*. Tim William Machan describes Norman ambiguity toward multilingualism: "Language and Society in Twelfth-Century England."
51. Herbert Schendl and Laura Wright, "Code-Switching in Early English: Historical Background and Methodological and Theoretical Issues," 33.

language, but on the contrary, "reflect the—often very high—multilingual competence of the authors and scribes who wrote them."[52] As Laura Wright illustrates in painstaking detail, London business texts from the thirteenth through fifteenth centuries not only juxtapose English, Anglo-Norman, and Latin, but create a register in which the three languages are "intermingled at a morphological level, indicating a much more integral relationship."[53] The presence of code-switching in numerous domains provides evidence for the use of English directly alongside Latin and French at various levels of medieval English society.[54] Proverbs and other alliterative phrases frequently participate in code-switching, sometimes in unexpected ways. For example, a macaronic sermon using Latin as its base language includes two alliterative English sayings—one proverbial, one not—within a single sentence:

> Si docebis aperte plebem tuam, hewe not supra caput tuum, ne capias altas materias trascendunt ingenium tuum, ne forte þou trippe beside þe truthe.[55]

> [If you teach your people publicly, hew not above your head, lest lofty matters surpass your abilities and perchance you trip beside the truth.]

Both English insertions occur at clausal boundaries, which is quite common, but the writer (somewhat unusually) returns to Latin halfway through the English proverb ("Hew not above your head"), thus losing its alliteration. He is not trying to avoid alliteration, as the second English clause proves, so the mixed-language citation of the proverb must serve some other purpose. Such passages will be discussed in chapter 3.

Einar Haugen's concept of language ecology distinguishes high-status from low-status languages based, in part, on the domains for which each language is used. For Romaine, such a hierarchized situation represents an example of "diglossia."[56] Post-Conquest England presents us with an instance of triglossia,

---

52. Schendl and Wright, "Code-Switching in Early English," 20.

53. Laura Wright, *Sources of London English*, 3.

54. The papers in Schendl and Wright, *Code-Switching in Early English*, examine the phenomenon in charters, wills, inventories, tax and customs rolls, business accounts, and medical textbooks, as well as in poetry and sermons. Alan John Fletcher discusses examples in correspondence, legal opinion, and Latin grammars: see his *Late Medieval Popular Preaching in Britain and Ireland: Texts, Studies, and Interpretations*, 50–59. Davidson, in her *Medievalism, Multilingualism, and Chaucer*, analyzes code-switching in writers like Langland and Chaucer.

55. This instance of code-switching is cited by Helena Halmari and Timothy Regetz, "Syntactic Aspects of Code-Switching in Oxford, MS Bodley 649," 127. The translation is mine, as are all translations in this book unless otherwise indicated.

56. See Romaine, *Bilingualism*, 31–37.

with English, French, and Latin possessing different levels of prestige and being used, by and large, for different functions or domains. The narrative of language history in England has grown more complicated and nuanced than it used to be: no longer a single-stranded tale of the sudden fall and slow but inexorable rise of English in the period c.1100–c.1500, it instead describes a long-term, fluid ecology of multilingualism wherein different languages are deemed appropriate for different domains at different times and places. For example, in the hugely important domain of religious practice, Latin remains the high-status language right up to the Protestant Reformation, but the vernaculars carve out spaces of their own. English served as a language of personal devotion from the Anglo-Saxon period on, and also enjoyed occasional status as a language of biblical translation for the Anglo-Saxons and, much later, the Lollards, who deliberately followed their example.[57] In the decades around 1400, English competed with Latin as a language of theological (and political) polemic.[58] Because French was a minority language in England, it persisted in use as long as it did by serving certain social functions, including the maintenance of social distance between the nobility and the commons. Ian Short describes Anglo-Norman French as a "class-exclusive" sociolect of the elite, and English as "the class-inclusive vernacular not only of the native population, but also for members of the French-speaking minority."[59] In other words, the nobility fostered the knowledge of French among themselves not as a matter of communicative necessity but as a token of class distinction. According to Susan Crane, this "hierarchizing function of French" increased as knowledge of the language became more difficult to acquire (i.e., as it needed to be learned as a second language) and resembled the ecclesiastical use of Latin in that it "limited access to the domains in which it was used."[60] Over time, maintaining a French (versus English) identity became more problematic as a way for nobles to advertise their rank, and they assimilated more fully into the majority culture, including greater use of the majority

---

57. Jill C. Havens, "'As Englishe is comoun longage to oure puple': The Lollards and Their Imagined 'English' Community," 101–3.

58. Fiona Somerset, *Clerical Discourse and Lay Audience in Late Medieval England*. I will pick up this topic again in chapter 3.

59. Ian Short, "*Tam Angli quam Franci*: Self-Definition in Anglo-Norman England," 156. Short offers a convenient overview of the history of French in medieval England in his *Manual of Anglo-Norman*, 17–42.

60. Susan Crane, "Anglo-Norman Cultures in England, 1066–1460," 48–49. On "the survival of Norman French in the thirteenth century as a prestige dialect in an overwhelmingly Anglophone environment," see R. A. Lodge, "Language Attitudes and Linguistic Norms in France and England in the Thirteenth Century."

language.[61] Nevertheless, French (and specifically, Anglo-Norman) remained an important element of England's language ecology up to and past the end of the Middle Ages. Recent studies stress the variety of domains in which French persisted in use, including not just the commonly cited areas of law and literature but also business writing, religious devotions, military communication, and municipal record-keeping.[62]

Thus, the statuses of all three languages—English, French, and Latin—and the domains in which they are deemed appropriate are subject to both synchronic variation and diachronic change. A study of the entire matrix of language use in medieval England would be impossibly huge, so my intent is to focus on the status of English as it is represented by the alliterative proverb, by which I mean simply a proverb displaying alliteration of at least two content words, ideally through multiple attestations. In a small way, the question of whether there is such a thing as the "alliterative proverb" parallels the debate regarding the Alliterative Revival: was either of these phenomena perceived as a distinct creation, or do they seem meaningful only through modern eyes? I will freely admit at the outset to have created the "alliterative proverb" as a category that seemed best to inform my study of literary and linguistic continuity in Old and Middle English. However, as I analyzed alliterative proverbs in situ, it became clear that their particular combination of alliteration and proverbial structure produced cultural connotations that were recognized and manipulated by many medieval writers. English proverbs are not unique in their use of alliteration as the device is also found (less frequently) in medieval Latin and French proverbs. However, in the language ecology of post-Conquest England, alliterative proverbs in English are doubly marked: first, by the choice of English as the language of expression, and second, because alliteration carries an inescapable cultural-historical significance in English that it does not possess in French or Latin. Of the three languages, only English had a history of using alliteration as an essential element of poetry. Furthermore, Stephen Yeager argues that the alliteration of Old English legal, homiletic, and wisdom texts served as a marker of traditional, vernacular authority that survived well into the Middle English period.[63] Thus,

---

61. For a detailed study of this process of assimilation, see Hugh M. Thomas, *The English and the Normans: Ethnic Hostility, Assimilation, and Identity 1066–c.1220*. Laura Ashe argues that Anglo-Norman writers of the twelfth century used their French texts to develop a sense of national identity: *Fiction and History in England, 1066–1200*.

62. See Jocelyn Wogan-Browne, ed., *Language and Culture in Medieval Britain: The French of England c.1100–c.1500*; idem, "'Invisible Archives?' Later Medieval French in England"; and Richard Ingham, ed., *The Anglo-Norman Language and Its Contexts*.

63. Yeager, *From Lawmen to Plowmen*. For other studies on the cultural significance of alliteration, see the essays in Jonathan Roper, ed., *Alliteration in Culture*.

the alliteration of the proverb calls attention to its Englishness, and vice versa. Combining these elements, the alliterative proverb serves as a robust indicator of language choice. In the chapters that follow, I will explore some of the meaningful results of that language choice.

Viewing proverbs as part of a language ecology represents a broader approach than has heretofore been taken in medieval paroemiology. The most basic (and indispensable) type of research has been the collection of medieval proverbs and the editing of proverb collections.[64] One also finds some analyses of proverb use in particular authors or texts.[65] Rarer still are studies of proverbs in an entire genre of medieval literature.[66] Many or most medieval genres still await such treatment. Medieval paroemiology continues to suffer from the perception that its proverbs are too literate for the folklorist but too banal for the literary scholar. The field is not helped by the antiproverbial bias inherent in many technologized, literate (especially Western) societies, which often reject the wisdom rooted in the past in favor of that created by new forms of knowledge. Such an attitude may often lead to social good, but it makes it more difficult to overcome the alterity of medieval proverbs and the culture that valued them. In sum, the Middle Ages offer us a culture that held the proverb in (mostly) high esteem, like an oral culture, but also included some determinedly literate domains. Examining the movement of proverbs through a number of those domains provides a better picture of the wider intellectual, linguistic, literary—and paroemiological—world of medieval England.

In dealing with proverbs from the distant past, the greatest methodological problem lies in simple recognition: how do we know, without native competence, which statements are proverbial? Three factors, in various combinations, help to mark a sentence as proverbial: its form, whether it appears

---

64. A few important examples include *Thesaurus proverbiorum medii aevi*; Bartlett Jere Whiting with Helen Wescott Whiting, *Proverbs, Sentences, and Proverbial Phrases from English Writings Mainly before 1500* (hereafter *Proverbs . . . before 1500*); "The Durham Proverbs"; *Disticha Catonis*; James Woodrow Hassell Jr., *Middle French Proverbs, Sentences, and Proverbial Phrases*; Hans Walther, *Proverbia sententiaeque latinitatis medii aevi*; and Richard L. Harris, *A Concordance to Proverbs and Proverbial Materials in the Old Icelandic Sagas*.

65. As in Marcelle Altieri, *Les Romans de Chrétien de Troyes: Leur perspective proverbiale et gnomique*; D. V. Ives, "The Proverbs in the 'Ancren Riwle'"; and Susan E. Deskis, *"Beowulf" and the Medieval Proverb Tradition*.

66. See Dave L. Bland, "The Use of Proverbs in Two Medieval Genres of Discourse: 'The Art of Poetry' and 'The Art of Preaching'"; Claude Buridant, "Les proverbes et la prédication au Moyen Age"; and Bartlett Jere Whiting, *Proverbs in the Earlier English Drama*. For an extremely useful account of scholarship on proverbs in Old English, see Johanna Kramer, "The Study of Proverbs in Anglo-Saxon Literature."

in other texts, and direct contextual pointing.[67] Formal features of proverbs (ancient, medieval, or modern) include repetition, ellipsis, temporal adverbs (always, never), modalities (good, bad, must), and syntactic parallelism (better x than y). Furthermore, the proverb will typically also express a greater generality than does its context.[68] In any text, the specific pointing or introduction of a sentence as proverbial is, of course, very helpful and usually to be trusted.[69] Finally, the secure identification of a proverb is greatly enhanced if it can be shown to be used by different writers. However, locating multiple uses of the same proverb can be a matter of art as much as science.[70] For Old and Middle English literature, the base collection of proverbs was compiled by Bartlett Jere Whiting, who read voluminously in the field and jotted down sentences and phrases that met his criteria for proverbiality.[71] I have found no better way of locating early English alliterative proverbs than by excerpting them from Whiting's collection. Of course, I have then been able to add further attestations of some proverbs by using tools unavailable to Whiting, such as the *Thesaurus proverbiorum* and digitized corpora of Old English and Middle English texts.[72] Still, one sometimes happens across a medieval proverb by accident and, in rare cases, can add a new item to Whiting's catalogue.

Medieval proverbs may strike a modern reader as being somewhat dull, often lacking the metaphorical imagery that helps to make modern proverbs memorable. As Cameron Louis points out, modern definitions of the proverb usually stress its origins among the nonlearned folk, but in Middle English (and in Old English, though Louis does not address that material), one is more likely to encounter the "learned" proverb. This type of proverb tends to be more literal and somewhat longer than a proverb of oral origin and has often been translated from a Latin work like the *Disticha Catonis* or a wisdom book of the Bible.[73] Whether a medieval proverb was oral or written in its origin,

---

67. I have addressed this problem with relation to *Beowulf* in Deskis, *"Beowulf" and the Medieval Proverb Tradition*, 3–9. See also *Introduction to Paremiology: A Comprehensive Guide to Proverb Studies*.

68. Shirley L. Arora, "The Perception of Proverbiality"; Arvo Krikmann, "On Denotative Indefiniteness of Proverbs."

69. Although, there are exceptions like *The Owl and the Nightingale* and Chaucer's *Troilus and Criseyde*, where the poets' uses of the proverb as a tool of characterization can lead to hyperidentification of the form.

70. Methodological criteria for recognizing two sentences as examples of the "same" proverb are treated in chapter 2.

71. Whiting, *Proverbs . . . before 1500*.

72. *Thesaurus proverbiorum medii aevi*; *Dictionary of Old English Web Corpus*; *Middle English Compendium*.

73. Cameron Louis, "The Concept of the Proverb in Middle English."

it comes to us only via written sources, regarding which Bartlett Jere Whiting offers a useful reminder:

> The medieval proverbs which survive do so only because they were written down by educated men, none of them collectors from the field. In most cases the sayings were incorporated in literary works by authors who did not hesitate to make changes suggested by context, application, and meter. . . . What we have in most quotations is the proverb, not as an author may have heard or read it, but in the form which suited his immediate convenience or whim.[74]

Helen Wicker has successfully found meaning in the ways in which proverbs and moral verses are manipulated in context; she works from the understanding that "these expressions may have fronted an apparently timeless moral code, but in their everyday repetition they represented constant dialogue and exchange."[75] For this current study, the fact that medieval English writers felt free to manipulate proverbial material may be treated as an advantage, as it will open windows into the purposes for which these writers intended their proverbs. Chapter 2 takes a philological approach to the questions: "Did any alliterative proverbs survive from Old English into Middle English?" and "How did the linguistic changes of Middle English affect the construction of alliterative proverbs?". In this chapter, I present evidence for the continuity of a number of alliterative proverbs by tracing the history of their alliterating elements. I also demonstrate the continued production of alliterative proverbs during the Middle English period, identifying post-Conquest proverbs by their Romance vocabulary. Having established the ongoing robustness of alliterative proverbs after the Conquest, I take a more literary-historical approach in chapters 3 and 4. Because the language ecology of medieval England can only be reconstructed from written texts, I use the specific genres of those texts as a defining element of that ecology. In other words, genre can provide information about both author and audience that pertains to the use of proverbs. Chapter 3 describes how the interplay of proverbial form, alliterative vocabulary, and the choice of the English language creates its own variety of historicized wisdom in such didactic genres as the proverb collection, the gnomic poem, and the sermon. In chapter 4, I explore the later-developing genres of romance, lyric, and drama. Of course, this chapter does not provide

---

74. Whiting, *Proverbs . . . before 1500*, x.
75. Helen E. Wicker, "Between Proverbs and Lyrics: Customization Practices in Late Medieval English Moral Verse."

a complete analysis of proverbs in Middle English imaginative literature, in large part because certain major authors and important text-groups seem to avoid the alliterative proverb. Thus, an author like Chaucer, who uses proverbs in a deft and sophisticated way, does not figure in this study because the proverbs he uses typically lack alliteration. The same is true for most of the alliterative poems of late Middle English. The literary genres that do make frequent use of the alliterative proverb—the popular romance, the biblical and moral drama—are those that are best served by the association of the alliterative proverb with the Anglophone classes. The significance of these findings, as well as possibilities for extending them, are addressed in chapter 5.

CHAPTER 2

Alliterative Proverbs in Time

AS I DISCUSSED in chapter 1, an important issue in the literary history of medieval England is the level of continuity—or lack thereof—informing the composition of alliterative poetry. The same question can be asked of alliterative proverbs, but because these represent a simpler form, the answer should be correspondingly clearer. This does not mean that the endeavor is without its difficulties, which include the small size of the preserved corpus of Old English and the formality of that corpus relative to everyday speech. Although proverbs enjoyed greater respect throughout the Middle Ages than they do now, they were, even then, primarily oral in their transmission and were very probably more common in spoken than written discourse.[1] Hence, the number of proverbs available to us is relatively small. The evidence becomes even sparser when we limit our inquiry to alliterative proverbs. I have endeavored to be fairly conservative in adducing proverbial analogues, whether from the same or different languages. Analogous proverbs should refer to the same ethical or practical point; if the analogues are from the same language, they should also share at least two or three lexical elements and, ideally though not always, a similar syntactic structure. Of meaning, vocabulary, and syntax,

---

1. On the written transmission of medieval proverbs, see Deskis, *"Beowulf" and the Medieval Proverb Tradition*, ch. 6.

the last is the least important in this study, because the literary settings of the proverbs have necessitated numerous syntactic adaptations to them.

There are numerous instances where the alliterating word-pairs of a Middle English proverb are well attested in Old English. These repetitions indicate either that the proverb already existed in Old English (most often without attestation as such in the written record) or that the alliterating words were so commonly linked that they became fixed in proverbial form at some later date. This chapter begins with some examples of such continuity. Because the surviving corpus of Middle English proverbs is larger than that of Old English, it can bear further interrogation. Thus, I investigate some proverbs that could have arisen in Old English because their vocabulary is entirely Germanic, but for which there is no trace in the earlier period. Some of these proverbs have analogues in French, Latin, and German, but the Middle English examples remain notable for their use of alliteration. The alliteration typically provides stability to the form of the proverb, but the pervasive lexical and semantic changes of Middle English do sometimes take their toll. On the other hand, the strength of alliteration as a proverbial marker meant that new alliterative proverbs were coined using newer, French loanwords, providing evidence for a particular type of linguistic assimilation and accommodation in the language ecology of medieval England.

MIDDLE ENGLISH PROVERBS REFLECTING OLD ENGLISH COLLOCATIONS

When the Cup is fullest bear it fairest (Whiting C633)[2]

This is a rare example of a proverb that appears in nearly identical forms in both Old English and Middle English. In the early eleventh-century *Durham Proverbs* we find "Swa fulre fæt swa hit mann sceal fægror beran"[3] [The fuller the cup the fairer it must be carried]. The Middle English *Proverbs of Hendyng* yields "When the coppe is follest, thenne ber hire feyrest."[4] The version from the *Proverbs of Hendyng* maintains the alliteration on "full" and "fair," but has lost one other alliterative element through its replacement of "fæt" by "coppe."

---

2. Whiting, *Proverbs . . . before 1500*, cited by lemma number.

3. The Latin is "Vas quantum plenior tantum moderatius ambulandum," "The Durham Proverbs," no. 42, 295. See also *The Durham Proverbs: An Eleventh Century Collection of Anglo-Saxon Proverbs Edited from Durham Cathedral MS. B.III.32*.

4. K. Böddeker, ed., *Altenglische Dichtungen des MS. Harl. 2253*, 293. Samuel Singer notes analogues to the proverb in medieval Latin, Middle High German, and Old Danish, but none use the alliteration found in Old and Middle English: "Die Sprichwörter Hendings," 35.

As J. P. Oakden points out, alliteration in the *Proverbs of Hendyng* "is almost entirely due to the presence of certain traditional expressions and phrases."[5] In this case, the "traditional expression" dates back to the Old English period.

All Hights should be held (Whiting H378)
What you Hight see you hold (Whiting H379)
Bartlett Jere Whiting records two variants of this proverb, both from fifteenth-century Middle Scots texts. In his *Fables,* Robert Henryson writes "all hechtis suld haldin be."[6] The lyric beginning "Do way fore that may nocht awailghe" yields "Quhar thow hechtys se thow hald."[7] Despite their grammatical differences, these are clearly two expressions of the same proverb.

The Old English sentences that link *hatan* and *healdan* likewise exhibit small variations in form, but perfect consistency in meaning:

ðæt he meahte gehealdan ðæt ðæt he ær gehet [ond] swor[8]
[So that he might hold to what he had promised and sworn]

And þonne bið þæt fulluht, swylce hit wedd sy ealra þæra worda and ealles ðæs behates, gehealde, se ðe wille.[9]
[And that is baptism, as it were a pledge of all the words and all the vow, hold to it who will.]

Like the lyric, but unlike Henryson, the Old English examples use both alliterating words as verbs. The first example bears the closest semantic and grammatical similarity to the Middle English proverbs. The second, from Wulfstan's *Institutes of Polity,* also includes the modifier "all" found in Henryson. Though both examples derive from Old English translations of Latin texts, the fact that two different Anglo-Saxon translators chose to employ the same alliterative language in their prose may itself imply that the *hatan/healdan* collocation was common and familiar. That the proverb is found only in Middle Scots for the later period tantalizes, rather than discourages, considering the cultural conservatism of Scots literature.

---

5. J. P. Oakden, *Alliterative Poetry in Middle English: The Dialectal and Metrical Survey,* 2.8.

6. Robert Henryson, *The Fables,* line 2276, in *The Poems of Robert Henryson,* 86.

7. "A Ballad of Good Counsel" in *The Scottish Metrical Romance of Lancelot du Lak,* 169.

8. Alfred the Great, *King Alfred's West-Saxon Version of Gregory's Pastoral Care,* 465, lines 26–27.

9. Wulfstan, *Die "Institutes of Polity, Civil and Ecclesiastical": Ein Werk Erzbischof Wulfstans von York,* nos. 122 and 241.

Much will have more (Whiting M786)
Of Much they made more (Whiting M787)
The collocation "much" and "more" is very common and productive in the early English proverbial tradition.[10] Whiting locates at least five relevant examples of type M786 between 1400 and 1500, and one example of M787 from the turn of the sixteenth century:

Bot ay mekill wald haue mare, as many man spellis[11]

Have thai never so mekyl mok he wyl have more[12]

Haue he neuere so mykyl, ȝyt he wold haue more[13]

Mykull wulle more[14]

Nedeles moche wolde have more[15]

And as the maner is, of mych thay mad more. *Fama de magnis semper majore, vulgante*[16]
[As commonly said, the fame of the great becomes always greater.]

All of Whiting's examples exhibit strong proverbial form, and some are marked as current proverbs—for example, "as many man spellis" and "vulgante." Later collections add more examples, extending the currency of the proverb into the twentieth century.[17]

The proverbial pairing is equally common in Old English, occurring at least ten times. It is especially well attested in the Old English gloss to

---

10. See, for example, G. L. Apperson, *The Wordsworth Dictionary of Proverbs*, 433; and Morris P. Tilley, *A Dictionary of the Proverbs in England in the Sixteenth and Seventeenth Centuries*, M1287.

11. *The Wars of Alexander*, 144, line 4526.

12. John Audelay, "De concordia inter fratres et rectores ecclesiae" in *The Poems of John Audelay*, ed. James Orchard Halliwell, 14.

13. *The Castle of Perseverance*, line 89, in *The Macro Plays: The Castle of Perseverance, Wisdom, Mankind*, 5.

14. Max Förster, "Die mittelenglische Sprichwörtersammlung in Douce 52," 49, no. 65.

15. Karl Brunner, "Proverbs of Salamon," in "Spätme. Lehrgedichte," 195.

16. *The English Conquest of Ireland*, 41.

17. *The Oxford Dictionary of English Proverbs*, 550; Bartlett Jere Whiting, *Modern Proverbs and Proverbial Sayings*, M304, 431.

Defensor's *Liber scintillarum*,[18] where we find a version closest to the Middle English: "[ond] swa micele mare swa he begytt swa micele mare he secð"[19] [and as much more as he receives, so much more he seeks]. Other examples from Defensor, as well as from Ælfric, Alfred's translation of Gregory's *Pastoral Care*, and elsewhere, adjust the proverb to specific conditions by detailing exactly what a person has or seeks "much" and "more" of:

> swa micele maran eadmodnysse þu sy þurhbeorht swa micele swa maran wurþnysse forsett.[20]
> [The more radiant you are in humility, the more advanced you are in honor.]

> swa micelem swa on stowe hegra ys swa micelum on frecenysse maran wunað.[21]
> [The higher a place is, the more one stands in danger.]

> lar swa micele swa heo rumlicor geseald byþ swa micele mara heo genihtsumað.[22]
> [The more generously teaching is given, the more it abounds.]

> swa micele maran susla hi syllaþ swa micele swa hi maran synd.[23]
> [The greater they are, the more trouble they give.]

> ðætte sua micle sua hira onwald bið mara gesewen ofre oðre menn[24]
> [As much as their power is seen to be greater over other men]

> swa micele witodlice swa mara wurðmynt swa micele maran beoð fræcednisse.[25]
> [Verily, the greater the glory, the more the dangers.]

> and micele yrmða becumað ... maran and maran[26]
> [And much misery becomes more and more]

---

18. Defensor of Ligugé, "An Edition with Commentary of the Latin/Anglo-Saxon *Liber scintillarum*," cited from the Dictionary of Old English Web Corpus.
19. Ibid., ch. 30, #20.
20. Ibid., ch. 4, #46.
21. Ibid., ch. 32, #53 and ch. 58, #35.
22. Ibid., ch. 32, #100.
23. Ibid., ch. 58, #56.
24. Alfred the Great, *King Alfred's West-Saxon Version of Gregory's Pastoral Care*, 119, line 14.
25. Friedrich Kluge, "Zu altenglischen Dichtungen," 473, line 7.
26. Ælfric, *Ælfric's Catholic Homilies: The Second Series*, II.19, 188, lines 266–68.

swa micela swa se heofenlica cyning is . . . swa micele mara[27]
[As great as the heavenly king is . . . , so much greater.]

Based on its abundant attestations, I would argue that the structure "micel . . . mara" existed in Old English perhaps as a proverb, but certainly as what we could call a proverbial template, a traditional phrasing with a stable core and variable particulars.[28] The Middle English proverbs show the continuation of the tradition with but a stripping away of the particulars.

From Heaven comes help (Whiting H308)
This saying occurs only once in Middle English (according to Whiting), but it is explicitly marked as a proverb: "Ffrom heuen cometh helpe ys an old prouerbe."[29] Because the *Life of Saint Anne* dates from the fifteenth century, the "oldness" of this proverb might be called into question, but the collocation of "heaven" with "help" is fairly common in Old English literature:[30]

>   þe sende waldendgod,
> þin hearra / þas helpe   of heofonrice[31]
> [God, your lord, sent you help from heaven]

>   hu he, rodera þrim,
> heofona heahfrea,   helpe gefremede
> monna cynne[32]
> [How he, the glory of the skies, high lord of heaven, gave help to mankind.]

---

27. Basil, *The Anglo-Saxon Version of the Hexameron of St. Basil, or, Be Godes six daga weorcum. And the Anglo-Saxon Remains of St. Basil's Admonitio ad filium spiritualem*, ch. 2, line 53.

28. For a Middle English example of such a template, consider the word-pair "weal" and "woe," which forms the basis for Whiting W132, W133, W135, W137, W138, W140, and W432. This pairing is found only twice in Old English: *Genesis B*, line 466a; and *The Old English Apollonius of Tyre*, 42.

29. *The Middle English Stanzaic Versions of the Life of Saint Anne*, 91, line 29.

30. For a nonproverbial instance of the collocation in Middle English, see *The Romance of Sir Beues of Hamtoun*, version x, 212, line 4210: "He thankyd god omnipotent / That hym helpe ffro hevyn sent."

31. *Genesis B*, in *The Saxon Genesis: An Edition of the West Saxon "Genesis B" and the Old Saxon Vatican "Genesis,"* 219, lines 520b–21.

32. *Advent Lyric* 12 (*Christ I*), lines 423b–25a, in *The Exeter Anthology of Old English Poetry: An Edition of Exeter Dean and Chapter MS 3501*, I.62.

ond meotud bidde
þæt me heofona helm   helpe gefremme³³
[And I ask the Lord that he, heaven's helm, might bring me help]

Uton clypian to heofonum þæt god ure helpe³⁴
[Let us call out to heaven, that God may help us]

Hig clipodon þa swiðe on heora geswencednisse to þam heofonlican Gode, his helpes biddende.³⁵
[In their affliction, they called out loudly to the heavenly God, beseeching his help.]

Israhela folc þa earmlice clipode to þam heofonlican Gode, his helpes biddende.³⁶
[The people of Israel then pitiably called out to the heavenly God, beseeching his help.]

Most of these examples are poetic or semipoetic, so one could argue that *heofon* and *help* are linked simply for the alliterative usefulness of the pairing. Still, the examples are numerous enough that they bear closer examination.

The position of *help* is very stable in these sentences: it is always the direct object of a verb except where Ælfric uses the verb form. *Heofon*, on the other hand, is more varied, occurring either as a genitive modifier—*heofona heahfrea, heofona helm*—or as a descriptor of the place from where God provides His assistance (as in the Middle English proverb). The first two Old English sentences describe how God in heaven actually did provide help, while the last four express a hope that it will happen. Despite the variations, all six of these Old English sentences express, in alliterative form, the belief that help comes from heaven, the same belief expressed in the Middle English alliterative proverb. We cannot say for certain that this "old prouerbe" existed in Old English, but its core can certainly be found there.

Lief Child behoves lore (Whiting C216)

This proverb is common and fairly stable in English from the thirteenth century on. Its proverbial status is reinforced by its earliest Middle English

---

33. *The Passion of Saint Juliana*, lines 721b–22, in *The Exeter Anthology*, I.214.
34. "Passio Machabeorum," in *Ælfric's Lives of Saints*, 88, line 349.
35. Judges 3.15 in *The Old English Version of the Heptateuch*, 402.
36. Judges 6.7 in *Old English Version of the Heptateuch*, 406.

manifestations among the *Proverbs of Hendyng* and by its tendency to appear in texts of a didactic nature.

> Lef child bihoveþ lore,
> And evere þe levere þe more[37]

> Lef child lore bihouet3[38]

> My sire seide to me, and so dide my dame,
> "[Lo], þe leuere child þe moore loore bihoueþ"[39]

> Lefe chylde lore be-hoveth[40]

> Seyd hit ys full yore
> That lothe chylde lore behowyyt,
> and leve chylde moche more[41]

> For, as þe wyse man sayth and preuyth,
> A leve chyld, lore he be-houyth[42]

Half of these examples are labeled as traditional wisdom, and the only real variation is the occasional expansion of the proverb from one line to two.

The belief that a beloved person (not necessarily a child) should be taught is widespread in Old English, but not, apparently, proverbial. The alliterative collocation takes one of two forms: *leof* may be paired with the noun *lar* (as in the Middle English proverb) or with the verb *læran*. Because the Middle English examples show no tendency toward the *læran* type, I will concentrate first on the Old English sentences that link *leof* and *lar*.

> Cornelius gelaðode his leofestan freond
> wolde þæt hi ge-hyrdon þa halgan lare æt petre[43]

---

37. H. Varnhagen, "Zu den Sprichwörtern Hending's (Cambridge und Oxford-Text)," stanza 4, 191 (Oxford; also stanza 3 in Cambridge MS.). Later manuscripts of the *Proverbs of Hendyng* show some variation of the proverb.

38. *The Good Wife Taught Her Daughter*, stanza 26, line 155, in *The Good Wife Taught Her Daughter; The Good Wyfe Wold a Pylgremage; The Thewis of Gud Women*, 168.

39. *Piers Plowman* B, passus V, lines 37–38, in *Piers Plowman: The B Version*, 307.

40. Förster, "Die mittelenglische Sprichwörtersammlung in Douce 52," 53.

41. *The Good Wyfe Wold a Pylgremage*, in *The Good Wife Taught Her Daughter*, 173.

42. *Symon's Lesson of Wysedome for Chyldryn*, lines 87–88, in *The Babees Book*, 402.

43. "Cathedra sancti Petri," in *Ælfric's Lives of Saints*, 228.

[Cornelius summoned his dearest friends; he wanted them to hear the holy teaching from Peter]

Nu lære ic ðe swa swa leofne sunu
þæt ðu þæra cristenra lare forlæte mid ealle[44]
[Now I counsel you like a beloved son, that you should altogether abandon Christian doctrine]

Leofen men, beorgað eow georne wið deofles lara.[45]
[Beloved people, guard yourselves zealously against the devil's teaching.]

Forþon wat se þe sceal   his winedryhtnes
leofes larcwidum   longe forþolian[46]
[Therefore he who must long forgo the teaching of his beloved lord knows]

These examples show little more in common than the use of the same alliterative collocation. In the Middle English proverb, lore is very much a good thing; in these Old English sentences, it may be good or bad. In the *læran* sentences, however, the teaching is always positive:

Nu lære ic þe   swa man leofne sceal[47]
[Now I will teach you as one should a dear one]

Ne meahton we gelæran   leofne þeoden[48]
[We could not counsel our beloved lord]

Forþon ic leofra gehwone   læran wille[49]
[Therefore I will teach every dear one]

Forþon ic, leof weorud,   læran wille[50]
[Therefore, beloved people, I wish to counsel you]

---

44. "Natale sancti Georgii martyris," in *Ælfric's Lives of Saints*, 314. Note that this hybrid form includes both *læran* and *lar*.
45. Wulfstan, "Sermo de baptismate," in *The Homilies of Wulfstan*, 183.
46. *The Wanderer*, lines 37–38, in *The Exeter Anthology*, I.216.
47. *Exhortation to Christian Living*, line 1, in *The Anglo-Saxon Minor Poems*, 67.
48. *Beowulf*, line 3079, in *Klaeber's Beowulf and the Fight at Finnsburg*, 104.
49. *The Ascension*, line 376, in *The Exeter Anthology*, I.76 (*Christ II*, line 815).
50. *The Passion of Saint Juliana*, line 647, in *The Exeter Anthology*, I.211.

Leofan men, nu bidde ic and lære ælcne cristene man[51]
[Beloved people, now I bid and teach every Christian]

Men þa leofestan, ic eow bidde and eaðmode lære[52]
[Beloved people, I bid you and humbly counsel]

Leofan men, doð swa ic lære[53]
[Beloved people, do as I teach]

Leofan man, on eornost ic lære[54]
[Dear one, earnestly I teach]

leofa, swa ic þe lære   læst uncre wel
treowrædenne[55]
[Dear one, as I instruct you, fulfill well our covenant]

Besides being more common, the *læran* form is more consistent in both form and content. It is useful for homilists, but can be found in both religious and secular literature, and in both poetry and prose. The teaching is always directed toward the *leof* person or persons (again, like the Middle English proverb). This collocation is firmly enough established in Old English to qualify as a proverbial template, or even as a rhetorical topos, but it is unlikely to be the source of the Middle English proverb for two reasons. First, the Middle English versions of the proverb all use the noun "lore" instead of the verb "leren"; and second, none of the Old English examples includes the nonalliterative pairing of "child" and "behoveth" that is shared by all of the Middle English proverbs. So in this case, despite the alliterative collocation of "leof" and "lar" in the first group of Old English clauses, no probable connection can be drawn with the Middle English proverbs.

I have included this negative finding here as a methodological caution: the mere attestation in Old English of the same (or etymologically related) alliterative collocation, even in large numbers, does not ensure proverbial continuity. In order to propose an Old English origin for a Middle English proverb

---

51. *Eleven Old English Rogationtide Homilies*, Homily 8, 109, line 18.
52. *The Vercelli Homilies and Related Texts*, Homily 4, 90, line 1.
53. Wulfstan, "Her ongynð be cristendome," lines 76–77, in *The Homilies of Wulfstan*, 203; cf. "Sermo Lupi," in *Wulfstan: Sammlung der ihm zugeschriebenen Homilien nebst Untersuchungen über ihre Echtheit*, 307.
54. Wulfstan, "Her ongynð be cristendome," line 118, in *The Homilies of Wulfstan*, 206.
55. *Genesis A*, lines 2306–7a, in *Genesis A: A New Edition, Revised*, 245.

we need to see at least some syntactic regularity combined with a consistent semantic sense. Syntactic regularity may trump content, as in "Much will have more," but in an instance where semantic content fails to match (the Middle English positive and Old English mixed valences of *lar*) and syntactic form clashes as well (the noun "lore" versus the verb *læran*) shared collocations alone cannot tell us much about proverbial origins.

Full hard is Hunger in hale maw (Whiting H635)
There Hunger is hot, hearts are feeble (Whiting H645)
Each of these Middle English proverbs contains triple alliteration, but we can trace an alliterative pair in each back to an Old English collocation.

Whiting offers two fifteenth-century examples of H635, one of which is marked as proverbial:

fore It is sad in elderys saw:
"ful harde is hungyre in hale maw"[56]

For hym thoucht that ane hard thraw,
Hungyr than in til hail maw.[57]

In both of these Scottish examples, the alliterative proverb has been adapted to an end-rhymed text.

The collocation of "hunger" with "hard" is found fairly commonly in compact form in the Old English corpus:

Hunger se hearda[58]
[That hard hunger]

ond þu me mid þy heardan   hungre gebunde[59]
[And you bound me with that hard hunger]

ond þu me þy heardan   hungre gebunde[60]
[And you bound me with that hard hunger]

---

56. "Jacobus (Minor)" in *Legends of the Saints in the Scottish Dialect of the Fourteenth Century*, I.169.
57. Andrew of Wyntoun, *The Original Chronicle of Andrew of Wyntoun*, lines 199–200, II.159.
58. *Genesis A*, 215, line 1815.
59. *Soul and Body I*, line 31, in *The Vercelli Book*, 55.
60. *Soul and Body II*, line 28, in *The Exeter Anthology*, I.277.

þonne hy heardne   hungor þoliað[61]
[When they suffer hard hunger]

ac þær bið se hearda hungor[62]
[But there is hard hunger]

forðon ðe we þoliað þone heardestan hungor.[63]
[Because we suffer the hardest hunger.]

These examples indicate that *heard* is a frequent, perhaps even formulaic, modifier to *hungor*.

Whiting offers one Middle English proverb linking "hunger" and "hot," also from the early fifteenth century: "And þere hongur is hote, hertis ben febill."[64] The two words can also be found linked as a simple metaphor: "Withyn hunger so hote þat neȝ our herte brestyþ."[65] The collocation is more common in Old English:

hungor se hata[66]
[That hot hunger]

þæs hatan hungres[67]
[Of that hot hunger]

mid þam hatan hungre[68]
[With that hot hunger]

oððe ic mid hungre hate þe acwellan[69]
[Or I will kill you with hot hunger.]

---

61. *Paris Psalter*, 58.6, in *The Paris Psalter and the Meters of Boethius*, 11; see also Ps. 58.14: "and heardne eac hungor ðoliað" (12).
62. Homily 11 in *Eleven Old English Rogationtide Homilies*, 142, lines 88–89.
63. *The Old English Apollonius of Tyre*, 14.
64. *The Gest Hystoriale of the Destruction of Troy*, 168, line 5171.
65. *The Siege of Jerusalem*, 74, line 1086.
66. *Phoenix*, line 613a, in *The Exeter Anthology*, I.185.
67. Ælfric, Homily 28: "Dominica Undecima Post Pentecosten," in *Catholic Homilies: The First Series; Text*, 411.
68. Ælfric, "On the Old and New Testament," lines 1248–49, in *The Old English Version of the Heptateuch*, 74.
69. "Þære Halgan Rode Gemetnes," in *Legends of the Holy Rood*, 11.

As with "hard hunger," we see that *hat* appears in close proximity to *hungor* to form a compact collocation. I am fairly certain that both Middle English proverbs have their origins in the Old English collocations. What is less certain, considering the small number of Middle English examples and their relative lateness, is whether (a) the collocations circulated in proverbial form through the Middle English period but are not frequently attested, or (b) "hard hunger" and "hot hunger" circulated primarily as collocations that were only occasionally expanded with proverbial syntax. The labelling of "full hard is hunger in hale maw" as an "elderys saw" leads me to favor option (a) in that case; the proverbial history of "hot hunger" is more open to question.

In the Heart is the hoard of ilk man's word (Whiting H283)
This proverb appears as a two-line passage in the fourteenth-century *Ywain and Gawain*:

> And in þe hert þare es þe horde
> And knawing of ilk mans worde.[70]

However, the Old English parallels will show that the alliterative first line contains the proverb itself, with the second line representing an expansion to fill out a rhyming couplet.

> Eorl oðerne   mid æfþancum
> ond mid teonwordum   tæleð behindan,
> spreceð fægere beforan,   ond þæt facen swa þeah
> hafað in his heortan,   hord unclæne[71]
> [One man slanders another behind his back with insults and abuse;
> he speaks fairly before him, but he holds that treachery in his heart,
> an unclean hoard]

> Ne magun hord weras,   heortan geþohtas,
> fore waldende   wihte bemiþan[72]
> [Men cannot at all conceal their hoard, the thoughts of their hearts, before the Lord]

---

70. *Ywain and Gawain*, 5, lines 147–48. See also Whiting, *Proverbs... before 1500*, H278: "Heart on the hoard and hands on the sore."
71. *Homiletic Fragment I*, lines 3–6, in *The Vercelli Book*, 59.
72. *Christ in Judgement*, lines 181–82, in *The Exeter Anthology*, I.85 (*Christ III*, lines 1047–48).

>   ac se mæra dæg
> hreþerlocena hord,   heortan geþohtas,
> ealle ætyweð[73]
>
> [But that great day will reveal all, the hoard of the breast and the thoughts of the heart.]

Numerous characteristics link these Old English passages to the Middle English proverb. First is the simple proximity of *heort* and *hord* and the fact that the *hord* is consistently described as being contained within the *heort*. Second is the flexibility of the hoard: in both Old and Middle English it may be morally good or bad. Furthermore, all three of the Old English examples state or imply a potential disjuncture between the heart's true hoard and one's outward mien, as does the Middle English proverb. Finally, we might note that all but the last Old English text assume a generalized, sentential form. Based on this evidence, I believe that the Old English texts present a common, perhaps proverbial, sentiment that, through the accidents of preservation, occurs only in Middle English in a concise, proverbial form.

My next example of a Middle English alliterative proverb with a possible Old English origin is amply attested, but must be treated cautiously because all of the Old English collocations are found in poetic texts. Thus, we may be looking at the Old English roots of a Middle English proverb, but the absence of the collocation in prose makes the connection a little less certain.

After Bale comes boot (Whiting B18)

> How after bale hem com bote[74]

> After bale cometh boote[75]

> So after bale cometh bote, whoso byde conne[76]

> After bale, boot thou bringes[77]

> But aftre bale ther may come bote[78]

---

73. *Christ in Judgement*, lines 188b–90a, in *The Exeter Anthology*, I.85 (*Christ III*, lines 1054b–56a).
74. *Floris and Blancheflour: A Middle English Romance*, 680, line 1308.
75. *Gamelyn*, line 631, in *Middle English Verse Romances*, 173.
76. "The Tale of Beryn," line 3954, in *The Canterbury Interlude and Merchant's Tale of Beryn*. Note the addition of a third alliterative element ("byde") in a nonalliterative poem.
77. *The Last Judgment*, line 113, in *The Chester Mystery Cycle*, I.442.
78. *A Royal History of the Excellent Knight Generides*, 14, line 434.

Ffore after bale ther comyht bote[79]

After bate [sic] comyth bote[80]

When Bale is highest boot is nighest (Whiting B22)
For Aluered seide of olde quide—
An ȝut his nis of horte islide—
"Wone þe bale is alrehecst,
Þonne is þe bote alre necst"[81]

Bote þer þe bale was alre meast. swa was te bote nehest[82]

Þere þe bale is mest,
þere is þe bote nest[83]

Lo, an olde pro[v]erbe aleged by many wyse, "Whan bale is greatest, than is bote a nyebore"[84]

for whon þe bale was most. þen was þe bote next[85]

Whenne bale ys aldermest, bote ys ful hende[86]

When bale is most, bote is nexte.[87]

These two proverbs are ubiquitous in the Middle English corpus: both are very stable, both are very common, and both contain the alliterative collocation "bale" and "boot."[88] That pairing is similarly common in Old English:

---

79. Rossell Hope Robbins, "Speculum Misericordie," 943, line 106.
80. Sanford B. Meech, "A Collection of Proverbs in Rawlinson MS D 328," 120.
81. *The Owl and the Nightingale*, lines 685–88, in *The Owl and the Nightingale: Text and Translation*, 17.
82. "The Wohunge of Ure Laverd," in *Old English Homilies and Homiletic Treatises of the Twelfth and Thirteenth Centuries*, 277.
83. *Proverbs of Hendyng*, stanza 13 (Oxford), Varnhagen, "Zu den Sprichwörter Hendings," 193 (also in Cambridge MS., stanza 21, 186).
84. Thomas Usk, *Testament of Love*, Book 2, ch. 9, 109, lines 129–30.
85. *A Talkyng of þe Loue of God*, 38, lines 13–14.
86. *Firumbras*, lines 423, in *Firumbras and Otuel and Roland*, 15.
87. "The Proverbis of Wysdom," 244, line 14.
88. The ubiquity of these proverbs is further evidenced by the number of proverb collections in which they appear; see, for example: *The Wordsworth Dictionary of Proverbs*, 60; *Oxford*

in uprodor   eadigra gehwam
æfter bealusiðe   bote lifes,
lifigendra gehwam   langsumne ræd[89]
[In heaven above, to each of the blessed the reward of life after the baleful journey, to each of the living, long-lasting gain]

gyf him edwenden   æfre scolde
bealuwa bisigu,   bot eft cuman[90]
[If he should ever experience change or relief from his evil affliction]

se þe him bealwa to   bote gelyfde[91]
[He who expected from him relief from troubles]

    gif we sona eft
þara bealudæda   bote gefremmaþ[92]
[If we immediately make restitution for those sinful deeds]

Habbað wræcmæcgas   wergan gæstas,
hetlen helsceaþa,   hearde genyrwad,
gebunden bealorapum.   Is seo bot gelong
eall æt þe anum,   ece dryhten.[93]
[Wicked spirits, hostile devils, have hard beset the exiles, bound them with evil fetters. The remedy depends entirely on you alone, eternal God.]

Forgif me to lisse,   lifgende god,
bitre bealodæde.   Ic þa bote gemon,
cyninga wuldor—cume to, gif ic mot.[94]
[Mercifully forgive me, living God, for my bitter, evil deeds. I ask for the remedy, glory of kings; let me come to it, if I may.]

ond eal þæt mancynn   þe him mid wunige,
elþeodigra   inwitwrasnum,

Dictionary of English Proverbs, 28; *A Dictionary of the Proverbs in England*, B59; Bartlett Jere Whiting, *Proverbs in the Earlier English Drama*, 193.

    89. *Exodus*, lines 4–6, in *The Junius Manuscript*, 91.
    90. *Beowulf*, lines 280–81, in *Klaeber's Beowulf*, 12.
    91. Ibid., line 909, 32.
    92. *Elene*, line 514b–15, in *The Vercelli Book*, 80.
    93. *Advent Lyric 10 (Christ I)*, lines 363–66, in *The Exeter Anthology*, I.59.
    94. *Contrition A (Resignation A)*, lines 19–21, in ibid., I.337.

bealuwe gebundene.   Him sceal bot hraðe
weorþan in worulde[95]
[And (free) all the people who dwell with him, bound in trouble, from the hostile fetters of their foes. They shall quickly have help in this world.]

The germ of the Middle English proverbs is present in these Old English collocations, as they all assume, logically, that "bale" necessitates or is followed by "boot." However, the Old English examples show significant variation in the ways that they deploy the two terms. In four of the examples (over half), *bealu* appears as part of a compound, which gives it a more specific meaning. For example, *bealodæde* ("sinful deeds") is more specific than simple *bealu* ("trouble"). In another three examples, the two words appear together in the same line, but in different sentences. Whiting's B18 regularly (though not exclusively) links "bale" and "boot" with the verb "come," which we also see in the first of the Old English examples, while the regular use of the adverb "after" is paralleled by the use of *æfter* in *Exodus* and of *eft* in the second and third Old English examples. However, B22, which relies not only on the alliteration of "bale" and "boot" but also on the rhyme, or near rhyme, of "mest" or "hest" with "nest," is more lasting; I've merely cut off my examples in the early sixteenth century. Thus, I would conclude that the alliterative collocation of *bealu* and *bot* was not proverbial in Old English, but that its frequent use led to the fixing of proverbial form sometime later on. Whether or not I am correct in this assessment, we can observe that the example of "bale and boot" illustrates a continuity of thought and expression linking the Old and Middle English periods.

Wine and women make wise men go backwards (Whiting W358)
Some proverbs maintain alliteration from the Old English to the Middle English period, but may owe their consistency of meaning across that span to reinforcement by Latin authority. For example, the Bible warns the "wise man" against the dangers of wine and women: "Vinum et mulieres apostatare faciunt sapientes" (Ecclus. 19.2). Both Old and Middle English versions of this *sententia* adorn it with alliteration:

Win [and] wif awedan doð witan[96]
[Wine and woman drive the wise man mad]

---

95. *Andreas*, lines 945–48a, in *The Vercelli Book*, 29.
96. Defensor of Ligugé, *Defensor's Liber scintillarum: With an interlinear Anglo-Saxon Version*, 105; the Latin is "Uinum et mulieres apostatare faciunt sapientes."

Win [and] druncene wif gedoð hwilon þæt witon maffiað[97]
[Wine and a drunken woman sometimes make the wise man go astray]

Wine and women into apostasie
Cause wise men to fall[98]

The wyse man sayth that by wyn and by wymmen comen many evyls and inconvenyents.[99]

In all of the examples, we find triple alliteration on "wine," "women," and "wise," despite some variable expression of the specific problems to be caused. Defensor offers the briefest sentence, while Chrodegang adds some interesting modifiers in specifying that a *drunken* woman may *sometimes* exert a bad influence. The version from the Middle English *Remedie of Love* is clearly related to the Wycliffite translation of Ecclus. 19.2: "Wyn and wymmen maken also wise men to go bacward."[100] Caxton's *Cato* moves farthest from the others by refiguring the wise man from victim to speaker, but his sentence maintains the alliteration and the core idea nonetheless, despite deriving from a French, prose version.

Not surprisingly, this proverb seems most popular among Anglo-Saxons in a monastic environment, where warnings against drunkenness and lust were fairly common. Because we lack an Old English translation of Ecclesiasticus, we cannot say whether the alliteration began there or arose because translators of Defensor and Chrodegang found it easy and desirable to create alliterative *sententiae* using what are, after all, very common words. The Wycliffite translator of Ecclus. may have felt the same impulse, or may have inherited a verbal tradition in which the alliteration already inhered. In any case, what we seem to have here is a sententia or proverb that owes its origin and much of its transmission to Latin textual authority, but derives its form from the vernacular, alliterative tradition.

The Apple of one's eye (Whiting A156)

Roughly the same process that warned the wise against wine and women provides us with the phrase "the apple of one's eye." Here we are dealing not with a

---

97. Chrodegang, *The Old English Version of the Enlarged Rule of Chrodegang Together with the Latin Original*, ch. 60, 74; the Latin is "Uinum et mulieres ebriose apostatare faciunt sapientes" (72).

98. Attributed (mistakenly) to John Lydgate, *The Remedy of Love*, in W. Gurney Benham, *A Book of Quotations, Proverbs, and Household Words*, 199, and by Philip Hugh Dalbiac, *Dictionary of Quotations*, 346.

99. William Caxton, *Distichs of Cathon*, cited from Whiting, *Proverbs . . . before 1500*, W358 (649).

100. Ecclesiasticus 19.2 in *The Holy Bible . . . in the Earliest English Versions Made . . . by John Wycliffe and His Followers*, 3.158.

proverb per se, but with a "proverbial phrase," to use Whiting's term. The persistence of this particular phrase is assisted by its association with translations of Psalm 16.8: "A resistentibus dexterae tuae custodi me, ut pupillam oculi"[101] [Like the apple of your eye, keep me from those who resist your right hand]. The earliest example of this translation appears in the prose of the Old English *Paris Psalter*: "Geheald me, Drihten, and beorh me, swa swa man byrhð þam æplum on his eagum mid his bræwum"[102] [Hold and protect me, Lord, just as one protects with his brows the apples of his eyes]. King Alfred employed the phrase for his translation of Boethius: "hi scilde swa geornlice swa (swa) mon deð þone æppel on his eagan"[103] [I shield them as zealously as one does the apple of his eye]. Much later, Richard Rolle maintains the vocalic alliteration in his *Psalter*: "kepe me as the appile of the eghe,"[104] but by the fifteenth century, the phrase has lost both its biblical context and its association with the idea of protection: "he was more tender than is the apple of þe eye."[105] Henceforth, the phrase simply indicates anything that is personally precious.[106] The history of this collocation provides a clear example of how proverbial expressions can originate in one language domain—Latin ecclesiastical—and end up in a different language—English—and free from association with any specific domain.

These, then, are the Middle English alliterative proverbs for which I can discuss an Old English origin with some confidence. Later in this study, I will examine the contexts of these proverbs, which will tell us more about how they were transmitted (at least in writing), but for now, we may observe simply that some Old English alliterative proverbs and phrases continued to be used in the Middle English period. Some of these proverbs were linked to the written Latin tradition while others seem to have moved about more freely.

MIDDLE ENGLISH PROVERBS WITHOUT OLD ENGLISH PARALLELS (GERMANIC VOCABULARY)

Far more numerous than the proverbs discussed above are alliterative proverbs in Middle English that could be of Old English origin based on their

---

101. On the historical development of the translation of "pupillam" as "apple," see Marbury B. Ogle, "The Apple of the Eye."
102. Psalm 16.8, in *Liber Psalmorum: The West-Saxon Psalms*, 30–31.
103. *King Alfred's Old English Version of Boethius De Consolatione Philosophiae*, 133.
104. Psalm 16.9, in Richard Rolle, *The Psalter or Psalms of David and Certain Canticles*, 56.
105. *The Tretyse of Loue*, 64; see Whiting, *Proverbs . . . before 1500*, A156.
106. For later examples, see Archer Taylor and B. J. Whiting, *Dictionary of American Proverbs and Proverbial Phrases, 1820–1880*, 8; Tilley, *Dictionary of the Proverbs in England*, A290; Whiting, *Modern Proverbs and Proverbial Sayings*, A105.

vocabulary, but for which there is no evidence of historical continuity. Two contingencies account for their alliteration: (a) These proverbs (or collocations) did exist in Old English, but do not appear in the small corpus of Old English text that survives; and (b) during the Middle English period, alliteration continued as a popular element—both structural and ornamental—for newly minted proverbs. There is not much more to be said about point (a), but point (b) is amply illustrated in the examples that follow.

I have already discussed one Middle English alliterative proverb that could be descended from an Old English version, but probably is not: "Lief child behoves lore." In that case, the Old English corpus yielded the appropriate lexical items in close proximity, but not linked in such a way as to prove a clear connection to the Middle English proverb. In many other Middle English proverbs, the alliterative word pairing, though Germanic in origin, is not matched in Old English. It would be tedious and pointless to list all of these examples, so I will treat only those of some special interest.

Words are but wind (Whiting W643)
"Words are but wind" tantalizes with hints of a late Old English or early Middle English origin. Ælfric phrases the comparison as a simile, which is an accepted proverbial structure—"Eower word syndon winde gelice"[107]—but the second-person pronoun gives the sentence a nonproverbial specificity. It is not until the mid-fourteenth century that we find this idea expressed in a generalized, declarative sentence: "Bot word fares als dose the wind."[108] The connection of words with wind continues to be made with a variety of sentence structures through at least the seventeenth century,[109] but it also settles in as a consistently formulated proverb:

For word is wynd[110]

Word is but wynde[111]

---

107. Ælfric, Nonis Februariis VIII: "Natale Sancte Agatha Uirginis," in *Aelfric's Lives of Saints*, I.196, line 19.
108. *Ywain and Gawain*, 5, line 143.
109. See Morris Palmer Tilley, *Elizabethan Proverb Lore in Lyly's "Euphues" and in Pettie's "Petite Pallace" with Parallels from Shakespeare*, #713, 338; *Wordsworth Dictionary of Proverbs*, 710–11; and *Oxford Dictionary of English Proverbs*, 915.
110. John Gower, *Confessio Amantis*, Book 3, line 2768, in *The Complete Works of John Gower*, II.300.
111. John Lydgate, *Troy Book*, Book 1, line 4383, cited from Whiting, *Proverbs . . . before 1500*, W643, 670.

for wordis are as þe wynde[112]

For as it is sayd wordes is nothynge but wynde[113]

Wordes are but wynd.[114]

The linking of words and wind seems to have begun as a figurative image, one that became very popular and lasting, and also one that gave rise to a proverb which, like most expressions of this image, was held together by alliteration.

When Will oversties Wit, then Will and Wit are lost (Whiting W268)

Not every proverb takes the form of a declarative sentence; the imperative is somewhat less common but certainly well attested as a proverbial structure. Just as "word and wind" settled into a declarative proverb, "wit and will" found their most consistent form in an imperative sentence. The first two examples of proverbs using this alliterative pairing stem from the mid-thirteenth and late fourteenth centuries and take declarative form:

Hwenne-so wil wit ofer-stieð
Þenne is wil and wit for-lore[115]

Whan wille over wyt wryes,
Than gothe wille witt byforn.[116]

However, nearly all examples from the fifteenth century and later favor the imperative, introduced most often with the verb "let":

Let þi witt passe þi wille[117]

Bot set thi wyt thi will to dant[118]

---

112. "Christ before Pilate I: The Dream of Pilate's Wife" (Tapiteres and Couchers), line 236, in *The York Plays,* ed. Richard Beadle, 261.
113. William Nevill, *The Castell of Pleasure,* 102, line 659.
114. "The Beauty and Good Properties of Women, or Calisto and Melibæa," cited from Whiting, *Proverbs in the Earlier English Drama,* 184.
115. "Will and Wit," lines 1–2, in *English Lyrics of the XIIIth Century,* 65.
116. *Titus and Vespasian, or, The Destruction of Jerusalem,* xxvii, cited from Whiting, *Proverbs . . . before 1500,* W268, 642.
117. G. Schleich, "Die Sprichwörter Hendings und die Proverbis of Wysdom," 221: *Proverbis of Wysdom;* Whiting, *Proverbs . . . before 1500,* W408.
118. *The Consail and Teiching at the Vys Man Gaif his Sone,* in *Ratis Raving and Other Early Scots Poems on Morals,* 70; Whiting, *Proverbs . . . before 1500,* W408.

Let no3t þi wille passe þi witte[119]

Lett never thi wyll overcome thi wytte[120]

Lett never þi wyll þi wytt over-lede[121]

Let not your will over-gang your wit[122]

Lete neuere þi wil þi witt ouer lede[123]

And let not will vsurpe, where wit should rule[124]

Bot witt pas wylle
Vyce wil vertewe spylle.[125]

The persistent use of the imperative for this proverb may derive, to some degree, from its popularity with authors of explicitly didactic texts, but these examples are all independently derived and so must reflect an established and ongoing proverbial tradition. The alliteration of "will" and "wit" forms a very compact and stable contrast that finds its niche in being exploited by an imperative opening.

Well Fights that well flees (Whiting F141)

Some Middle English sententiae are clearly marked as proverbs from their earliest appearances, even if there is no surviving evidence for the proverb's currency before the Conquest. The proverbiality of an utterance may be stated explicitly, or may be implicit in the context in which the sentence is found. One example of such a proverb is "Well fights that well flees" (Whiting F141).[126] This proverb first appears in English in the thirteenth century:

---

119. "Always Try to Say the Best," line 20, in *Religious Lyrics of the XIVth Century*, ed. Carleton Brown, 192.
120. *The Epistle of Othea to Hector*, cited from Whiting, *Proverbs . . . before 1500*, W268, 642.
121. *Proverbs of Good Counsel*, in *Queene Elizabethes Achademy*, 69.
122. *Eger and Grime*, 261, line 1305.
123. "Of the Manners to bring one to Honour and Welfare," line 7, in *The Babees Book*, 34.
124. Thomas Hughes, *The Misfortunes of Arthur: A Critical, Old-spelling Edition*, 78, scene 2, line 18; see Whiting, *Proverbs in the Earlier English Drama*, 298.
125. "Fyrst þou sal luf god and drede," lines 5–6, in Karl Brunner, "Me. Disticha (aus Hs. Add. 37049)," 87.
126. The collocation "fleo oððe feohte" appears twice in Old English, both times in a legal, but not proverbial, setting; see Felix Liebermann, *Die Gesetze der Angelsachsen*, II Æthelred 11 and II Cnut 114.

Wel fi3t, þat wel fleþ[127]

"Wel fi3t þat wel fli3t," seiþ þe wise.[128]

The first example is found in *The Proverbs of Hendyng*, so it is contextually marked as proverbial; the second version appears in *The Owl and the Nightingale*, a poem that is famous as a repository for early Middle English proverbs, and it is marked as a sentence spoken by "the wise." Clearly, then, "Well fights that well flees" was an alliterative proverb firmly established in English by the mid-thirteenth century. The proverb remained known in its alliterative form through to the end of the Middle English period, as Whiting cites this example from around 1450:

for it is an olde sawe, he feghtith wele that fleith faste.[129]

Besides its early attestations and its temporal longevity, "Well fights that well flees" is further interesting for being an international and multilingual proverb. Earlier than any of the Middle English examples, the proverb is found in the twelfth-century romance *Ipomedon*, by Hue de Rotelande:

Suvent ad l'um dit en dedut: Ben se cumbat cil, ki ben fut[130]
[Often it has been said in jest: He fights well who flees well.]

For Hue, an Anglo-Norman writer, the proverb is already established, though in French or English first we cannot say. The fourteenth century yields two Middle High German versions of the proverb, both alliterative, though one has been expanded into a rhyming couplet:

Wer wol gevluhet der hât wol gevochten[131]
[Who flees well has fought well]

Wer vliuhet daz man vliehen sol,

---

127. *Proverbs of Hendyng* (Oxford), Varnhagen, "Zu den Sprichwörtern Hendings," stanza 10, 193 (Cambridge MS., stanza 9, 183).

128. *The Owl and the Nightingale*, 6, line 176.

129. *The Early English Versions of the Gesta Romanorum*, 374; Whiting, *Proverbs . . . before 1500*, F141.

130. Hue de Rotelande, *Ipomedon*, line 7409, cited from *Thesaurus proverbiorum* Fliehen 4.1.2.3 (vol. 3, 307).

131. Hermann von Fritzlar, *Heiligenleben*, cited from ibid.

Sicher der hât gevochten wol.¹³²
[Who flees when he ought has truly fought well.]

Because medieval proverbs traveled easily from one vernacular language to another (and between Latin and the vernaculars), it is impossible to pin down the origin of this proverb. It is enough to note that as one of its changes this international saying finds early and stable expression in English, in alliterative form.

Mastery mows the meadow down (Whiting M413)
"Mastery mows the meadow down" is a proverb that enters English later than "Well fights that well flees" but has a similarly interesting relationship with versions in other languages. This proverb seems to be of French origin, as variants of "Force paist le pré" [Power grazes the lea] appear as early as the twelfth century and are very common thereafter,¹³³ but the earliest English examples are not found until the fifteenth century. A Latin version, expanded to add rhyme, appears as early as the French: "Vis pascit pratum, vis prati fert dominatum"¹³⁴ [Force grazes the meadow, force rules the meadow]. The French and Latin versions of the proverb, brief as they are, both employ alliteration; when the proverb is translated into English, the alliteration is maintained (sometimes even expanded from two elements to three), even though this necessitates a change of vocabulary:

Bot it is said in commone sawis
That mastry mawis þe medow doune aye¹³⁵

Strenght moweth the medowe¹³⁶

Strenhgth mowes down þe medow.¹³⁷

The English proverb, with its new alliteration, continues into the nineteenth century.¹³⁸

---

132. Ulrich Boner, *Der Edelstein*, cited from ibid.
133. See *Thesaurus proverbiorum* Wiese 2 (vol. 13, 98–99); and James Woodrow Hassell Jr., *Middle French Proverbs, Sentences, and Proverbial Phrases*, F113 (116).
134. Jakob Werner, *Lateinische Sprichwörter und Sinnsprüche des Mittelalters aus Handschriften gesammelt*, V63 (124).
135. Andrew of Wyntoun, *Original Chronicle of Andrew of Wyntoun*, III.314, lines 1498–99.
136. W. A. Pantin, "A Medieval Collection of Latin and English Proverbs and Riddles, from the Rylands Latin MS. 394," 104.
137. Förster, "Die mittelenglische Sprichwörtersammlung in Douce 52," 54.
138. *Oxford Dictionary of English Proverbs*, 518.

Cold Rede is quean rede (Whiting R66)

The exigencies of translation also affect alliterative patterning in "Cold rede is quean rede." The proverb (which in Old Norse is "Köld eru kvenna ráð") is almost certainly of Scandinavian origin, being found in Old Norse poetry as early as the ninth or tenth century and in numerous of the sagas.[139] The Old Norse examples consistently alliterate on "köld" and "kvenna," which is also where we find the alliteration in the earliest Middle English version of the proverb:

> for hit is said in lede.
> Cold red is quene red.[140]

By Chaucer's day, "quene" was no longer much used as a synonym for "woman," so his version of the proverb replaces both it and "red":

> Wommennes conseils been ful ofte colde.[141]

The lexical change and the end-rhymed context of "The Nun's Priest's Tale" have given this fourteenth-century variant a new vocabulary and rhythm, but the fact that it remains alliterative shows the strength of the tradition.

Better is List than lither strength (Whiting L381)

Of course, not every proverb lasts forever, and lexical change does claim its victims. "Better is list than lither strength" or "better is cunning than evil strength" appears fairly commonly in texts from c.1200-c.1400:

> Betere is wis liste þen luðer strengðe[142]

> ȝuse, ȝuse, lauerd king. Hit wes ȝare iqueðen
> þat betere is liste þene ufel strenðe[143]

> ffor better liste þen lythere strenght[144]

---

139. For a useful discussion of this proverb, see Richard L. Harris, "'(opt) eru köld kvenna ráð'—a Critically Popular Old Icelandic Proverb and Its Uses in the Íslendingasögur and Elsewhere."
140. *The Proverbs of Alfred*, line 444, ed. O. Arngart, II.118.
141. Geoffrey Chaucer, "The Nun's Priest's Tale," VII.3256, *The Riverside Chaucer*, 259.
142. *Ancrene Wisse, Edited from Ms. Corpus Christi College Cambridge 402*, 138.
143. Laȝamon, *Brut or Hystoria Brutonum*, 442, lines 8589-90.
144. Richard of St. Victor, *Benjamin Minor* [anon. English trans.], in *Yorkshire Writers: Richard Rolle of Hampole, an English Father and His Followers*, I.170.

betyr is list þen liþer strengþe[145]

Betir is list þan leþir strengþe[146]

bot wirche more wiþ a list þen wiþ any liþer strengþe[147]

Betere is red thene rap, and liste thene lither streingthe.[148]

As these examples make clear, the alliterative pairing of "list" and "lither" helped to give this proverb a consistent form for about two hundred years. However, the use of "list" to mean "cunning" faded out of English sometime around the first half of the fifteenth century,[149] and the proverb lost both alliteration and consistent form. The basic idea that cleverness or wisdom can prevail over brute strength continues to be expressed proverbially, but without any fixed form.[150] In this instance, then, change of vocabulary neither killed nor really transformed the proverb, but left it without its most consistently structured form.

Be Ware ere you be woe (Whiting W45)
Sometimes proverbs are not just victims of lexical change, but also markers of that change. For example, the word "beware" has a complicated history. It begins as a phrase, but is found written as a single word as early as 1300; however, up until around 1600, "it was used only in those parts of the vb. where *be* is found, viz. the imper., infin., and pres. subj."[151]—so grammatically, it still behaved as a phrase rather than a single word. The most common Middle English proverb using "be ware" happens to be an alliterative one: "Be ware ere you be woe." In this proverb, which appears from 1381–1506 but seems to have been especially popular in the fifteenth century, the sound pattern requires the parsing of "ware" as a separate, stressed word that alliterates with "woe":

---

145. "A Tretyse of þe Stodye of Wysdome þat Men Clepen Beniamyn," in *Deonise Hid Diuinite and Other Treatises on Contemplative Prayer Related to "The Cloud of Unknowing,"* 41.
146. "Pistle of Preier" in *Deonise Hid Diuinite*, 58.
147. *The Cloud of Unknowing*, ch. 46, in *The Cloud of Unknowing and the Book of Privy Counselling*, 87.
148. Giraldus Cambrensis, *Descriptio Kambriae*, Book 1, ch. 12, in *Giraldi Cambrensis Opera*, VI.188.
149. See OED list, *n*.2.
150. See Whiting, *Proverbs . . . before 1500*, M281 and S833, and *Oxford Dictionary of English Proverbs*, 898; for Medieval Latin examples expressing the same idea, see Deskis, *"Beowulf" and the Medieval Proverb Tradition*, 122 and 132.
151. OED beware, *v*. 1.

be war or þe be ye wo¹⁵²

He is wys ȝat kan be war or him be wo¹⁵³

Eche man be war, er hym be wo¹⁵⁴

He has wysdam and wyt, I tel ȝow trewly,
Þat can be ware or he be wo and leue in clene lyue¹⁵⁵

In wele be ware or þou be wo¹⁵⁶

In wele be ware or ye be woo¹⁵⁷

That folowyth counseyle of hys frende
He may be war or hym be woo¹⁵⁸

But well were he that ware so wyse,
That coude be ware or he be wo.¹⁵⁹

In this instance, then, the alliterative proverb exerts a conservative linguistic influence by treating "be ware" as a phrase (no matter how the two elements might be spaced). As we saw with the pair "list/lither," proverbs often protect archaic vocabulary (at least as long as the vocabulary can still be comprehended), and the use of such archaic words or phrases in an alliterative pattern assists in that preservation.

Old Sin makes new shame (Whiting S338)

Our next proverb is also frequently attested and shows the stability that alliteration can provide to a proverb. "Old sin makes new shame" appears in medieval English texts from roughly 1300–1500. Technically, "sin" and "shame"

---

152. "John Ball's Letter, II (1381)," in *Historical Poems of the XIVth and XVth Centuries*, 55.
153. "Poetical Scraps" in *Reliquiae Antiquae*, II.120.
154. The line serves as a refrain in the poem "Man, be warre er the be woo," in *Twenty-Six Political and Other Poems*, 60–64.
155. John Audelay, "Marcolf and Solomon," (Poem No. 2), lines 42–43, in *The Poems of John Audelay*, ed. Ella K. Whiting, 11.
156. Ibid., Poem No. 18 (*incip.* "Here I conclud al my makyng"), 140, line 218.
157. *The Early English Carols*, no. 338, 231; see also no. 355, 239.
158. *Proverbs of Salamon*, stanza 18, lines 1–2, in Brunner, "Spätme. Lehrgedichte," 179.
159. *The Kalender of Shepherdes*, III.66, lines 14–15.

should not be treated as a pair, as /s/ and /ʃ/ do not alliterate in classical Old English or Middle English poetry,[160] but proverbs do not need to be classical in their stylistic features, and it seems very clear that the (near) alliteration of these two words helps this compact proverb maintain a consistent form over two centuries of use.[161]

The earliest example comes from the late thirteenth century—"Old sinne makes newe shame!"[162]—followed by three more from the fourteenth century, one of which is marked as a common saying:

Senne makeþ nywe schame,
þaȝ hy for-ȝete be;[163]

Men sein, "Old Senne newe schame"[164]

So that the comun clamour tolde
The newe schame of Sennes olde.[165]

By the middle of the fifteenth century, the proverb appears in several manuscript collections of English proverbs, sometimes with Latin versions alongside.[166] In that century, it continues to prove popular in didactic poetry, chronicle, and romance:

Old syn makes newe schame[167]

---

160. "Sin" and "shame" are treated as an alliterative pair once in Old English, in the late *Lord's Prayer II* (line 84): "Forgif us ure synna, / þæt us ne scamige eft" as seen in *Anglo-Saxon Minor Poems*, edited by Elliott Van Kirk Dobbie, 73. Dobbie suggests that *scylda* might be a better reading in line 84a, "But *synna* makes satisfactory sense" (186).

161. The proverb is less stable in other languages. For Latin and Dutch versions, see *Proverbia Communia: A Fifteenth Century Collection of Dutch Proverbs Together with the Low German Version*, #582 and note, 252–53. For Middle French examples of the fourteenth and fifteenth centuries, see Hassell, *Middle French Proverbs*, P100 (195).

162. *Havelok*, 67, line 2462.

163. William of Shoreham, "De septem mortalibus peccatis," lines 17–18, in *The Poems of William of Shoreham*, 98.

164. John Gower, *Confessio Amantis*, Book 3, line 2033, in *The Complete Works of John Gower*, II.281.

165. Gower, *Confessio Amantis*, Book 7, lines 5115–16, in *The Complete Works of John Gower*, III.377.

166. Meech, "Collection of Proverbs," 121; Förster, "Die mittelenglische Sprichwörtersammlung in Douce 52," 55; and Pantin, "A Medieval Collection of Latin and English Proverbs and Riddles," 104 (with "Elde" for "Olde").

167. "Fyrst thou sal luf god and drede," line 117, in K. Brunner, "Me. Disticha (aus Hs. Add. 37049)," 90.

> Thus synnes olde, make shames come full newe¹⁶⁸
>
> I now perceyue wel & see that the proverbe that is said commonly is trew, that is "that olde synne reneweth shame"¹⁶⁹
>
> ffor men seyen in olde speche,
> Grene wounde nys bote game,
> and ole synne maketh newe schame.¹⁷⁰

In the last two of these citations, the saying is explicitly marked as proverbial; in the very last, it is also linked in rhyme to another proverb cast in alliterative form.¹⁷¹ With its consistency and longevity, "Old sin makes new shame" provides an excellent example of how alliteration (or perceived alliteration) assists proverbial cohesiveness in the Middle English period.

Ever at the End wrong will wend (Whiting E82)
The lexical stability afforded by alliteration is even more remarkable for the proverb "Ever at the end wrong will wend," as this proverb is not only longer than the last in most of its variants, but consistently links two alliterating (or assonant) pairs of words in two phrases tied together by end rhyme. In short, this proverb constitutes a tightly bound, two- or four-line poem. The "Englishness" of the proverb is established by around 1300, when Walter of Henley cites it in his French-language (and proverb-studded) *Husbandry*:

> kar hom dit en englyse On ȝeer oþer to wro[n]ge wylle on hone go. Ant euere aten hende wrong wile wende¹⁷²
> [As is said in English, wrong will go in hand one year to the next, and ever at the end, wrong will wend.]

Around the same time, the couplets appear in the *Arthour and Merlin* of the Auchinleck Manuscript:

---

168. John Hardyng, *The Chronicle of Iohn Hardyng*, ch. 114, 213.
169. *Melusine*, compiled (. . .) by Jean D'Arras, Englisht about 1500, ch. 19, 79.
170. "God of hefne, þat sittest in trone," lines 217–19, in Frank A. Patterson, "A Sermon on the Lord's Prayer," 411.
171. For other examples of "A green wound is soon healed" (none before the sixteenth century), see *Oxford Dictionary of English Proverbs*, 337.
172. Walter of Henley, *Walter of Henley's Husbandry, together with an anonymous Husbandry, Seneschaucie, and Robert Grosseteste's Rules*, 4.

> Men seyt ȝere and oþer to
> Wrong wil an hond go
> And euer at þe nende
> Wrong wil wende.¹⁷³

Not surprisingly, a century later, the sentence has been shortened to its semantic core—"Euer att end wrong wyll wend"¹⁷⁴—which is also how it appears in the mid-fifteenth century:

> Ever at the ende wrong wil out wende.¹⁷⁵

The latest version (c.1500) located by Whiting (or myself) has reexpanded the proverb and replaced the final word in a way that maintains both rhyme and alliteration in the sentence:

> A ȝere or a wronge will onne goo,
> And euer at the ȝynde wronge will haue woo.¹⁷⁶

As evidenced by these examples, the structural feature of alliteration (sometimes with rhyme) helps to maintain the form of this proverb over a long period of time, in both prose and poetic texts.

When the Steed is stolen make fast the stable door (Whiting S697)

Alliteration also assists the coherence of "When the steed is stolen make fast the stable door," which was a well-cited proverb in Britain from about 1400–1700.¹⁷⁷ The syntax of the sentence can vary somewhat from instance to instance, but the triple alliteration of "steed, stolen, stable" provides a consistent core:

> ... for whan the grete Stiede
> Is stole, thanne he taketh hiede,

---

173. *Of Arthour and of Merlin*, I.139, lines 1895–98.
174. "The Proverbis of Wysdom," 244, line 29.
175. "Fyrst thou sal luf god and drede," line 33, in Brunner, "Me. Disticha (aus Hs. Add. 37049)," 88.
176. R. H. Bowers, "Hichecoke's 'This Worlde is but a Vanyte' (HM 183)," 333, lines 33–34.
177. For instances dating from the sixteenth through eighteenth centuries, see *Wordsworth Dictionary of Proverbs*, 598–99. For examples from drama of the mid-sixteenth century, see Whiting, *Proverbs in the Earlier English Drama*, 130, 144, and 283.

And makth the stable dore fast[178]

When þe stede ys stole hit ys tyme to schette þe stabell' doyr[179]

Whan the stede ys stole, than shytte the stable-dore[180]

Whan the stede is stolen, shit the stabill dore[181]

Whan the stede is stolyn to shyt the stable dore[182]

When the stede is stolyn, spar the stable dur[183]

Whan the stede is stolne, shut the stable durre.[184]

The alliterative pattern of the basic proverb proved too much to resist for two Scottish (nonalliterative) poets of around 1500, who added a fourth alliterating element, "ste(i)k":

Bot all to late to stek þe stable nowe;
Begane I quhane þe stede Is stollin away[185]

The steid is stollin, steik the dure; lat se
Quhat may avale; God wait! the stall is tume![186]

Other writers or proverb collectors of the fifteenth century reduce the amount of alliteration by replacing "steed" with "horse":

---

178. Gower, *Confessio Amantis*, Book 4, lines 901–3, in *The Complete Works of John Gower*, II.325.
179. Meech, "Collection of Proverbs," 118.
180. Max Förster, "Kleinere Mittelenglische Texte," 204.
181. Richard Hill, *Songs, Carols, and other Miscellaneous Poems from the Balliol Ms. 354, Richard Hill's Commonplace-Book*, ed. Roman Dyboski, 128.
182. Alexander Barclay, *The Ship of Fools*, I.76.
183. John Skelton, *Garlande or Chapelet of Laurell*, line 1435, in *John Skelton: The Complete English Poems*, 352.
184. John Heywood, *John Heywood's "A Dialogue of Proverbs,"* 116, line 633.
185. *Lay of Sorrow*, lines 84–85, in Kenneth G. Wilson, "*The Lay of Sorrow* and *The Lufaris Complaynt*: An Edition," 717.
186. Gavin Douglas, *King Hart*, lines 25–26, in *The Poetical Works of Gavin Douglas*, I.107.

When þe hors is stolyn, steyke þe stabul dore[187]

When þe hors is stole, steke þe stabull-dore[188]

It is a comyn proverbe and trouthe it is. whan the hors is stolen. it is to late to shete the stable.[189]

Despite the variation found in some versions of this proverb, its alliteration is noteworthy not only for its frequency but also for the fact that it seems to arise quite late in the Middle English period: no examples appear before the late fourteenth century. Two of the alliterating words—"steed" and "stolen"—are of Old English origin, but "stable" is borrowed from French and does not appear in English texts until the mid-thirteenth century. The proverb itself is probably French in origin, though in that language it does not alliterate. The twelfth-century proverb-poem *Les proverbes au vilain* (upon which the Middle English *Proverbs of Hendyng* was partially modeled) offers: "A tart ferme on l'estable, quant li chevaus est perduz"[190] [Too late to close the stable, when the horse is lost]. J. W. Hassell has collected more French examples from the thirteenth through the fifteenth centuries.[191] Medieval Latin versions first appear in the thirteenth century.[192] The frequent appearance of this proverb allows us to postulate a history for it: the proverb seems to have arisen in France around the twelfth century, whence it spread to England and, in French and Latin, elsewhere in Europe. In England, the proverb seems to have taken its decisively Germanic alliterative form from the beginning, despite its Romance origin, which confirms the robustness of alliterative patterning of proverbs in Middle English.

For the Less to lose the more (Whiting L207)
Attestations of this next proverb are also all late medieval, are also sometimes marked as proverbial, and also show a certain amount of variation. The alliterative wording of the proverb vacillates between "less/lose" and "less/leave":

---

187. Pantin, "Medieval Collection of Latin and English Proverbs and Riddles," 97.
188. Förster, "Die mittelenglische Sprichwörtersammlung in Douce 52," 46.
189. William Caxton, tr., *Ovyde, Hys Book of Methamorphose, Books X–XV,* 17. For an even less alliterative form of the proverb, see Caxton, *The Fables of Aesop as First Printed by William Caxton in 1484,* II.245: "how be it that it was not tyme to shette the stable whan the horses ben loste & gone"; see also the other examples listed in Whiting, *Proverbs . . . before 1500,* S697.
190. *Proverbes au vilain. Die Sprichwörter des gemeinen Mannes,* stanza 49, 22.
191. Hassell, *Middle French Proverbs,* C127, 23.
192. *Thesaurus Proverbiorum* STALL 2 (vol. 11, 100–103).

> For often times of scarsnesse
> It hath be sen, that for the lesse
> Is lost the more . . . [193]

> For dyne of doel of lureȝ lesse
> Ofte mony mon forgos þe mo[194]

> For the lesse me lefus the more[195]

> For þe lasse me lysed þe more[196]

> It is no wysemanys lore / to take þe las and leue þe more[197]

> In proverbs hyt ys seyde full yare:
> Mony for þe lesse forgoyþ þe mare.[198]

Expression of the basic semantic contrast between "less" and "more" remains quite stable; the variation comes in with respect to the verb linking those two elements ("lose" or "leave"), but the tendency toward alliteration limits the range of forms used. The brevity of this proverb allows it to fit easily into end-rhymed texts, which doubtless assisted in its literary transmission.

Seldom Seen soon forgotten (Whiting S130)

Another brief proverb maintained its alliterative form (in fact, triple alliteration) from the fourteenth into the eighteenth century, but in the latter part of that period came to be eclipsed by a nonalliterating rival. Judging by the results obtained by proverb collectors, the heyday of "Seldom seen soon forgotten" was roughly 1400–1550:

> þat selden I-seiȝe is sone forȝete[199]

---

193. Gower, *Confessio Amantis*, Book 5, lines 4777–79, in *The Complete Works of John Gower*, III.77.
194. *Pearl*, stanza 29, lines 339–40, in *The Works of the Gawain-Poet*, 225.
195. Förster, "Die mittelenglische Sprichwörtersammlung in Douce 52," 50.
196. Pantin, "Medieval Collection of Latin and English Proverbs and Riddles," 100.
197. Ibid., 93. Note the addition of end rhyme in this example, as well.
198. *The Romance of Guy of Warwick: The Second or 15th-century Version*, I.289, lines 1493–94.
199. "The Death of Edward III," line 8, in *Historical Poems of the XIVth and XVth Centuries*, 103.

Seld i-say ys sone fore-yete[200]

seldon seyn is sone for3ette[201]

Seldun sey, sone for-3ete[202]

Seldon seyen, son' for 3eton'[203]

for the wiseman saith: "Seldom seen, sone forgetyn"[204]

Zelde y-sey3e sone for3ete[205]

Seld y-sey & sone y-fryt[206]

Seld sene, sone forgotin[207]

She sayth that she hath seen hit wreten
That "seldyn seen is soon foryeten"[208]

... seldome sene, soone forgotten[209]

if ye loke hem lightly and see hem seld thei shall sone be fogete.[210]

Despite the quite evident popularity of this proverb, it eventually lost pride of place to another: "Out of Sight out of mind" (Whiting S307). "Out of sight out of mind" first appears in the sixteenth century and, with its parallelism and near rhyme, mostly overtakes the alliterative "Seldom seen soon forgotten." Still, the alliterative proverb clings to life alongside its successor, as in this

---

200. "Proverbis of Wysdom," 244, line 25.
201. "Ambulate," lines 31–32, in *Middle English Sermons Edited from British Museum MS. Royal 18 B. xxiii*, 77.
202. Förster, "Die mittelenglische Sprichwörtersammlung in Douce 52," 52.
203. Pantin, "Medieval Collection of Latin and English Proverbs and Riddles," 102.
204. *The Prose Ipomedon*, in *Ipomedon in drei englischen Bearbeitungen*, 326, line 36.
205. W, "Proverbs [From MS. Harl. 3362, of the end of the fifteenth century.]," 309.
206. Meech, "Collection of Proverbs," 118.
207. Hill, *Songs, Carols, and Miscellaneous Poems*, 129.
208. "Now wold I fayne," lines 19–20, in *A Literary Middle English Reader*, 416.
209. Heywood, *John Heywood's "A Dialogue of Proverbs*," 119, line 759.
210. John Paston I to Margaret Paston, 20 September 1465, in *Paston Letters and Papers of the Fifteenth Century*, I.145.

example from the twenty-first century: "Seldom seen, soon forgotten; out of sight, out of mind and all that."[211] As our next example will also show, alliteration remains common in English proverbs long after it ceases to serve as a structural element in English poetry.

First Look and afterward leap (Whiting L435)
For the twelfth through fifteenth centuries, one could argue that end rhyme was the most common and easily distinguished feature of most poetry, especially of courtly and/or literate poetry, but that alliteration persisted in an association with poetry in popular culture (or at least in some minority segment of culture). In the twenty-first century, this is no longer so: for most of the English-speaking populace, performed poetry entails end rhyme, as evidenced in genres like rap, hip-hop, country, and pop music, or slam poetry. Ironically, it is only the hyperliterate who, recognizing the roots of alliteration in English literary history, tend to use it in a structured (as opposed to ornamental) way. Proverbs, however, represent one locus of popular culture where alliteration still reigns as a structural element, and that is the point of my final example in this section: "First look and afterward leap," or, as it is more commonly known, "Look before you leap." Like some other Middle English alliterative proverbs, this one seems to have arisen late in the period, as its first recorded appearance is in a fifteenth-century collection, but in its longevity and frequency, it perhaps surpasses all others.[212] The early examples are these:

First loke and aftirward lepe;
Avyse the welle, or thow speke[213]

Loke or þu speke [*for* lepe] / and thynke or þu speke[214]

We say . . . "Look ere thou leap:" whose literal sense is, "Do nothing suddenly, or without advisement."[215]

---

211. Azar Nafisi, *Reading Lolita in Tehran: A Memoir in Books*, 319.
212. *Oxford Dictionary of English Proverbs*, 482, cites examples into the nineteenth century; *Wordsworth Dictionary of Proverbs*, 380, provides variants from the sixteenth through twentieth centuries; and Whiting himself collected a baker's dozen of examples from twentieth-century texts (*Modern Proverbs*, L216).
213. Förster, "Die mittelenglische Sprichwörtersammlung in Douce 52," 57.
214. National Library of Wales Peniarth MS. 356, p. 196, in Rosell Hope Robbins and John L. Cutler, eds., *Supplement to the Index of Middle English Verse*, 1941.5, 227.
215. William Tyndale, "The Interpretation of Scripture: The Four Senses of the Scripture," part 3 of *The Obedience of a Christian Man*, in *The Work of William Tyndale*, 340.

Although this proverb is very well known and generally understood in modern culture,[216] these earliest attestations, interestingly, surround it with explanation. In the first two, the metaphor of the proverb is defined and restricted as having to do with speech, whereas Tyndale employs the proverb in his general discussion of how figurative language functions, especially in the Bible. I cannot say who first coined this proverb, but we can follow by these examples the process by which it acquired its common meaning.

I began this section of my study by examining a Middle English alliterative proverb that may have begun quite early (Words are but wind), and I have concluded with one that began late but continues happily on. Along the way we have noted numerous features of the development of these proverbs. These alliterative proverbs may take the form of a declarative sentence (Cold rede is quean rede) or an imperative (Look before you leap). Some of them are multinational (Well fight that well flees), even if translation requires some changes to achieve alliteration (Mastery mows the meadow down). In most cases, their alliteration helps to maintain their form (Old sin makes new shame), although they are not immune to the vagaries of linguistic change (Better is list than lither strength). Some of these alliterative proverbs remain vibrantly current (Look before you leap), but others fall out of fashion (Seldom seen soon forgotten). All of the proverbs I have examined so far have relied on Germanic vocabulary for their alliteration, but, as we shall see next, the strength of the alliterative tradition in English proverbs is such that novel sayings continued to be created using the new French vocabulary with which English was infused following the Norman Conquest.

MIDDLE ENGLISH PROVERBS WITHOUT OLD ENGLISH PARALLELS (ROMANCE VOCABULARY)

Englishmen are envious (Whiting E107)

Although alliteration is much less common in French than in English proverbs, one can sometimes locate identical proverbs in both languages, as with "Englishmen are envious":

> we Englys men þeron shulde þynke,
> Þat enuyë vs nat blynk[217] (c.1303)

---

216. In one study, "Look before you leap" landed squarely in the top quartile for familiarity among 203 proverbs and sayings presented to American college undergraduates: Kenneth L. Higbee and Richard J. Millard, "Visual Imagery and Familiarity Ratings for 203 Sayings."

217. Robert Mannyng, *Handlyng Synne*, lines 4165–66, in *Robert of Brunne's Handlyng Synne*, 141.

these Inglisshemen most commonly have ever great envy at straungers[218] (1523)

Les Anglais sont envieux (Hassell, A153)[219]
[The English are envious]

Les Englès sont communement envieux sur tous estrangiers quant ilz sont à leur dessus (c.1352)
[The English are commonly envious of all strangers around them]

Li Englès sont communement envieus sour toutes estragnes gens (c.1380)
[The English are commonly envious of all foreigners.]

I have included approximate dates in this section because they show an interesting pattern. Based on the alliteration of the proverb and on the fact that it appears in English writings nearly fifty years before the French, one might conclude that we have here an English saying that was borrowed into French. On the other hand, "envy" and its adjectival form "envious" are French words that had to be loaned to English; furthermore, the sentiment of the proverb seems more likely to be French than English in its origin. A third possibility is that the "English" referred to in this proverb are the unwashed masses being disparaged by their noble, French-speaking superiors, in which case the proverb would be English (i.e., Anglo-Norman) in origin and available for appropriation by French writers on the continent. As so often happens when working with proverbs, the evidence is insufficient to allow us to reach a definitive conclusion, but the compactness of the French versions relative to the English, and the greater variation shown by the English versions, both make me suspect that, despite the "Englishness" of the alliteration, the proverb is a French (or Anglo-Norman) one to which the English authors simply allude.

The next example illustrates some stylistic differences between Middle English and Middle French proverbs. Both sets of proverbs warn against buying something sight unseen, but each uses a different barnyard image.

When the Pig is proffered open the poke (Whiting P192)
Wan man ȝevit þe a pig, opin þe powch[220]

---

218. Froissart, Jean, *The Chronicle of Froissart*, ch. 9, I.31.
219. Hassell, *Middle French Proverbs*.
220. *Proverbs of Hendyng* (Cambridge), Varnhagen, "Zu den Sprichwörtern Hendings," 189.

When me profereth þe pigge, opon þe pogh[221]

Whan I profir the pig, opin the poke[222]

It is sayd comenly, whan the pygge is profered: open the poughen[223]

Whan the pygge is proferd to holde vp the poke[224]

To buy a Cat in the sack (Whiting C102)
To bye a catte in tho sakke is bot litel charge[225]

Acheter chat in poche (Hassell C83)
[To buy a cat in a sack]

Comme cil qui chat achatera
El [sic] sac . . . [226]
[Like he who would buy a cat in a sack]

Veulz tu espouser chat en sac?[227]
[Would you marry a cat in a sack?]

The English examples begin around 1300; the French around 1375. In the English proverbs, "pig" is probably an Old English word, but "poke" enters English from French "poche." The two words are combined to create a fairly common alliterative pairing.[228] Middle French, however, does not have a "pig in a poke," it has a "chat en sac." With the exception of Wyclif, who seems to have adopted the French version, the English proverbs overwhelmingly favor the alliteration of "pig" and "poke" while the French variants prefer the near rhyme of "chat" and "sac."

---

221. Förster, "Die mittelenglische Sprichwörtersammlung in Douce 52," 54.
222. Hill, *Songs, Carols, and Miscellaneous Poems*, 128.
223. Robert Whittinton, *Vulgaria*, in *The Vulgaria of John Stanbridge and the Vulgaria of Robert Whittinton*, 107.
224. Heywood, *John Heywood's "A Dialogue of Proverbs,"* 101, line 140; see also 175, lines 2610–12.
225. John Wyclif, "De Blasphemia," in *Select English Works of John Wyclif*, III.422.
226. Gower, *Mirour de l'omme*, lines 7237–38, in *Complete Works of John Gower*, I.84.
227. Eustache Deschamps, *Le miroir de mariage*, line 8758, in *Œuvres complètes des Eustache Deschamps*, 9.284.
228. For other Middle English proverbs linking "pig" and "poke," see Whiting, *Proverbs . . . before 1500*, P187, P190, and P191.

Custom is the second kind (Whiting C646)

The proverb "Custom is the second kind" also shows a good bit of variation, but this time the changes have to do with Latin and English variation rather than any influence from French. The proverb has a long history, going back to Aristotle's *Ars Rhetorica*: "καὶ γὰρ τὸ εἰθισμένον ὥσπερ πεϕυκὸς ἤδη γίγνεται" ["habit is something like nature."][229] With its use of "quasi" and "quandam," Cicero's version maintains the same verbal latitude as Aristotle's: "deinde consuetudine quasi alteram quandam naturam effici" [later habit produces a sort of second nature].[230] In late antiquity, the idea is picked up by Macrobius—"consuetudo, quam secundam naturam pronuntiavit usus" [habit, which experience has called our second nature][231]—and is very popular with Augustine, who employs it at least twice in his *Contra Julianum* and once in *De musica*:

> secunda natura, sic enim a doctis appellari consuetudinem[232]
> [Thus custom is called second nature by the wise]

> [consuetudo] non frustra dicta est a quibusdam secunda natura[233]
> [Custom is not without reason called second nature by some]

> Non enim frustra consuetudo quasi secunda, et quasi affabricata natura dicitur[234]
> [For not without reason is custom said to be like a second, artificial nature.]

In these examples, we can see the proverbialization of the sentence: Augustine does not cite Aristotle or Cicero (least of all Macrobius) as a source, but ascribes the saying to "doctis" and "quibusdam" ["the wise" and "some people"]. Even at this early stage there is a certain amount of variation, as Cicero gives "altera natura" whereas both Macrobius and Augustine favor "secunda natura." In the High Middle Ages, only Roger Bacon cites Aristotle as a source for the saying; the fact that these later authors all use the wording "altera natura" argues against their borrowing the sentence directly from

---

229. Aristotle, *Ars Rhetorica*, Book 1, ch. 11 in idem, *On Rhetoric: A Theory of Civic Discourse*, 87.
230. Text and translation from Cicero, *De Finibus bonorum et malorum*, V.xxv.74, 476, 477. See also *Oxford Dictionary of English Proverbs*, 162; and A. Otto, *Die Sprichwörter und sprichwörtlichen Redensarten der Römer*, 90–91.
231. Text and translation from Macrobius, *Saturnalia*, VII.9.7, 3.228, 229.
232. Augustine of Hippo, *Contra Julianum*, Book 1, ch. 105, col. 1119.
233. Ibid., Book 4, ch. 103, col. 1398.
234. Idem, *De musica*, Book 6, ch. 7.19, col. 1173.

Augustine or from the most common Latin translation of Aristotle's *Ars rhetorica,* which also used "secunda":[235]

> Vsus enim, ut ait quidam, aegre dediscitur et consuetudo alteri naturae assistit[236]
> [For habit, as has been said, is difficult to unlearn, and custom becomes second nature]

> adeo ut dicatur non proprietate nominis, sed sedulitate officii, consuetudo altera natura[237]
> [So habit is not called by its own name, but is called second nature for its functions]

> Consuetudo enim est altera natura, ut dicit Philosophus[238]
> [For custom is second nature, as the Philosopher says]

> et consuetudo est altera natura, ut dicit Aristoteles[239]
> [And custom is second nature, as Aristotle says.]

To sum up the Latin examples, then, they seem to originate with Aristotle, but they are frequently cited without attribution (like a proverb) and show variation between the modifiers *secunda* and *altera*. They do not alliterate.

Versions of "Custom is the second kind" can be found in English from the fourteenth through the nineteenth centuries, but the heyday of the proverb was the fifteenth century, as in examples three through six below:

> costome is þe secounde fro kynde[240]

> Usage is the seconde kinde[241]

---

235. See the thirteenth-century translation by William of Moerbeke of *Aristotelis Ars Rhetorica,* I.219. On the popularity of this translation, see James J. Murphy, *Rhetoric in the Middle Ages: A History of Rhetorical Theory from Saint Augustine to the Renaissance,* 92–93.

236. John of Salisbury, *Policraticus,* Book 3, ch. 8, in *Ioannis Saresberiensis Policraticus I-IV,* 192.

237. Petrus Cellensis, *Commentaria in Ruth,* commentary 1, part 1, in *Commentaria in Ruth; Tractatus de tabernaculo,* 54.2.

238. Roger Bacon, *Opus maius,* Pars prima. Causae erroris, ch. 4, 3.9, line 3. On Bacon's (unadmiring) knowledge of a different Latin translation of Aristotle, see Murphy, *Rhetoric in the Middle Ages,* 93.

239. Ibid., Pars quinta, Perspectivae pars secunda, Distinctio tertia, ch. 7, 2.123, line 7.

240. John of Trevisa, *Higden's Polychronicon,* Book 7, in *Polychronicon Ranulphi Higden Monachi Cestrensis; Together with the English Translations of John Trevisa and of an Unknown Writer of the Fifteenth Century,* 7.339.

241. Gower, *Confessio Amantis,* Book 6, line 664, in *The Complete Works of John Gower,* III.185.

For as ypocras Sayth, "costome is the seconde nature or kynde"[242]

And þe wolde prouerbe seithe: custome & vse is a noþer nature or kynde[243]

usage is ane othir nature[244]

The secund natur Is callit conswetud.[245]

The major variations in English are between "custom" and "usage"—for which I can perceive no meaningful pattern—and between "kind" and "nature." Both "usage" and "nature" disrupt the alliteration of the proverb, but "nature" does so in a more historically conditioned way. According to the OED, the use of "kind" to mean "basic nature" is rare after 1600;[246] with these examples, we can see the process of semantic change beginning as early as the mid-fifteenth century, as Yonge and Bokenham feel compelled to gloss "kind" with "nature" and the later writers switch to "nature" entirely. Over its long history, this short proverb showed variant forms in both Latin and English, but it is noteworthy for our study that the vernacular version begins alliteratively and loses that form only when a more general lexical change makes it untenable.

Oft Rape rues (Whiting R32)

A similar instance of semantic change affecting a proverb can be seen with "Oft rape rues." For the apparent lifespan of this proverb, from the thirteenth through the fifteenth century, "rape" denoted, among its other meanings, "haste." According to the citations collected for the OED, "rape" loses this meaning by around 1500,[247] which is also about the time that the proverb disappears.

Ofte rape reweþ[248]

Biþenk hou oft rape wil rewe[249]

---

242. James Yonge, *The Governaunce of Prynces*, 238.
243. Osbern Bokenham, *Mappula Angliae*, 33–34.
244. Sir Gilbert Hay, *The Buke of the Governaunce of Princis*, in *Gilbert of the Haye's Prose Manuscript (AD 1456)*, II.126.
245. *The Contemplacioun of Synnaris*, in *The Asloan Manuscript: A Miscellany in Prose and Verse*, II.197.
246. OED kind, *n.* I.3.a; see also I.6.
247. OED rape, *n.*2.
248. *Proverbs of Hendyng*, stanza 40, Varnhagen, "Zu den Sprichwörtern Hendings," 199.
249. *Amis and Amiloun*, 29, line 656.

60 • CHAPTER 2

> Men sen alday that rape reweth[250]

> Fore ofte rape rewyþe at last[251]

> for oftyn tyme rape rueth.[252]

This proverb is not reformulated, like "Custom is the second kind"; instead, it simply falls out of use when one of its elements becomes linguistically unavailable. The alliteration seems to have provided not just form, but some part of the meaning of this proverb which, having lost its alliteration, also loses its authority and ceases to function.

Praise at the Parting (Whiting P39)
Sometimes an alliterative proverb simply falls out of fashion, as seems to have been the case with "Praise at the parting." This compact proverb remained very stable in its form, but had a clearly delineated lifespan, from the fifteenth to the seventeenth century. There is, as far as I can tell, no linguistic or paroemiological reason why this saying should have faded away by the mid-seventeenth century, but so it did.

> "Preyse at þe parting," seide þe knyʒt, "And bihold wele þe ende"[253]

> Now prayse at the partyng[254]

> No, bot prase at the partyng[255]

> Pryse at the parting, how that thow dois[256]

> And prayse at the parting euyn as ye fynde[257]

> He shall have no cause to prayse to his frendes at the partynge[258]

---

250. Gower, *Confessio Amantis*, Book 3, line 1625, in *Complete Works of John Gower*, II.270.
251. "The Proverbis of Wysdom," 244, line 40.
252. Margaret Paston to John Paston II, 12 March 1469, in *Paston Letters*, I.337. See also her letter to James Gloys, 18 January 1473 (I.370).
253. *The Early English Versions of the Gesta Romanorum*, 39.
254. *First Shepherds' Play*, line 385, in *The Towneley Plays*, I.117.
255. *Judgment*, line 782, in ibid., I.423.
256. *Rauf Coilʒear*, line 86, in *Scottish Alliterative Poems in Riming Stanzas*, 85.
257. Henry Medwall, *Fulgens and Lucres*, a.iv.
258. Whittinton, *Vulgaria*, in *The Vulgaria of John Stanbridge*, 100.

if she praise at the parting[259]

It is an old saying: praise at the parting[260]

praise at the parting[261]

Praise in departing[262]

"But proue att parting," Spencer sayes.[263]

Perhaps the proverb became too "popular," in the elitist sense, for authors to use without irony, and Shakespeare's pun pokes fun at its old-fashioned alliterativeness. Whatever the reason for its demise, the proverb thrived in the late medieval and Renaissance eras, which should remind us that such sayings do not obey our boundaries of periodization: just as some proverbs spanned the divide between Old English and Middle English, others, like this one, do the same in Middle English and early modern English, even if they do not survive much beyond that time.

By now it should be clear that alliteration was an important structural component in medieval English proverbs. This fact has allowed us to trace some proverbs from their pre-Conquest origins to their post-Conquest afterlives, demonstrating an intellectual and linguistic link between the two periods. Even proverbs that were coined later in Middle English maintain the alliterative tradition. Although alliteration is more often associated with Old English, the evidence of the proverbs shows that it remained a viable, active, and adaptable feature of English verbal culture through the entire Middle Ages. The following chapters will explore some of the cultural connotations of that attachment to alliteration in the realm of the proverb.

---

259. Richard Mulcaster, *Positions*, 10.
260. *Tom Tyler and His Wife*, 313, line 667. See *Wordsworth Dictionary of Proverbs*, 509.
261. John Lyly, *Euphues and His England*, in *Euphues: The Anatomy of Wit; Euphues & His England*, 348. See Tilley, *Elizabethan Proverb Lore*, no. 501, 252; and *Oxford Dictionary of English Proverbs*, 643.
262. William Shakespeare, *The Tempest*, III.iii.38, in *The Riverside Shakespeare*, 1677. See Tilley, *Elizabethan Proverb Lore*, no. 501, 252; and *Oxford Dictionary of English Proverbs*, 643.
263. "Hugh Spencer's Feats in France," stanza 27, line 1, Child no. 158, in *The English and Scottish Popular Ballads*, 379. This ballad was found in the Percy Manuscript of the seventeenth century. See Whiting, "Proverbial Material in the Popular Ballad," 24.

CHAPTER 3

Alliterative Proverbs in Didactic Texts

IN ANY CULTURE, the proverb derives much of its meaning from the way it interacts with its context. This interaction is perhaps most evident in the case of metaphorical proverbs, which are interpreted as metaphors based largely on the content surrounding them. For example, the admonition to "Look before you leap" is intended quite literally when delivered as part of a bungee-jumping lesson, but becomes metaphorical when a lawyer advises a client to read a contract before rushing into a business deal. The context of advice-giving can provide meaning to a nonmetaphorical proverb as well, by establishing a situation where a proverb is expected, thus allowing any sententia to be interpreted as a proverb or potential proverb.

However, proverbs do not merely receive interpretative input from their contexts; they, in turn, help to shape those contexts. In the case of medieval England, the only contexts we can recover for the proverbs explored in chapter 2 are written documents, so it is impossible to determine the various ways in which alliterative proverbs must have contributed forms of meaning in daily discourse. Nevertheless, the variety of written genres in which alliterative proverbs appear is quite broad. Each genre created meaning in its own way, so it will be the function of this chapter to explore the numerous interactions of alliterative proverbs with certain literary (or simply literate) genres in the English Middle Ages. The major genres addressed in this chapter—proverb collection, gnomic poem, devotional prose, sermon—are alike not only in being instructional in intent but also in having been produced in both the Old English and Middle English periods. This generic stability provides a framework within which we can use the alliterative proverb to trace numerous features of language ecology and cultural connotation.

PROVERB COLLECTIONS AND GNOMIC POEMS

The most widespread, and probably the most influential, genre for the distribution of proverbs was the simple proverb collection. Only a few of these collections survive from the Anglo-Saxon period, but they are very numerous in later centuries. The proverb collection has little artistic pretention, but serves a consistently pedagogical function. The pedagogy is frequently related to language study, as the proverbs in a collection may inculcate moral values, but their more immediate purpose is usually to teach Latin. Such collections contribute very deliberately to the complex language ecology of medieval England. As pedagogical tools in a multilingual environment, many of the proverb collections of the English Middle Ages are at least bilingual, and sometimes trilingual, texts.[1] The usefulness of such collections for teaching both literacy and morality, and for providing salutary reading material generally, ensured that they multiplied in a variety of forms: verse and prose; monolingual and multilingual; anonymous and ascribed.[2] Likewise, the manuscript contexts in which proverb collections appeared were also varied, ranging from pedagogical collections to literary anthologies to religious miscellanies to handbooks for preachers.[3]

The earliest independent (that is, noncontinental) proverb collection in English is the so-called Durham Proverbs. This collection contains forty-six pairs of Latin and Old English proverbs. Most of the other texts in this eleventh-century manuscript also seem designed to assist in language study: they include Latin hymns and canticles with Old English interlinear glossing and a version of Ælfric's *Grammar*. Inge Milfull interprets the manuscript as a type of handbook for a teacher in a monastic school, as it contains both a grammar section and a text section.[4]

---

1. For descriptions of some trilingual (Latin, English, Anglo-Norman) collections, see Förster, "Frühmittelenglische Sprichwörter," 3, 13–15.

2. For a general characterization of such collections, see Sarah M. Horrall, "Latin and Middle English Proverbs in a Manuscript at St. George's Chapel, Windsor Castle," 346–48.

3. See Cameron Louis, "Manuscript Contexts of Middle English Proverb Literature."

4. Inge B. Milfull, "Formen und Inhalte lateinisch-altenglischer Textensembles und Mischtexte: Durham Cathedral B. III. 32 und 'The Phoenix,'" 471.

In the Durham Proverbs, some of the Latin / Old English pairings reflect vernacular translation of Latin *sententiae*, but others result from the juxtapositioning of independently existing proverbs in the two languages or even of Latin translation of English proverbs.[5] In support of this last possibility, Olof Arngart points out that in some instances the Latin mistranslates the English or translates only part of the English proverb; in one case, the Latin rendering retains an Old English word. Furthermore, numerous of the Old English proverbs are highly patterned using alliteration and sometimes metrical rhythm to a degree not found in the Latin.[6] Quite a few of the proverbs correspond to strictly vernacular analogues from the continent. So, the Durham Proverbs reside in a bilingual manuscript of religious content, but unlike the other works in that manuscript, for which Latin is the high-status language of truth, the Durham Proverbs present sentences of vernacular wisdom as authoritative texts in their own right. Even if they were used to teach Latin, the Durham Proverbs had to possess sufficient cultural status to make them worth translating.

Arngart notes that "The O. E. proverbs are copiously adorned with alliteration": according to my count, thirty-two of the forty-six Old English proverbs display alliteration of content words.[7] This astonishing concentration of alliteration in a nonpoetic text seems to indicate that alliteration served as a primary marker of proverbiality in the Anglo-Saxon period. As Arngart points out, many of the Durham Proverbs have analogues in Scripture, in the classics, and in Old English poetry,[8] but I would argue that the variants recorded here are given alliterative form to mark them as proverbial sentences worthy of being translated into Latin and perhaps even memorized. Recently, Stephen Yeager has made a compelling argument that alliteration is one feature that distinguishes what he calls "sententiousness" in Old and Middle English texts. For Yeager, "sententiousness" may inhere in proverbs or maxims, but he defines it more broadly as "a quality of statements that implies their self-evident truth."[9] Thus, he locates sententiousness in genres ranging from Anglo-Saxon laws and homilies to late Middle English alliterative allegories. In this study, I am interested in a more specific link between alliteration and proverbial form. As we will see, that link does produce some of the same cultural effects that

---

5. "The Durham Proverbs," 288; Thijs Porck, "Treasures in a Sooty Bag?."
6. *The Durham Proverbs*, 6.
7. Based on Arngart's 1981 edition of "The Durham Proverbs," numbers 2, 4, 6–9, 11–13, 15–21, 23–27, 29–31, 35, 37–38, 40–44.
8. Ibid., 289.
9. Yeager, *From Lawmen to Plowmen*, 39.

Yeager finds for sententiousness, including an attempt by Middle English authors to make use of the Old English past.

Looking at Latin proverbs translated into English (or any other medieval vernacular), the most widely circulated collection was, without doubt, the *Disticha Catonis*.[10] This collection of Latin hexameter couplets, a pagan product of late antiquity, served as a basic schoolbook for the Carolingians and subsequently for the Anglo-Saxons and the rest of Christendom.[11] As part of the pedagogical process, the *Disticha* were often translated into the vernacular, mostly, one presumes, by students but sometimes by more accomplished Latinists. As a result, we possess glosses and translations of the *Disticha Catonis* in nearly every medieval vernacular language.[12]

England was no exception to this pattern. Several Latin manuscripts of the *Disticha Catonis* survive from Anglo-Saxon England, as well as three late Old English translations found in twelfth-century manuscripts. The Old English prose versions of the *Disticha Catonis* are fairly loose translations of the Latin.[13] Unlike the Durham Proverbs, the Old English translations of the *Disticha* do not employ significant alliteration. This point of contrast between the two collections arises from the difference in the ways they deploy Latin and the vernacular. In the Durham Proverbs, the vernacular *sententiae* are the "originals," so they are enhanced with alliteration to lend them proverbial authority. With the *Disticha Catonis*, the Latin text arrives already invested with authority—linguistic, poetic, and pedagogical—so the Old English translators feel no need to formalize the vernacular. The Anglo-Saxon translators were not awed by the Latin text, as evidenced by the way in which they introduced Christian elements into their translations,[14] but there is no question that the Old English version is secondary to the Latin.

---

10. The standard edition of the Latin text remains the *Disticha Catonis* edited by Marcus Boas.

11. For a clear and concise overview of medieval Latin school-texts, including the *Disticha Catonis*, see Jill Mann, "'He Knew Nat Catoun': Medieval School-texts and Middle English Literature," 42–52. For a more detailed description of instructional manuscripts in Anglo-Saxon and early Norman England, see Patrizia Lendinara, "Instructional Manuscripts in England: The Tenth and Eleventh Century Codices and the Early Norman Ones." On the use of the *Disticha Catonis* by Christian teachers and students, see Richard Hazelton, "The Christianization of 'Cato': The *Disticha Catonis* in the Light of Late Mediaeval Commentaries."

12. For an overview of such translations, see Ingrid A. Brunner, "On Some of the Vernacular Translations of Cato's Distichs."

13. For an edition of the Old English *Disticha Catonis*, see R. S. Cox, "The Old English Dicts of Cato." For further commentary, see Treharne, "Form and Function of the Twelfth Century Old English Dicts of Cato."

14. See Cox, "Old English Dicts of Cato," 37–38.

The history of the *Disticha Catonis* in England is still woefully understudied; as Stephanie Hollis and Michael Wright point out, "There is, surprisingly, not even a comparative examination of OE and ME versions of *Disticha Catonis* which aims to discover whether there are historically significant differences in the rendering of what was a staple text of elementary education throughout the Middle Ages and beyond."[15] Certainly, translations of the *Disticha Catonis* continued in England through the Middle English and Early Modern periods.[16] The surviving Old English translations were actually copied in the twelfth century for probable monastic use.[17] The first new post-Conquest translations, also from the twelfth century, are not English, but Anglo-Norman, as might be expected for a text linked to formal schooling. The earliest Middle English translation dates from the thirteenth century, followed by several more in the fourteenth and fifteenth centuries. By the end of the Middle Ages, public demand for English versions of the *Disticha Catonis* had risen so high that William Caxton published two versions in four editions.[18] As is usual for proverb collections, the text of the *Disticha Catonis* and its translations was very fluid: Middle English versions were sometimes translated from a Latin original, but at least as often from the French.[19] This shift in translation practices provides information about all three languages. First, it shows that by the late Middle Ages, the authority of this particular proverb collection no longer depended on the Latin language. Second, it reflects a change in pedagogical practice: the *Disticha Catonis*, with its simple sentences, had long been a textbook for the most elementary learning. Thus, the demand for English versions of the *Distichs* in the fifteenth century reflects the growing practice of teaching basic literacy in English, rather than in French or Latin.

Nearly every Middle English translation of the *Disticha Catonis* expanded each distich into a rhymed stanza of four to eight lines, so much extraneous material (and filler) was introduced by necessity. By this process, vernacular versions of the *Disticha Catonis* less resemble actual translations and take on more of the character of semi-independent gnomic poems. Of the alliterative proverbs examined in chapter 2, only one has a presence in a Middle English version of the *Disticha Catonis*.[20] Most vernacular translations of the *Disticha*

---

15. Stephanie Hollis and Michael Wright, *Old English Prose of Secular Learning*, 10.

16. For a convenient overview of such translations, see I. Brunner, "On Some of the Vernacular Translations," 119–20. For a Middle English version omitted by Brunner, see Sarah M. Horrall, "Christian Cato: A Middle English Translation of the *Disticha Catonis*."

17. Treharne, "Form and Function," 471 *et passim*.

18. I. Brunner, "On Some of the Vernacular Translations," 101.

19. Ibid., 113–18.

20. From Caxton's edition of Benedict Burgh's translation: "The wyse man sayth that by wyn and by wymmen comen many evyls and inconvenyents"; see p. 36.

seem to have been fairly independent projects, without very much recourse to other versions or to preexisting, circulating proverbs. Furthermore, most Middle English versions of the *Disticha Catonis* were end-rhymed. However, the study of alliteration in the *Disticha Catonis* does repay some attention, as Middle English translators, despite their commitment to end rhyme, also exploited the connection between proverbs and alliteration. As Sarah Horrall observes, alliteration occurs in roughly 20 percent of the lines in one Middle English *Disticha* (in MS. Bodl. 3894 [Fairfax 14]), though only 10 percent of another (MS. Bodl. Engl. Misc. C. 291).²¹ Alliteration as a marker of proverbial wisdom also figures prominently in the opening stanzas of a third version (MS. Bodl. 29003 [Add. A. 106]):

> All chylder þat wyll clergy kon,
> Take hed how Catoun kenned his son
>   Of lely lyuing to lere;
> For to hym he told many a skyll
> To lere þe gud & leue þe yll
>   Be ways many & sere.
>
> Son (he sayd) sen it is so
> Þat a God is withowtyn mo,
>   Maker of all mankind,
> Als bukes says, & wit þerby
> Hym sal þou serue all soueranly
>   With clen hert & clen mynd.²²

Although Horrall does not think highly of this translator's skill,²³ there can be no doubt that his use of alliteration here is not accidental, but purposeful, establishing his poem as a work of wisdom. Thus, the history of the *Disticha Catonis* in England involves different metrical forms—the hexameters of the Latin, the end-rhymed stanzas of the Middle English—but alliteration, even if only ornamental, persists as a signal of the proverbial nature of the text, adding a vernacular weight to the authority of the pseudonymous Roman.

It may have possessed the longest pedigree, but the *Disticha Catonis* is not at all the only model for proverb collections in the Middle English period.²⁴

---

21. Horrall, "An Unknown Middle English Translation of the *Distichs* of Cato," 27–28.
22. Horrall, "Christian Cato," 162; emphasis added.
23. Ibid., 159.
24. See Louis, "Proverbs, Precepts, and Monitory Pieces." See also his "Authority in Middle English Proverb Literature."

Like the *Disticha Catonis,* the earliest Middle English proverbial texts relied on a named figure of authority, but unlike the *Disticha,* these works were (almost) fully vernacular in their origins and structure. I refer, of course, to the *Proverbs of Alfred* and *Proverbs of Hendyng.*

According to Olof Arngart, the *Proverbs of Alfred* was composed (in its earliest form) in Sussex around the mid-twelfth century.[25] It must have been somewhat popular in its day, as it survives (in various versions) in four manuscripts from the thirteenth century.[26] The *Proverbs of Alfred* is arranged in stanzas that use an unordered combination of alliteration and end rhyme. Because it is one of the few surviving English-language poetic texts from the early Middle English period; because its extensive use of alliteration recalls the techniques of pre-Conquest poetry; and, most of all, because the poem sets up King Alfred as the speaker of its wisdom, the *Proverbs of Alfred* has proven of interest as a potential link between the Old English and Middle English periods. I have already discussed (in chapter 1) the status of English-language texts before and after the Norman Conquest, so I will simply note here that the prosody of the *Proverbs of Alfred* is generally seen to fall between that of Old English and the new forms of Middle English. In its unregulated but frequent use of both alliteration and rhyme—sometimes favoring one, sometimes the other, occasionally neither—and in its use of stanzaic rather than stichic structure, the *Proverbs of Alfred* is, as its dating might suggest, transitional between the older and the newer, the Germanic and the Romance traditions.[27]

The use of King Alfred as the speaker of the poem raises interesting issues of cultural continuity. Even Arngart's relatively early dating of the *Proverbs of Alfred* places it a century after the Norman Conquest and 250 years after the death of Alfred himself. Nevertheless, the poem begins with a mise-en-scène in which Alfred is addressing a gathering of politically important men (a *witenagemot*) at Seaford:

At Seuorde
séte þeynes monye.
fele Biscopes.
and feole. bok-iléred.
Eorles prute.
knyhtes egleche.

---

25. *Proverbs of Alfred,* II.55–62.
26. For summary descriptions, see ibid., II.11–39. Volume 1 of Arngart's edition comprises a complete study of the manuscript filiations.
27. Ibid., II.225–32; Minkova, "The Credibility of Pseudo-Alfred: Prosodic Insights in Post-Conquest Mongrel Meter."

þar wes þe eorl Alurich.
of þare lawe swiþe wis.
And ek Ealured
Englene durlyng:
on englene londe he wes kyng.
Heom he bi-gon lére.
so ye mawe i-hure.
hw hi. heore lif
lede scholden.
Alured. he wes in englene lond.
an king. wel swiþe strong.
He wes king. and he wes clerek.
wel he luuede godes werk.
He wes wis on his word.
and war. on his werke.
he wes þe wysuste mon:
þat wes englelonde on.[28]

The reputation of King Alfred as a dispenser of wisdom may be a local survival, as all four manuscripts of the *Proverbs of Alfred* were copied in the southern Midlands.[29] Arngart favors "popular" or oral transmission of the Alfredian reputation,[30] but André Crépin sees it as transmitted through knowledge of Alfred's own writings and translations.[31] Robert Rouse argues for a monastic origin for the *Proverbs of Alfred*, but still explains the frame as inspired by a "local oral tradition of Alfred holding councils in the Seaford area."[32] Whatever the structural model or mode of transmission, Alfred's reputation is clearly (here and in *The Owl and the Nightingale*) one of great wisdom and authority, making him an appropriate speaker of gnomic sententiae.

One potential relationship between the Old English and Middle English periods on which the *Proverbs of Alfred* might shed some light is the favoring of gnomic poetry in each. Most of the scholars who have written on the *Proverbs of Alfred* seem to agree that the major inspirations for its structure lie in written sources, like the biblical Book of Proverbs. Alfred, like Solomon,

---

28. *Proverbs of Alfred*, stanza 1 (lines 1–24), II.71–73. For a normalized text (omitting stanzas 30–34) and modern translation, see *The Proverbs of Alfred: An Emended Text*.
29. *Proverbs of Alfred*, II.17, 29, 33, and 37.
30. Arngart, "The Distichs of Cato and the Proverbs of Alfred," 99.
31. André Crépin, "Mentalités anglaises au temps d'Henri II Plantagenêt d'après les *Proverbs of Alfred*."
32. Robert Allen Rouse, *The Idea of Anglo-Saxon England in Middle English Romance*, 38.

is presented as a wise and pious king who taught his people in memorable sayings. So, according to Arngart, for example, the composition of the *Proverbs of Alfred* proceeded by the poet borrowing his frame from the Book of Proverbs, then filling it out with material from a variety of sources: the Bible, the *Disticha Catonis*, oral proverbs, and his own invention.[33] Christopher Cannon notes the similarity between Alfred's role and those of Cato (*Disticha*), Solomon (Proverbs, Wisdom, and Ecclesiastes), and Jesus ben Sirach (Ecclesiasticus), but concentrates on a comparison between the structure of the stanzas in the *Proverbs of Alfred* and the strictures of the classical rhetorical exercise known as the *chria*.[34] I believe that the biblical model, being better known at the time, is more apt than the rhetorical one, but in any case, both argue for a literate inspiration. Stephen Yeager draws a parallel to a different sort of document: the late Old English collection of laws known as *I-II Cnut*.[35] The exception to this trend would be Rouse, who, despite supporting a monastic milieu for the poem, believes that its frame was adopted from local legend, as I have quoted him above. I would add one further complication to this debate: there are examples of gnomic wisdom spoken by figures of authority that are not connected to the Christian, legal, or school-rhetoric traditions. Some of these examples occur far afield: in his discussion of the ancient Greek *Phocylides* (itself an example of the genre), M. L. West mentions the Sumerian *Instructions of Šuruppak*.[36] However, he also adduces analogues that are closer to home for our study: the Old Norse *Loddfáfnismál* (part of *Hávamál*) and *Sigrdrífumál*, both of which use a refrain in the manner of the repeated "Þus quaþ Alured" of our Middle English poem.[37] Neither of the Old Norse poems is considered biblical or classical in its origin or inspiration. For an earlier and insular example of a sententious king, famous for his learning and piety, there is the eighth- or ninth-century Irish *Bríathra Flainn Fhína maic Ossu*, a collection of maxims attributed to Aldrith of Northumbria.[38] So, the stanzaic structure of the *Proverbs of Alfred* may not result from a rhetorical exercise, and the use of Alfred as a speaker of wisdom may derive from a vernacular, legendary tradition.

Only one of the Old English wisdom poems employs a frame similar to that of the *Proverbs of Alfred*, and that is *Precepts*, which portrays a father

---

33. Arngart, "The Distichs of Cato and the Proverbs of Alfred," 118.

34. Christopher Cannon, "Proverbs and the Wisdom of Literature: The *Proverbs of Alfred* and Chaucer's *Tale of Melibee*."

35. Yeager, *From Lawmen to Plowmen*, 116–17.

36. M. L. West, "Phocylides," 164.

37. Ibid., 165.

38. *Old Irish Wisdom Attributed to Aldfrith of Northumbria: An Edition of Bríathra Flainn Fhína maic Ossu*.

instructing his son. This type of parental instruction is very common in later Middle English poetry, but it also makes an appearance toward the end of the *Proverbs of Alfred*. The last five stanzas of the poem (in its longest version) each begin with the familiar "Þus quad alured," but they add an address to a specific listener: "sone min swo leue."³⁹ Although stanza 30, which introduces a son as the audience for Alfred's wisdom, marks the most evident structural shift in the poem, Arngart notes that some scholars have also perceived a break at stanza 12:

Þus queþ Alured.
Lvsteþ ye me leode.
ower is þe neode.
And ich eu wille lére.
wit and wisdom.
þat alle þing ouer-goþ.⁴⁰

The refrain-like first line, which connects each stanza to the others, is here followed by five lines of general introduction, or reintroduction. As a whole, then, the *Proverbs of Alfred* comprises three sections: the first, introduced with the scene at Seaford; the second, reintroduced as a presentation of wisdom to the people; and the last, set up as a father's advice to his son. This tripartite structure might account for the diversity of scholarly opinion regarding the most relevant models for the poem: it may be that each section reflects a different derivation. In any case, the structure calls to mind another gnomic poem in three parts: the Old English *Maxims I*. It is instructive, I think, to compare the two poems.

Some of the similarities between *Maxims I* and the *Proverbs of Alfred* are obvious, others more subtle. Both poems use alliteration. Both are didactic works constructed mainly out of generalized statements of wisdom. Both acquire those statements from a variety of sources: Latin and vernacular, written and oral.⁴¹ Arngart's description of the compositional process for the *Proverbs of Alfred* also describes that of *Maxims I* with unintended accuracy:

[The poet] selects his sources and adapts them to his plan; he endeavors, though perhaps not always successfully, to join his teachings together in a

---

39. *Proverbs of Alfred*, stanza 30, II.128.
40. Ibid., stanza 12, lines 187–92, II.93 (commentary on II.2).
41. On the sources of the *Proverbs of Alfred*, see Arngart, "The Distichs of Cato and the Proverbs of Alfred" and *Proverbs of Alfred*, II.7. On the sources of *Maxims I*, see Deskis, "Proverbs and Structure in *Maxims I. A*."

proper sequence and coherence of thought; and he manages to present them in a form that is by no means lacking in literary merit.[42]

The sources to which Arngart refers may be individual proverbs or *sententiae*, or larger components like sectional divisions. Arngart and Crépin agree that it is characteristic of gnomic poetry to be able to amalgamate such pieces of available material ("found art," one might say) into the whole.[43] I have argued elsewhere that the same process of amalgamation accounts for the structure of *Maxims I*.[44] Gnomic poetry, whether Old English or Middle English, is flexible by nature; its relatively loose frame allows for ease of expansion or contraction. In fact, neither *Maxims I* nor the *Proverbs of Alfred* ever actually closes its frame.

The two poems do not overlap very much (hardly at all) in their specific contents, but they do share certain themes. Following the opening frame, each offers a religious lesson:

Maxims I, lines 4b-12a:
    God sceal mon ærest hergan
fægre, fæder userne,   forþon þe he us æt frymþe geteode
lif ond lænne willan;   he usic wile þara leana gemonian.
Meotud sceal in wuldre,   mon sceal on eorþan
geong ealdian.   God us ece biþ,
ne wendað hine wyrda   ne hine wiht dreceþ,
adl ne yldo   ælmihtigne;
ne gomelað he in gæste,   ac he is gen swa he wæs,
þeoden geþyldig.

[One must first praise God, our father, because he, from the beginning, gave us life and earthly joy; he will remind us of that loan. The Lord must dwell in glory, man dwell on earth, the young must grow old. Our God is eternal, fate does not change him nor does anything—sickness nor old age—vex him, the Almighty. He does not grow old in spirit, but he is ever as he was, the constant Lord.]

Proverbs of Alfred, stanza 2, lines 37-60:
Mildeliche ich munye.
myne leoue freond.

---

42. Arngart, "The Distichs of Cato and the Proverbs of Alfred," 118.
43. *Proverbs of Alfred*, II.51; Crépin, "Mentalités anglaises," 54–55.
44. Deskis, "Proverbs and Structure in *Maxims I. A*."

poure and riche.
leode myne
þat ye alle a-dréde.
vre dryhten crist.
luuyen hine and lykyen.
for he is louerd of lyf.
He is one. god;
ouer alle godnesse.
He is one gleaw.
ouer alle glednesse.
He is one. blisse.
ouer alle blissen.
He is one monne.
Mildest mayster.
He is one. folkes
fader. and frouer.
He is one. rihtwis.
and so riche king.
þat him ne schal beo wone.
nouht of his wille.
wo hine her on worlde.
wrþie þencheþ.[45]

The focus is different in each passage: *Maxims I* stresses God's eternal and unchanging nature, while the *Proverbs of Alfred* iterates His uniqueness. Still, each poet begins his presentation of wisdom with God, implying a divine source for all wisdom.

Maxims I and the *Proverbs of Alfred* share other themes, as well. Each advises a cautious use of speech, discusses the matter of friendship, and describes some features of relationships with women. A detailed comparison of each poem's treatment of these topics would doubtless prove interesting, but would be digressive here. It is enough to note that these are topics commonly addressed in wisdom poetry directed toward a male audience.[46] A monastic audience specifically has been proposed for each of the present poems. Much current thought regarding the Exeter Book, in which *Maxims I* appears, places

---

45. *Maxims I(A)*, lines 4b–12a, in *The Exeter Anthology of Old English Poetry*, I.248; *Proverbs of Alfred*, stanza 2, lines 37–60, II.75–77.

46. The same themes are found in *Hávamál*, for example. West points out that the topics of women and marriage are also common in gnomic poetry from ancient Greece and the Near East (West, "Phocylides," 166–67).

it in the context of the Benedictine Reform in England.[47] However, no convincing argument has been made that *Maxims I* is an exclusively monastic product. Rouse argues for a monastic origin for the *Proverbs of Alfred*, citing a general monastic interest in Old English in the twelfth century, along with a sense that the poem's particular version of kingship might reflect a monastic view of the subject.[48] On the other hand, several stanzas of the *Proverbs of Alfred* address the criteria by which a man should choose a wife, so at some point the poem became directed toward a lay (though still male) audience.

Maxims I and the *Proverbs of Alfred* diverge somewhat in the ways that they address their audiences. For example, the opening frame of each poem implies a different relationship between speaker and listener. In the *Proverbs of Alfred*, the relationship is plainly hierarchical: the king addresses his subjects. *Maxims I*, on the other hand, offers a greater possibility for dialogue in its opening:

> Frige mec frodum wordum.   Ne læt þinne ferð onhælne,
> degol þæt þu deopost cunne.   Nelle ic þe min dyrne gesecgan,
> gif þu me þinne hygecræft hylest   ond þine heortan geþohtas.
> Gleawe men sceolon gieddum wrixlan.[49]

> [Question me with wise words. Do not conceal your spirit or hide what you know most deeply. I will not tell you my secrets if you hide your own wisdom from me along with the thoughts of your heart. Wise men should exchange sayings.]

The addressee is singular, rather than plural, and is encouraged to offer thoughts of his own. This potential exchange of ideas, though common in dialogue poems of both the Old English and Middle English periods, never actually occurs in *Maxims I*, but nevertheless, the opening presupposes a meeting of the minds between equals. Thus, the *Proverbs of Alfred* presumes the audience to be junior in some way, either in age or in rank, whereas *Maxims I* was either planned for an audience of monastic peers or (as I think more likely) was appropriated from a nonmonastic origin.

There are other differences between the two poems. Unlike *Maxims I*, the *Proverbs of Alfred* makes frequent (though irregular) use of end rhyme and arranges its lines into stanzas, each introduced by the refrain "Þus quaþ

---

47. Michael D. C. Drout, "Possible Instructional Effects of the Exeter Book 'Wisdom Poems': A Benedictine Reform Context"; Brian O'Camb, "Bishop Æthelwold and the Shaping of the Old English *Exeter Maxims*."

48. Rouse, *Idea of Anglo-Saxon England*, 37–40.

49. *Maxims I(A)*, lines 1–4a, in *Exeter Anthology*, I.248.

Alured." The *Proverbs of Alfred,* with its four surviving manuscripts, seems to have enjoyed wider circulation than *Maxims I,* though I would not want to hazard a guess why. More important than any of those features, though, in contrasting the two poems, is the fact that *Maxims I* makes much greater use of the flexibility we have noted in the genre of gnomic poetry. Both poems provide wisdom to help a man function in the world—that is, practical and social wisdom—but the *Proverbs of Alfred* does so in a simpler and more direct fashion. The poet alternates between third-person, descriptive sententiae (for example, "Wyþ-vte wysdome / is weole wel vnwurþ") and second-person, prescriptive statements ("Yf þu seoluer and gold. / yefst and weldest in þis world. / Neuer vpen eorþe. / to wlonk. þu ny-wrþe").[50] Nearly every statement has direct applicability to the audience. Outside of its frame, *Maxims I* does not use the second person, but it does offer both descriptive and prescriptive sententiae, formatting the latter with "sceal"-clauses: "Þing sceal gehegan / frod wiþ frodne"[51] [Wise man ought to meet with wise man]. However, unlike the *Proverbs of Alfred, Maxims I* makes significant use of nongnomic discourse types, especially narrative.[52] *Maxims I* also includes sententiae of a descriptive but non-ethical nature, like "Umbor yceð, þa æradl nimeð" [The child grows, then is taken by illness] or "Forst sceal freosan, fyr wudu meltan"[53] [Frost must freeze, fire must destroy wood]. These nongnomic discourse types play important roles in the structure of *Maxims I,* but that type of structure is not a feature of the *Proverbs of Alfred.* The discourse complexity of *Maxims I* resembles that of Old Norse wisdom poems like *Hávamál* and may reflect a background in oral poetics. The *Proverbs of Alfred,* despite containing some proverbs that circulated orally, seems less adventuresome, hence less confident, in its structure.

Ultimately, the *Proverbs of Alfred* occupies an indeterminate space among competing (and collaborating) traditions. From the Anglo-Saxon past, it appropriates the authority of King Alfred, the alliteration linked to proverbial wisdom, and some of the structural features of the gnomic poems. By its implied parallel between King Alfred and King Solomon, and in some of its content, the poem borrows biblical authority. Its use of end rhyme and stanzaic structure reflects both Latin influence and Norman fashion. The implied audience of the poem is similarly eclectic: monastic or lay, or both, but definitely English-speaking and, ideally, conversant in and thus appreciative of the various cultural trends that nurture this text.

---

50. *Proverbs of Alfred,* stanza 6, lines 96–97, and stanza 9, lines 138–41, II.83 and 87.

51. *Maxims I(A),* lines 18b–19a, in *Exeter Anthology,* I.248.

52. See Deskis, "Exploring Text and Discourse in the Old English Gnomic Poems: The Problem of Narrative."

53. *Maxims I(A),* line 31; *Maxims I(B),* line 1, in *Exeter Anthology,* I.249 and 252.

The *Proverbs of Alfred* uses alliteration to forge a link with the Anglo-Saxon past and to underscore, in its metrically casual way, the proverbial nature of its wisdom. Nevertheless, it does not actually contain many alliterative proverbs. The *Proverbs of Hendyng*, another early Middle English gnomic poem, also uses alliteration, but with less emphasis on meter and more on the proverbs themselves.

The *Proverbs of Hendyng* was probably composed in the Midlands sometime around 1250.[54] Considering that it arose roughly a century after the *Proverbs of Alfred*, it is no surprise that the *Proverbs of Hendyng* exhibits stronger Romance influence. Like the *Proverbs of Alfred*, the *Proverbs of Hendyng* is structured in stanzas, but those of the later work are fairly consistently end-rhymed in an AABCCB pattern. The stanzas are rhythmically regular (for the most part), with the A and C lines consisting of four stresses and the B lines of three stresses. Each stanza concludes with a proverb (usually prose) and the tag "Quod Hending."[55] The model for the structure of the *Proverbs of Hendyng* is no secret: it is generally assumed to derive from the Old French *Proverbes au vilain*, which, in one instance, can be found in the same manuscript.[56] Like the *Proverbs of Alfred* and the *Proverbs of Hendyng*, the late twelfth-century *Proverbes au vilain* exists in multiple, quite varied, versions, but its stanzaic structure is identical to that of the *Proverbs of Hendyng*, except that each stanza ends with the tag "Ce dit li vilains"[57] [So says the peasant].

The poet of the *Proverbs of Hendyng* works one interesting change on the structure he borrowed from the *Proverbes au vilain*: in selecting the proverb that defines and punctuates each stanza, he frequently chose alliterative forms in contrast to the end rhyme of the stanza proper. Nearly half of the proverbs alliterate in a nonincidental manner. By choosing alliterative proverbs, the poet links his Romance-structured text to the English-speaking culture of his readers or listeners. In fact, of the six proverbs from this poem that we examined in chapter 2, three are found exclusively in English—Lief child behoves lore; After bale comes boot; Oft rape rues—and two have links to the Old English period—After bale comes boot; When the cup is fullest, bear it fairest.[58] Alliteration is once again a signifier of Englishness and of wisdom.

---

54. John Edwin Wells, *A Manual of the Writings in Middle English, 1050–1400*, 377.

55. For edited text of two versions of the *Proverbs of Hendyng*, see Varnhagen, "Zu den Sprichwörtern Hendings."

56. Louis, "Manuscript Contexts of Middle English Proverb Literature," 221; see *Facsimile of Oxford, Bodleian Library, MS Digby 86*.

57. *Proverbes au vilain*.

58. For a fuller commentary on analogues to the *Proverbs of Hendyng*, see Singer, "Die Sprichwörter Hendings."

The significance of the name "Hending" or "Hendyng" is less clear. Juliette de Caluwé-Dor suggests that it might draw on its etymology to connote "courtly or noble" and thus offer a contrast to the "vilain" of the poem's model.[59] One version of the *Proverbs of Hendyng* describes Hendyng as the son of Marcolf, which links the poem to the debate-poem tradition of Solomon and Saturn/Marcolf. Because Marcolf is decidedly nonaristocratic, de Caluwé-Dor also suggests that the name of his son Hendyng could be ironic (this, I suppose, would make him a "vilain"). Deciding not to reconcile these competing interpretations, de Caluwé-Dor goes on to explore the ways in which the *Proverbs of Hendyng*, though not a debate-poem, still resembles the Solomon and Marcolf pieces by offering competing forms of wisdom: Christian wisdom (focused on Providence and charity), pagan wisdom (centered on the immutability of fate), and bourgeois realism (amoral and discourteous).[60] If one accepts de Caluwé-Dor's interpretation, it seems unlikely that the *Proverbs of Hendyng* would make an appropriate school-text; even Wells calls it "worldly and bitter."[61] Perhaps, like *Maxims I* (and maybe the *Proverbs of Alfred*), the *Proverbs of Hendyng* was meant for a somewhat more mature audience, better able to contemplate and weigh the often contradictory ways of the world. The *Disticha Catonis* was used as an elementary school-text, despite its uneasy fit with Christian doctrine, because its form made it useful for teaching Latin. The *Proverbs of Alfred* and *Proverbs of Hendyng* are strictly vernacular texts and lack that linguistic application. They represent the ongoing tradition of wisdom poetry (for adults) in the vernacular and they stress, by their use of alliteration, the Englishness of both their wisdom and their language.

The twelfth century is, of course, the age of great growth in vernacular literature. For example, the genres of romance and courtly lyric develop in France and spread quickly across Europe and Britain. I believe, however, that the vernacularization of proverb literature may have moved in the opposite direction, or was, at least, more bidirectional. Anglo-Saxon England seems to have possessed a mature tradition of proverbial or gnomic poetry in the vernacular. Biblical influence can be perceived to some degree in these poems, but overall, such gnomic poems as *Maxims I* and *Maxims II* derive from an ancient and native tradition of wisdom poetry. The established authority of such a tradition helps to explain the dominance of the vernacular in a text like the Durham Proverbs.

---

59. Juliette de Caluwé-Dor, "Les Proverbes de Hendyng: Héroïsme païen, charité chrétienne et réalisme bourgeois," 57–58.
60. Ibid., 61.
61. Wells, *Manual*, 377.

For French, the situation was different. Elisabeth Schulze-Busacker is able to trace the beginning of French proverb literature only as far back as the mid-twelfth century and locates its origin not in France, but in England. Around 1150, Sanson de Nanteuil translated the Proverbs of Solomon into French at the request of Alice de Condet, who belonged to an intellectual circle around Bishop Alexander of Lincoln. Sanson's text comprises a translation of the biblical Book of Proverbs, plus a commentary into which he inserts numerous French proverbs of vernacular origin.[62] Within twenty years of Sanson's work, Serlo of Wilton created the first deliberate collection of French proverbs; though he was probably living in Paris at the time, his collection takes a specifically Anglo-Norman form, containing proverbs in French and English, accompanied by Latin paraphrases. By the late decades of the twelfth century, French proverb literature is being composed in poetry, as in the Anglo-Norman translations of the *Disticha Catonis*.[63] From its Anglo-Norman origins, medieval French proverb literature grows in the entire range of French-speaking places, like the court of Philip of Flanders, where the *Proverbes au vilain* was composed. This would not be the only instance of Anglo-Norman textual innovation spreading eastward: Laura Ashe points out that the earliest French-language chronicle, law text, bestiary, lapidary, and heraldic treatise originated in post-Conquest England.[64] Like these other text types, French proverb literature owes much to the multilingual and multicultural environment of Anglo-Norman England. The Anglo-Saxon tradition of gnomic poetry persisted into the twelfth century, as evidenced by a work like the *Proverbs of Alfred*. The triglossia of twelfth-to-thirteenth-century English clerical and aristocratic culture made translation an almost constant activity. Putting these two trends together yields a fertile ground for the creation of a new, French proverb literature that subsequently flowed easily into the continental stream of vernacularization of literary culture.

Returning to the topic of the English language: in Bodleian Library, Digby 86, the *Proverbs of Hendyng* and *Proverbes au vilain* are accompanied by an excerpt from the *Proverbs of Alfred*. This trilingual anthology also contains devotional material in both Latin and French: prayers, psalms, and a Life of the Blessed Virgin. In English, Digby 86 augments the proverb collections with literary works of satire and entertainment like the fabliau *Dame Sirith* and the

---

62. Elisabeth Schulze-Busacker, "Au Carrefour des Genres: les 'Proverbes au vilain,'" 82; see also her "Proverbs and Maxims in Medieval French Literature."

63. Idem, "Au Carrefour des Genres," 84–86. For a list of Anglo-Norman proverb texts, see Ruth J. Dean with Maureen B. M. Boulton, *Anglo-Norman Literature: A Guide to Texts and Manuscripts*, 143–56.

64. Laura Ashe, *Fiction and History in England, 1066–1200*, 23.

beast fable *The Fox and the Wolf.* The secular end of the cultural continuum is further represented by French texts ranging from fabliaux and romances to a treatise on the care of hunting birds.⁶⁵ The inclusion of poeticized proverb collections in such an impressive anthology shows that, in the words of Cameron Louis, "proverb literature was throughout the Middle English period seen very much as part of the canon of respected mainstream literature which was read by aristocrats and wealthy members of the middle class."⁶⁶ In Digby 86, we see further evidence of the status of the English language upheld through the medium of the proverb: this manuscript offers a rich banquet of intellectual, devotional, and entertaining materials (alongside some purely practical instructions), but its gnomic poems present the most encompassing ethical directions for adult readers. The *Proverbs of Alfred* is morally straightforward, the *Proverbs of Hendyng* and *Proverbes au vilain* somewhat more complex in the ethical world they reflect, but the choice of language for these texts—English in two of the three—demonstrates the persistent power of English proverbial discourse. In Digby 86, a high-status, trilingual collection, the English language, especially when voiced proverbially, is deemed suitable for both simple and sophisticated issues of individual and social ethics. This domain of wisdom or advice typically gets little attention from modern readers, but it formed an essential component of personal and social development in the Middle Ages.

Works like the *Disticha Catonis* (in Latin, English, and French), the *Proverbs of Alfred,* and the *Proverbs of Hendyng* remained available through the thirteenth and fourteenth centuries, but very few new collections of English proverbs were compiled during that period. This lull is not surprising, considering that French surpassed English as the literary vernacular at that time. As a result, numerous French and Anglo-Norman proverb collections originated and/or circulated in England, some including Latin parallels for teaching purposes, others including allegorical expositions for the aid of preachers or even legal commentaries for the training of lawyers.⁶⁷ The use of these French-language collections in England increased the cross-fertilization of proverbs between the two languages. Just as English proverbs were translated into Latin as school exercises going back to the Anglo-Saxon period, English proverbs of oral or written origin would find transformed life in French collections and, of course, French proverbs encountered in schoolroom contexts would become part of the English repertoire.

---

65. *Facsimile of Oxford, Bodleian Library, MS Digby 86.*
66. Louis, "Manuscript Contexts of Middle English Proverb Literature," 223.
67. J. Morawski, "Les recueils d'anciens proverbes français analysés et classés."

The production of proverb collections in English picks up considerably in the fifteenth century. Some of these collections follow the familiar schooltext pattern of pairing Latin and vernacular sentences,[68] while others contain only vernacular proverbs but arrange and rewrite them into rhymed couplets or stanzas.[69] The learned enthusiasm for proverbs grows even greater in the sixteenth and seventeenth centuries as the study of rhetoric becomes more influential. Following the example of Erasmus with his compendious *Adagia*, Renaissance scholars produced numerous collections in both Latin and English.[70] Like the Renaissance collections, those of the fifteenth century seem to use mostly written sources in their composition. For example, the English/Latin collections found in Rylands Latin MS. 394 and Douce MS. 52 "may . . . be regarded practically as two versions of the same collection" as they overlap considerably in both contents and structure.[71] Rawlinson MS. D 328 shares more than a third of its eighty-three proverbs with Rylands 394 and Douce 52.[72] All three of these are curricular tools for teaching Latin, so a written transmission is to be expected. Scholars of the fifteenth century were not early folklorists striving to preserve a proverbial heritage, but teachers in search of lesson plans for instruction in both Latin language and rhetoric. Nevertheless, in their search for literacy tools they doubtless passed along some genuinely oral proverbs that from then on also became part of the written tradition. Alliterative proverbs, which were English in form even when not in origin, remained part of that oral/written mélange.

Proverb collections, then, constitute an informative element of the language ecology of medieval England by illustrating the complexity of linguistic relationships over a long period of time. It is easy enough to state that in the Anglo-Saxon period, Latin was a higher-status written language than English, but then we find a text like the Durham Proverbs, in which the English portion sometimes carries more authority than the Latin. The presence of Latin in medieval proverb collections reflects the role of the church in literacy education; this role wanes a bit in the late Middle Ages, but the Renaissance sees a resurgence of Latin proverb collections, this time based on the pursuit of humanistic studies. The Middle English period likewise resists a simplified narrative not only in the relationship between Latin and the vernacular, but

---

68. See, for example, Pantin, "Medieval Collection of Latin and English Proverbs and Riddles"; Meech, "Collection of Proverbs in Rawlinson MS D 328"; and Joanna Bellis and Venetia Bridges, "What shalt thou do when thou hast an english to make into Latin?"
69. See Zupitza, "The Proverbis of Wysdom"; and K. Brunner, "Spätme. Lehrgedichte."
70. See Heywood, *John Heywood's "A Dialogue of Proverbs,"* 8–28.
71. Pantin, "Medieval Collection of Latin and English Proverbs," 89.
72. Meech, "Collection of Proverbs," 114–15.

also in the constantly shifting roles of the two vernaculars, English and French. It surprises no one to see English proverb collections outnumber French ones in the fifteenth century, but the earlier, deliberate assertion of Englishness in the thirteenth-century *Proverbs of Hendyng* or the English origins of French proverb poems are perhaps more unexpected. The importance of these proverb collections cannot be overestimated: they were part of the education of nearly every literate person in the Middle Ages and thus both influenced and reflect attitudes toward language throughout that period.

Not all didactic genres make use of alliterative proverbs. From the fourteenth and fifteenth centuries arose a rash of what we might call "moral poems" in Middle English. These works seem directed toward the laity—sometimes children, sometimes adults—and are almost always end-rhymed in couplets or stanzas. Examples of this type of poetry include "The Good Wife Taught Her Daughter," "A Ballad of Good Counsel," Alexander Barclay's version of "The Ship of Fools," and "Symon's Lesson of Wysedome," along with numerous shorter works found in miscellanies and commonplace books.[73] Alliterative proverbs are not common in these poems, perhaps because the poets—who are typically not of the highest caliber—found them difficult to work into their metrical schemes, but perhaps also because these poems offer an *alternative* to proverb collections in the educational process and thus strive not to duplicate them too closely. Furthermore, the audience for these "moral poems" was often made up of social strivers who would perhaps rather not teach their children using metrical or proverbial forms that were sometimes linked more closely with peasants than with princes.[74] Only aristocratic readers, insulated by greater socioeconomic distance, enjoyed the freedom to arch an eyebrow at the reported sayings of the underclass.

DEVOTIONAL PROSE

One vernacular genre that grows considerably between the Old English and Middle English periods is religiously didactic (but nonhomiletic) prose. In the Anglo-Saxon period, such works were directed almost exclusively toward the clergy, with the sad assumption that not all of them could read Latin with ease.

---

73. *The Good Wife Taught Her Daughter*; *The Good Wyfe Wold a Pylgremage*; *The Thewis of Gud Women*; "A Ballad of Good Counsel" in *The Scottish Metrical Romance of Lancelot du Lak*, 169–70; Barclay, *The Ship of Fools*; "Symon's Lesson of Wysedome," in *The Babees Book*, 399–402.

74. For further discussion of these texts and their readership, see the introduction to *The Good Wife Taught Her Daughter* and A. Leslie Harris, "Instructional Poetry for Medieval Children."

The famous preface to King Alfred's translation of Gregory's *Regula Pastoralis* addresses the bishops of the realm in English—partly so that its message might be disseminated more widely but also to support by example the teaching of English literacy for which it calls.[75]

The body of religious prose grows considerably during the Middle English period as the laity are added to its audience.[76] There is, in fact, a certain amount of overlap as texts that were written for certain varieties of religious—recluses, for example—would be read more widely among both cloistered and laypeople. Conversely, treatises directed toward pious laypeople also found a clerical audience. The rise of women readers among both lay and religious fertilized this growth.[77]

In fact, the first Middle English didactic prose text that I wish to address was written for women—the *Ancrene Riwle* or *Ancrene Wisse*. This thirteenth-century treatise was initially addressed to a trio of anchoritic sisters, but the author had in mind and included material for a wider audience, as well. The *Ancrene Wisse* was revised, adapted, and translated (into French and Latin) very quickly for a variety of audiences: anchoritic and nonanchoritic, female and male, religious and lay.[78] Alliteration serves multiple roles in this text, as we can explore through the career of a particular alliterative proverb.

In a description of the deceitful ways of the devil, the author of the *Ancrene Wisse* explains that the evil one may try to trick a person by advocating an attitude generally favored by God (e.g., just discipline) but pressing for its misapplication: "Rihtwisnesse he seið mot beo nede sturne ant þus he liteð cruelte wið heow of rihtwisnesse."[79] Authoritative warnings against such behavior follow, one drawn from the Bible and cited in both English and Latin, and one in the form of an English proverb:

> Me mai beon al to riht wis. Noli esse iustus nimis. In ecclesiate. Betere is wis liste þan luðer strengðe.[80]

> [One may be entirely too righteous. Do not be overly strict in justice. In Ecclesiastes (7.16). Better is wise cunning than evil strength.]

---

75. On the cultural context of Alfred's translations, see Carolin Schreiber, *King Alfred's Old English Translation of Pope Gregory the Great's "Regula Pastoralis" and Its Cultural Context*, 11–22.
76. Vincent Gillespie, "Vernacular Books of Religion."
77. See Alexandra Barratt, "English Translations of Didactic Literature for Women to 1550."
78. Bella Millett, "The *Ancrene Wisse* Group," 2–3.
79. *Ancrene Wisse*, ed. Tolkien, 138 [punctuation omitted].
80. Ibid. The version in Cotton Cleopatra C. VI omits the Latin (*The English Text of the Ancrene Riwle: Edited from British Museum Cotton MS. Cleopatra C.vi*, 197).

The alliteration of the proverb provides it with sufficient authority to stand beside a biblical quotation. It is, according to D. V. Ives, a specifically English proverb;[81] in fact, its Englishness is nearly iconic in other texts. Here, then, the proverb combines with the biblical quotation to reinforce the desired lesson using authorities from both the Latin and English realms of the anchoress's cultural world. By juxtaposing the English proverb and quotation—in both languages—the author of *Ancrene Wisse* unites the vernacular milieu from which the anchoress comes with the sacred life to which she aspires. Bella Millett suggests that the time (around the 1230s) and place (West Midlands) of the *Ancrene Wisse*'s origin make it a likely candidate for syncretic composition. Religious institutions of the West Midlands maintained an interest in Anglo-Saxon manuscripts, but the bishops seem also to introduce new Franco-Latin preaching methods from Paris. As Millett argues, these older and newer trends were not necessarily in opposition to each other, but could be combined in a work like the *Ancrene Wisse*.[82] It is not surprising, then, to see the author of *Ancrene Wisse* experimenting with forms of linguistic authority.

The same proverb continues to prove popular with writers and translators of Middle English literature for contemplatives. Many of these texts were heavily influenced by Richard of St. Victor, whose works they frequently translate, summarize, or paraphrase. In transforming Richard's words and ideas from Latin into English, the later writers vernacularize their texts in ways that go beyond the strictly linguistic. For example, in his so-called *Benjamin Minor*, Richard presents lengthy allegorical readings of the sons of Rachel. Joseph represents discretion:

> Sed post natam Dinam et quasi per confusionis ignominiam fratres sui inveniunt, et per experimentum addiscunt, nihil melius esse quam consilio regi: *Quia melior est vir prudens viro forti* (Prov. XVI). *Vir enim prudens loquitur victorias, et qui cum consilio cuncta agit, in aeternum non poenitebit* (Prov. XXI). Cum igitur consilii necessaria utilitas per experimentum cognoscitur, et per studium attentius quaeritur et invenitur, Joseph quodammodo nascitur, per quem virtus discretionis intelligitur.[83]
>
> [But after Dina's shameful birth his brothers searched for him (Joseph) confusedly, and discovered through their efforts that he had risen to become

---

81. D. V. Ives, "The Proverbs in the 'Ancren Riwle,'" 265.
82. Millett, "*Ancrene Wisse* Group," 9–10.
83. Richard of St. Victor, *De Praeparatione animi ad contemplationem, liber dictus Benjamin Minor*, ch. 47, *PL* 196.48C–48D.

consul to the king. Because a wise man is better than a strong one (Proverbs 16). For a wise man speaks of victories, and he who does all things by good counsel will not be punished in eternity (Proverbs 21). When, therefore, useful counsels are necessarily found through experience, and are sought and found through attentive study, in this way is Joseph discovered, who stands for the virtue of discretion.]

A Middle English version of the *Benjamin Minor* (not close enough to be called a translation) was written in the fourteenth century. It omits Richard's quotation of Prov. 16 and paraphrases Prov. 21:

> & þerfor it is þat after am all & last is Dyna borne, for oft after a sodeyn fal comes sone schame. And þus after mone fallynges & failynges, & schame foloande, a man lers be þe prof þare is noying better þen to be rewlede be counsell, þe wilk is þe redist geytyng of discresion. Forwy he þat dus all yng with consaile, hym sall newere forynk it—ffor better liste þen lythere strenght.[84]

Alliteration figures prominently in this passage, with the clusters of "sodeyn, sone, schame" and "fallynges, failynges, foloande." The authoritative wisdom of alliteration becomes apparent when our proverb is used not in passing or as a simple supplement, but, introduced with "ffor" (that is, "because"), as a logical prerequisite to the biblical paraphrase. Rhetorically, the English proverb forms the base of knowledge on which the biblical proverb expands. If the reader were to recognize the biblical reference, the English proverb would still appear (almost) equally authoritative; if the reader missed the allusion, the alliterative proverb would stand out even more for its authority and memorableness. A different redaction of the Middle English *Benjamin Minor* (Harley 674 versus Harley 1022) uses the same clusters of alliteration but treats the biblical passages a little differently:

> For whi he þat doþ alle þing by counsel, he schal neuir forþink it. For betir is a sley man þan a strong man, 3e, and betyr is list þen liþer strengþe. And a sley man spekiþ of victories.[85]

This version breaks up the two biblical verses into three sententiae, reorders them, and places the English proverb in the middle. By this disruption, the

---

84. Richard of St. Victor, *Benjamin Minor*, in *Yorkshire Writers*, I.170.
85. *A Tretyse of þe Stodye of Wysdome þat Men Clepen Beniamyn*, in *Deonise Hid Diuinite*, 40–41.

biblical sentences lose some of their superior authority and are rendered further equivalent to the English proverb by being adorned with such alliterative language as "sley, strong, sekiþ." Alliteration is a commonly used device in this text, as in another, the *Pistle of Preier,* probably by the same author.[86] Our proverb is found in that work, and in *The Cloud of Unknowing,* a more famous treatise perhaps from the same pen.[87] According to Phyllis Hodgson, who edited the entire cluster of texts, their use of alliteration

> is abundant, but unobtrusive, for it is neither perfunctory nor merely decorative. It sharpens the outline of the thought and reinforces the rhythm of the sentence. Often it serves to point an antithesis or to weight a balance, and it gives to many a phrase the pithiness of epigram.[88]

Hodgson's explanation, while accurate, is based entirely on the principles of rhetoric. The fourteenth-century author might also have been influenced by the prevalence of alliteration in early Middle English religious prose like the works of the Katherine Group.[89] He is intellectually indebted to Latin writers like Richard of St. Victor, but endeavors to create a specifically English literature of Christian devotion. He does this partly through his vocabulary, continuing the use of words from earlier English religious texts and introducing new lexemes.[90] He makes good use of the teachings of Latin rhetoric, but the frequency with which he employs alliteration gives his style an especially English flavor. Like William Langland—who was writing at around the same time—he finds alliteration (including alliterative proverbs) to be an appropriate and forceful mode for the expression of religious wisdom. However, the appreciation of English as a language of religious discourse was not permanent. Nicholas Watson describes the second half of the fourteenth century as a period in which the appropriateness of English for theological discourse became increasingly contested.[91] As the audience for English texts became wider, ecclesiastical authorities were less able to exert control over them; the rise of the Lollard movement added to the sense of crisis. According to

---

86. See introduction to *Deonise Hid Diuinite.*

87. *A Pistle of Preier,* in ibid., 58; *The Cloud of Unknowing and The Book of Privy Counselling,* 87.

88. *Deonise Hid Diuinite,* l.

89. The phrase "liste ne luðer strengðe" appears in the *Life of St. Katherine;* see *Seinte Katerine,* 79–80 (lines 1031–32 in the Titus MS.; the phrase also appears in the Royal and Bodley MSS.).

90. *Deonise Hid Diuinite,* xxx–xxxiv.

91. Nicholas Watson, "Censorship and Cultural Change in Late-Medieval England," 837–46.

Watson, Arundel's *Constitutions*, which banned the making or owning of new Bible translations, created a climate in which the development of "vernacular theology" was stifled.[92] Existing religious texts in English continued to circulate, but Latin recovered its status as the language of *translatio studii*.[93]

Nevertheless, religious prose is one domain in which English flourished as a written language for a time after the Norman Conquest. For this use, Latin would have represented a higher-status language choice, but would have excluded the lay audience and even some part of the clerical audience. French was another option, as the high-status vernacular, but its use may not have extended far enough from centers of power. Thus, there existed a niche exploited by writers of English religious prose, who chose English very consciously in this three-way linguistic competition. The incorporation of alliteration, and specifically, of alliterative proverbs in these works of religious prose reflects the desire of the authors to highlight their linguistic choice and advertise the strength of their native linguistic tradition.

ETHNOGRAPHY

Having mentioned, albeit briefly, the influence of Latin rhetorical training on the use of alliteration, I will digress to consider another text that includes the proverb "Better is list than lither strength," but is not a piece of devotional prose. This is the *Descriptio Kambriae* by Giraldus Cambrensis. Giraldus wrote the *Descriptio* in 1194 and revised it twice in the first decades of the thirteenth century. He was, besides an ambitious ecclesiastic, an interested observer of language who commented, for example, on dialect features of both Welsh and English.[94] In Book I of the *Descriptio Kambriae* he describes the great intelligence of the Welsh people, concentrating on their various means of expression. Giraldus praises their musicianship and their oratory, then moves on to speak of their poetry, which he finds noteworthy for its use of alliteration. This section is worth quoting in full:

> Præ cunctis tamen rhetoricis exornationibus, annominatione magis utuntur; eaque præcipue specie, quæ primas dictionum literas vel syllabas convenientia jungit.

---

92. For some responses to Watson's highly influential article, see the forum on vernacular theology in *ELN* 44 (2006).
93. See also Alastair Minnis, *Translations of Authority in Medieval English Literature*, 25–37.
94. Mark Faulkner, "Gerald of Wales and Standard Old English."

Adeo igitur hoc verborum ornatu duæ nationes, Angli scilicet et Kambri, in omni sermone exquisito utuntur, ut nihil ab his eleganter dictum, nullum egregium, nullum nisi rude et agreste censeatur eloquium, si non schematis hujus lima plene fuerit expolitum. Sicut Britannice in hunc modum;

Dychaun Dyu da dy unic.
Erbyn dibuilh puilh paraut.

Anglice vero sic;

Godis to gedere gamen and wisdom.
Ne halt nocht al sor isaid, ne al sorghe atwite.
Betere is red thene rap, and liste thene lither streingthe.

In Latino quoque haud dissimiliter eloquio, eandem exornationem frequens est invenire. In hunc modum Virgilius;

Tales casus Cassandra canebat.

Et illud ejusdem ad Augustum;

Dum dubitet natura marem faceretve puellam,
Natus es, O pulcher, pene puella, puer.

In nullis tamen linguis, quas novimus, hæc exornatio adeo ut in prioribus duabus est usitata.

Mirum autem quod Gallica lingua, alias tam ornata, hunc verborum ornatum, ab aliis tam usitatum, prorsus ignorat. Nec ego tamen id crediderim, quod priores populi duo, tam diversi ab invicem et adversi, in hoc verborum ornatu ex arte conveniant, sed potius ex usu longo: qui, quia placuit solum, et facili similium ad similia transitu aures demulcet, per succedentia tempora inolevit.[95]

[More than any other rhetorical figure they delight in alliteration, and especially that which links together the initial letters or syllables of words. The two peoples, both English and Welsh, make such play with this literary device when they are trying to speak elegantly, that any pronouncement is condemned as rough and uncouth if it is not so polished and adorned. Here are two examples in Welsh:

Dychaun Dyu da dy unic. (God can provide for the lonely man.)
Erbyn dibuilh puilh paraut. (Guard thyself against evil desire.)

Here are three in English:

God is togedere gamen and wisdom.
Ne halt nocht al sor isaid, ne al sorghe atwite.
Betere is red thene rap, and liste thene lither streingthe.

---

95. Giraldus Cambrensis, *Descriptio Kambriae*, Book 1, ch. 12, 187–89.

It is much the same in Latin literature, where you often find this figure. Virgil wrote:

Of such calamities Cassandra sang.

It was Virgil again who addressed the following lines to Augustus:

A boyish girl? Dame Nature is inscrutable!

You're born, a girlish boy, a boy, but beautiful.

In no other of the languages which I know is this device of alliteration used as much as in English and Welsh. It is remarkable, for instance, that French, which is so richly adorned with other figures, should never make use of this particular one, whereas other languages are full of it. I cannot believe that the Welsh and the English, so different from each other and so antagonistic, could ever consciously agree about the rhetorical device. It must be just habit: the facile jump from like to like has appealed to each of them separately. It pleases the ear and so it has been used more and more down the years.][96]

Of immediate interest is the fact that Giraldus, of a noble Welsh-Norman family, writing at the very end of the twelfth century, finds English poetry noteworthy for its alliteration. It would be tempting to draw from this connection the conclusion that alliteration was still a widely recognized feature of English poetry at this point, or even less ambitiously, that poetry in English was familiar even to the nobility and higher clergy. However, Giraldus is probably not a reliable informant on these points. Yoko Wada argues that Giraldus's command of Welsh (language and literature) was not likely very strong and points out that his vernacular examples of alliteration "appear to be such as might have been taken from a language-workbook, whereas his example from Latin is from Vergil."[97] In fact, Ian Cornelius points out that "casus Cassandra canebat" is not just from Vergil, but was a common phrase used to illustrate alliteration in medieval schools. According to Cornelius, Giraldus's perception of alliteration takes place entirely through the lens of his knowledge of Latin rhetoric, which colors much of this passage of the *Descriptio Kambriae*.[98] Certainly, the vernacular examples cited by Giraldus show no great depth of poetic knowledge; instead, they are proverbial. Thomas Jones believes that the

---

96. Giraldus Cambrensis, *The Journey through Wales and The Description of Wales*, 240–42.

97. Yoko Wada, "Gerald on Gerald: Self-Presentation by Giraldus Cambrensis," 241. See also Ad Putter, "Multilingualism in England and Wales, c.1200: The Testimony of Gerald of Wales."

98. Ian Cornelius, "Classical Rhetoric and the Perception of Alliterative Verse." I am extremely grateful to Professor Cornelius for his generosity in forwarding to me a copy of his paper.

lines in Welsh "seem to come originally from gnomic poems"[99] and it is clear that the English examples take proverbial form. It is almost certain that Giraldus found them in a proverb collection. For example, Giraldus cites the compound sentence "Ne halt nocht al sor isaid, ne al sorghe atwite." As pointed out by Lewis Thorpe, a similar sentence appears in the Durham Proverbs: "Ne deah eall soþ asæd ne eall sar ætwiten"[100] [It does not avail to speak every truth or lament every sorrow]. Thorpe does not comment on a significant difference between the two versions: the substantive of Giraldus's first clause is "sor," whereas the Durham Proverbs reads "soþ." The difference extends to the Latin glosses to each text. The Durham Proverbs glosses only the first clause, with "Non omnia uera dicenda sunt" [not every truth should be spoken] while MS D (Dimock's base manuscript) of the *Descriptio Kambriae* glosses the entire sentence, giving the substantives as "malum" and "incommodum."[101] It is likely that the Durham Proverbs records the proverb more accurately, first, because the initial clause becomes a common proverb by the end of the fourteenth century,[102] and second, because Giraldus's version is essentially redundant, which proverbs typically are not. Either Giraldus misread his source, or the proverb collection that he used was itself faulty. Whichever the case might be, the error reflects Giraldus's reliance on a written source and an imperfect familiarity with the proverb itself, and to some degree, with proverbial idiom more generally.[103]

Despite his inability to cite solid examples, Giraldus does seem to understand—to some extent—the basic position of alliteration in the vernacular traditions he discusses. He overstates his case, but it was true that both Welsh and English poets used alliteration as a significant feature of their metrics, while French poets did not. Of course, Giraldus misleads his readers regarding the prevalence of alliteration in Latin poetry. He sets a clear line with Welsh, English, and Latin on one side, and French on the other. By doing so, he lends the status of Latin to Welsh and English, without necessarily debasing French poetry, which he describes as "alias tam ornata." His implicit praise and elevation of Welsh and English poetry does not seem to stem from

---

99. Thomas Jones, "Gerald the Welshman's 'Itinerary through Wales' and 'Description of Wales': An Appreciation and Analysis," 221, note 51.

100. Giraldus Cambrensis, *The Journey through Wales and The Description of Wales*, 241, note 539; "The Durham Proverbs," #19.

101. Ibid.

102. See Whiting, *Proverbs . . . before 1500*, S485: "All sooth is not to be said."

103. A. A. Goddu and R. H. Rouse describe how Giraldus relied on another type of collection—the florilegium—for many of his quotations; see their "Gerald of Wales and the *Florilegium Angelicum*."

personal experience—he can't actually cite any—but is part of his structural program for the *Descriptio* in which Book 1 is full of praise for Wales while its faults are deferred to Book 2.[104] In sum, Giraldus must have known a little bit about alliteration in the poetry of his day, but when he needed to find examples of it he turned to the types of materials that came most readily to hand (or mind): school-texts for the Latin and alliterative proverbs for the vernaculars. He provides an interesting example of the strength of the connection between proverbs and alliteration in English, of the potential relationship between alliterative proverbs and poetry, and of the inventive uses to which proverb collections could be put by a creative medieval scholar.

SERMONS

The genre of didactic literature touching the largest medieval population—clerical and lay, aristocratic and common—was the sermon. The long history of the sermon and the necessity for sermons to address various types of audiences mean that medieval sermons appear in multiple forms. For example, the laity would typically be preached to in the vernacular, but the use of English in a sermon from the thirteenth century might imply a different social status for that lay audience than it would in the eleventh. A Latin sermon from the fourteenth century could have been intended for a clerical audience, or it could be the written record of a sermon preached in English or French. The proverb had its uses in addressing any audience, although those uses varied depending upon context, ranging from providing a note of familiarity for a lay audience, to marking structural divisions in a scholastic sermon for a group of university auditors.

Although a form of wisdom statement like the proverb might seem an inevitable component of a didactic genre like the sermon, the textual record indicates that the use of proverbs in medieval sermons in fact required a bit of a cultural push. In general, Old English homilies and sermons do not use many proverbs. One could read through quite a substantial number of Old English sermons before coming upon a sentence that we would classify as a proverb (although proverbial comparisons like "as dark as night" are more common). Proverbs become more plentiful in sermons beginning in the late twelfth to early thirteenth centuries.[105] This growth in the homiletic use of

---

104. Giraldus Cambrensis, *The Journey through Wales and The Description of Wales*, 47–48.
105. G. R. Owst, *Literature and Pulpit in Medieval England*, 41–46; Siegfried Wenzel, *Verses in Sermons: "Fasciculus morum" and Its Middle English Poems*, 73–74, 96–97; idem, "French Proverbs from the Mouths of English Preachers?"; Buridant, "Les proverbes et la prédication

proverbs comes thanks to two ecclesiastical developments. The first is the introduction of the "scholastic" or "modern" sermon, a style of sermon with a highly defined structure.[106] The scholastic sermon organized the explication of its theme into numerous *divisiones*; according to handbooks for the composition of such sermons, proverbs were useful rhetorical tools for introducing and demarcating these divisions.[107] As a result, proverbs appear fairly frequently in these texts.

Scholastic sermons are often associated with the universities, and are at least as likely to have been composed and received in Latin as in the vernacular. A second development, also around the turn of the thirteenth century, led to the greater use of proverbs in vernacular sermons directed toward the laity: the Fourth Lateran Council of 1215. Among other things, the Fourth Lateran Council called for the clergy to increase their efforts in instructing the laity in the principles of the faith.[108] This renewed emphasis on pastoral work resulted in the production of a wide range of English-language religious texts, sermons among them. The understanding that folk proverbs represented the familiar wisdom of the common people led to the use of such proverbs as rhetorical and didactic tools in sermons for the laity. Thus, the increased deployment of proverbs in sermons from the thirteenth through the fifteenth centuries advanced from two directions: the Latin and learned, on the one hand, and the appeal to the vernacular and oral, on the other. Of course, once set in motion, these two movements merged together and reinforced each other, so the presence of a specific proverb in a specific text cannot necessarily be attributed to one or the other trend.

Whether appearing in English, French, or Latin sermons, proverbs were used for their persuasive powers (as appeals to common wisdom or as proof texts), as vernacular touchstones of familiarity, and as summarizing statements

---

au Moyen Age: De l'utilisation des proverbes vulgaires dans les sermons." For a somewhat dissenting view, see Franco Morenzoni, "Les proverbes dans la prédication du XIIIe siècle."

106. On "ancient" and "modern" forms of sermons, see H. Leith Spencer, *English Preaching in the Late Middle Ages*, 228–47; for a concise description of the structure of a "modern" sermon, see Wenzel, *Preachers, Poets, and the Early English Lyric*, 66.

107. Wenzel, *Verses in Sermons*, 96; Buridant, "Les proverbes et la prédication," 26–28; Bland, "The Use of Proverbs in Two Medieval Genres of Discourse: 'The Art of Poetry' and 'The Art of Preaching.'" Morenzoni ("Les proverbes dans la prédication") gives numerous examples of these recommendations for proverb use, though he argues that they are uncommon.

108. For a succinct description of the development of pastoral materials in the wake of the Fourth Lateran Council, see Leonard E. Boyle, O. P., "The Fourth Lateran Council and Manuals of Popular Theology." On the use of English for such materials, see Judith Shaw, "The Influence of Canonical and Episcopal Reform on Popular Books of Instruction," 51–55. See also F. Donald Lagan, *A History of the Church in the Middle Ages*, 193–201; and Turville-Petre, *Reading Middle English Literature*, 123–24.

producing structural divisions. Sermons of all types drew from the authority of proverbs that were already in existence, but they also helped to create "new" proverbs when, as often happened, preachers or sermon writers promulgated brief quotations without reference to their written sources. In this manner, sentences from the Bible and the Fathers were offered and received in the same way as proverbs of anonymous origin. In medieval society, where proverbs still wielded social and intellectual authority, the very form of a didactic statement carried sufficient weight to render unnecessary any appeal to a named source.

Besides floating relatively freely between the literate and oral realms, proverbs in sermons also participated in the linguistic fungibility of the genre. English proverbs appear in Latin sermons; French proverbs appear in English sermons; Latin proverbs may appear almost anywhere. Both the proverb and the sermon are international forms; because Latin was the most common mode of international communication, it was the language in which many proverbs moved from place to place.[109] In fact, the Latin version of a sermon, with its attendant proverbs, could be created as a text specifically for convenient reference, even when the public, oral delivery of the sermon took place in some other language. The complicated web of languages in sermons is perhaps most evident in the macaronic sermons of late medieval England, a defined corpus the elements of which have been carefully examined.

The macaronic sermons studied by Siegfried Wenzel, Patrick Horner, and others, are composed primarily in Latin, with bits of English sprinkled throughout.[110] This code-switching sometimes occurs at sentence boundaries, but it is more frequently intrasentential. Thus, a proverb may be cited entirely in English—"Schal neuer cloc henne be wel crowing cok"[111]—but, more frequently, it will appear in a linguistically mixed form—"hewe not supra caput tuum"[112] [hew not above your head]. Such code-switching, curious as it is, can shed light on the performative and textual history of these sermons in the complex language ecology of medieval England. Wenzel suggests that the macaronic sermons could have been delivered orally to a bilingual audience, but he also describes them as written compositions meant to be read and studied by "fellow preachers."[113] Alan Fletcher rejects Wenzel's suggestion of macaronic preaching, arguing instead that these sermons may have been preached

---

109. Buridant, "Les proverbes et la prédication," 42–43.
110. Wenzel, *Macaronic Sermons: Bilingualism and Preaching in Late-Medieval England; A Macaronic Sermon Collection from Late Medieval England, MS Bodley 649* (ed. Horner).
111. Wenzel, *Macaronic Sermons*, 91.
112. Cited by Halmari and Regetz, "Syntactic Aspects of Code-Switching," 127.
113. Wenzel, *Macaronic Sermons*, 106, 124–25.

orally in English, but acquired Latin when they were written down.[114] Fletcher supports his hypothesis by pointing out that Latin was the standard language for ecclesiastical writing and that the audience for a written version of the sermons would be clerical, so the use of Latin, the language of the clergy, would create a bond between the sermon author and the audience. Wenzel describes the code-switching in the sermons as "a random phenomenon"; Halmari and Regetz find a syntactic "hierarchy of switching sites" but admit that the patterns of switching are "probabilistic" rather than predictable.[115] Such unpredictable, intrasentential code-switching implies writers who are highly proficient bilinguals,[116] a characterization on which everyone seems to agree. Fletcher's theory of oral presentation of the sermons in English, with subsequent inscribing of primarily Latin versions, agrees with the way we typically perceive the use of language in the relevant domains: English for oral teaching, Latin for ecclesiastical writing. If the sermons were preached in English, the potential audience would open up to include laypeople. However, all of the macaronic sermons in question are of the "modern" or scholastic structure, a type of sermon more often (though not exclusively) associated with the universities and other collections of clergy.[117] Both Wenzel and Horner support a university setting for these sermons (Fletcher does not suggest a venue); if they were, in fact, preached in English, we might need to reconsider some assumptions about language use among the clergy.[118] Perhaps the Latin competence of even the more highly educated clergy—those attending university—was sufficient for reading and writing but not necessarily for speaking or listening. In such a setting, the status of English would not have been high enough for written use, but it would gain strength as the language spoken by scholars. In any case, the written, macaronic versions of the sermons, in which, as Fletcher explains, "English is being allowed to contest Latin," demonstrate what he calls the "linguistic self-confidence" of both languages.[119] We might now examine specific instances of how proverbs fit into this homiletic context.

Because the rhetorical techniques of sermon writers are typically purposeful, the ways in which they introduce proverbs reliably indicate their attitudes

---

114. Fletcher, *Late Medieval Popular Preaching in Britain and Ireland*, 61–66.

115. Wenzel, *Macaronic Sermons*, 101; Halmari and Regetz, "Syntactic Aspects of Code-Switching," 116.

116. Romaine, *Bilingualism*, 112–14.

117. Wenzel, *Macaronic Sermons*, 74; *Macaronic Sermon Collection*, 7.

118. See, for example, the statement by the abbot of Bury St. Edmunds in the late twelfth century that his monks would benefit more if they were preached to, not in Latin, but "*Gallice uel pocius Anglice* 'in French or, preferably, in English,'" cited by Cecily Clark, "The Myth of 'The Anglo-Norman Scribe,'" 171.

119. Fletcher, *Late Medieval Popular Preaching*, 66.

toward them and the uses to which they intended to put them. One way that preachers emphasize the authority of proverbs is to point out their antiquity:

> ffor men seyen in olde speche,
> Grene wounde nys bote game,
> and ole synne maketh newe schame.[120]

In this poeticized sermon on the Lord's Prayer, the author has combined two alliterative proverbs into a rhyming couplet. His reference to "olde speche" may reinforce the time-honored value of these sententiae or may refer specifically to their alliteration. The latter seems more likely, as it would strain credulity to believe that the only two proverbs in this lengthy, end-rhymed poem just happened to alliterate by accident. For this sermonizer, "olde speche" equals alliterative and proverbial speech.

Sometimes, not just the antiquity, but the Englishness of the proverb's language is specified, even within texts that are English themselves:

> men seit on old Englisch that weneinge nis no wisdome[121]

> As me saiþ on hold Englis: "Wan deþ haþ i-bite and is last strok y-smite, þan ay loue ys lef forȝut."[122]

The first of these two quotations derives from its context at least some justification for referring to the English language: it comes from the prologue to a Middle English translation of a collection of French sermons. The alliterative proverb, explicitly labeled as English, endues the language choice of the (late fourteenth-century) translation with the authority of ancient wisdom: the translator's source material may be French, but English adds its own intellectual value to it.

In the second quotation, from a late Middle English sermon, the reference to "hold Englis" seems designed to impart the authority of ancient, alliterative proverbs to a mostly end-rhymed sentence that takes gnomic form, but in its length, rhyme, and rhythm seems more lyric than proverbial (and in its rhyme, newer rather than older). By the time this sermon was committed to writing in the mid-fifteenth century, the rhetorical authority of proverbs

---

120. Patterson, "A Sermon on the Lord's Prayer," 411.
121. Fletcher, *Late Medieval Popular Preaching*, 282.
122. Ibid., 228.

"in old English" was sufficiently established that the descriptor could be detached from an actual proverb and used to lend its authority elsewhere.

Sometimes the authority of a proverb is understood to inhere not in its language or antiquity, but in its familiarity. Siegfried Wenzel cites a Latin version of "Lief child behoves lore" from a fourteenth-century sermon collection: "Wlgariter dicitur: Carus filius caris indiget dogmatibus"[123] [It is commonly said: The beloved child needs precious teaching]. Elsewhere, an almost identical phrasing introduces a proverb in a macaronic sermon: "Vt vulgariter dicitur: 'He þat wil in curia nunc manere, he most couuray wel fouell' "[124] [As it is commonly said, He who wishes to remain at court must curry favel well]. In the first instance, the proverb and its described status as a common saying are simply carried over wholesale from English into Latin. As demonstrated in chapter 2, "Lief child behoves lore" is, in fact, a common proverb, and its translation here poses no great problem of recognition or comprehension. The second quotation, on the other hand, adds the complication of metaphor to the linguistic challenge. "To curry favel"—"favel" meaning a dun-colored horse—is a common metaphor for flattery first attested by Whiting around 1330.[125] In most instances, it occurs as a proverbial phrase rather than a complete, fixed sentence, but an alliterative, proverbial form does seem to have existed by the late fourteenth/early fifteenth century, as exemplified in the sermon and in the *Proverbis of Wysdom*:

> Who so wyll in cowrt dwell,
> Nedis most he cory fauell.[126]

The inclusion of this proverb in the sermon lends support to Fletcher's hypothesis that the original language of the macaronic sermons was English, because this proverb is essentially untranslatable and could not have appeared in a fully Latin version. Comparison with the version from the *Proverbis of Wysdom* sheds some light on the process of Latinizing the sermon: the untranslatable end of the proverb is recorded in English, but so is the beginning; thus, the English proverb is contained in a frame of English (the language in which it was "commonly said"). Retaining the English language at the beginning of an English proverb also accounts for the code-switching pattern of a proverb examined earlier: "Si docebis aperte plebem tuam, hewe not supra caput tuum"[127] [If you teach your people in public, hew not above your head].

---

123. Wenzel, *Verses in Sermons*, 146.
124. Idem, *Macaronic Sermons*, 91.
125. Whiting, *Proverbs . . . before 1500*, F85.
126. "Proverbis of Wysdom," 246, lines 91–92.
127. Halmari and Regetz, "Syntactic Aspects of Code-Switching," 127.

Besides being "commonly" said, an alliterative proverb may be "truly" said: "Et sicut veraciter dicitur, 'In trust is treason,' subito demon irruit in eum" [And just as it is truly said, "In trust is treason," suddenly the demon fell on him].[128] Here, the entire proverb appears in English, but a different sermon in the same collection mixes it with Latin, though maintaining the alliteration that is perhaps the proverb's guarantee of veracity: "Gile is circumquaque. Nunc in trist est treson" [Guile is everywhere. Now in trust is treason].[129] Still from the same collection of macaronic sermons, a proverb that alliterates in English is transmitted in Latin as a sentence that is simply "said," with no intensifying adverb: "vt dicitur, raro visus, cito oblitus" [as it is said, rarely seen, soon forgotten].[130] In a different, nonmacaronic sermon, the same proverb serves, without introduction, as an integrated element of a seamless argument: "Þus þou muste often tymes þenke on God, for-why on hym þat we þenke not on an seldon seyn is sone forʒette"[131] [Thus, you must frequently think about God, because he whom we think not of and seldom see is soon forgotten]. In this instance, the proverb is so thoroughly integrated into its context that it is recognizable as a proverb only by its alliteration.

In Middle English (and macaronic) sermons, then, alliteration highlights the antiquity, the Englishness, and the wisdom value of proverbs. These sermons also use alliteration ornamentally (in nonproverbial passages), as recommended by rhetorical manuals or in rhetorical moves of their own devising.[132] Perhaps, however, in light of the persuasive, didactic value associated with alliteration in proverbs, the ornamental type of alliteration also added to the reception of sermons as wisdom texts in a way that has hitherto gone undetected.

Sermons, religious instructions, biblical commentaries, gnomic poems, even ethnographic travelogues—all of these genres existed in both the Old English and Middle English periods. The very continuity of these genres reflects a level of intellectual consistency before and after the Norman Conquest. However, within that generic consistency, certain changes took place: for example, new types of religious instructions were devised for the female laity, but other forms like the gnomic poem eventually fell out of cultural production. Throughout these centuries of change, the alliterative proverb remained available to express certain ideas, especially that of the wisdom

---

128. Text and trans. from *Macaronic Sermon Collection*, 134, 135.
129. Ibid., 322, 323.
130. Ibid., 488, 489.
131. "Ambulate," in *Middle English Sermons*, 77.
132. For example, Shannon Gayk describes how alliteration links prose to poetry in the rhetoric of some Lollard sermons: "As Plouʒmen Han Preued."

inherent in the English-speaking past. From its early appearance in the Durham Proverbs through the linguistic complexities of macaronic sermons in the fifteenth century, the alliterative proverb allowed didactic writers to draw from a perceived well of vernacular wisdom and to use that perception to reach out to a growing Anglophone audience, not just by using the language of the majority but by appealing to their sense of community as it was rooted in the past. As we have seen, the increasingly complicated linguistic, political, and social ecologies of England demanded equally complex applications of such a small, but important, form as the alliterative proverb.

CHAPTER 4

Alliterative Proverbs in Romance, Lyric, and Drama

THE GENRES I ADDRESSED in chapter 3 existed in some form during both the Old English and Middle English periods. Proverb collections, gnomic poems, religious instructions, and sermons all underwent changes through the centuries, but all were available as proverb vectors from the beginnings of medieval English literacy through the end of the Middle Ages. In this chapter, I will explore the role of alliterative proverbs in three literary and performative genres that figured prominently during the Middle English period but had no real counterparts in Old English. Romance and vernacular drama are new creations of the high and late Middle Ages respectively, and although we possess some examples of Old English lyric poetry (e.g., the elegies and *Cædmon's Hymn*), the religious and secular lyrics of Middle English differ so significantly from them that it makes sense to treat the later lyrics as generically newborn. The simple fact that we are able to locate and examine alliterative proverbs in these new genres testifies to the cultural and linguistic strength of that segment of the tradition.

ROMANCE

An essential feature of medieval romance is its association with the ecology of the vernacular. As is well known and often told, the very word *romanz* first referred to a form of language, and only later narrowed its semantic sphere to certain narratives composed in that language. Of course, the vernacular language to which *romanz* referred and in which romances were written was French, rather than English (at least initially), but the connection between the romance genre and vernacular language and culture existed from the beginning and was never broken. Unlike sermons, which traveled across Europe from one language area to another primarily in Latin, romances, which enjoyed the same broad dissemination, remained functionally separate from the Latin sphere.[1] One could argue that in areas where French was spoken only by the sociopolitical elite, it was not a true vernacular, but in comparison to Latin, French always fell on the vernacular side of the line. For example, relying on the current, broader view of the vernacular as a language in a less secure position relative to another allows Katharine Breen "to treat French . . . as vernacular in relation to Latin but not in relation to English."[2] According to William Rothwell, French had ceased to be a vernacular language in England by the beginning of the thirteenth century; at that point, it was learned as a second (or third) language. However, Rothwell also illustrates how, at the same time, French was often chosen as a more accessible language than Latin.[3] Throughout Europe, the romance was introduced using the medium of the French language but ultimately adopted the local vernacular in both language and form. In England, this process resulted in Middle English romances both rhymed and alliterative. The romance genre also adheres frequently to vernacular culture in its subject matter and sources. Certain romances may be bookish in a historiographic or even ecclesiastical way, but in general, the genre welcomed and included characters, plots, and motifs from oral traditions of secular background. The need to claim some sort of "authority" for their tales led many romance authors to invent "old books" as their sources, but in practice they continued to visit the vernacular well. This simultaneous desire for the comforts of authority coupled with immersion in vernacular language and culture produced a genre ripe for the inclusion of proverbs, which served both needs. Even the decidedly nonvernacular school-rhetoric absorbed and deployed by some romance authors included a space for the use of proverbs, as we saw in chapter 3.

In a romance, as in any third-person narrative, a proverb may be delivered by a character or by the narrator. Whoever presents the proverb, it functions

---

1. Matilda Tomaryn Bruckner explains that the roots of romance reside in the translation of Latin epics into French "to give lay audiences access to the matter of Antiquity": "The Shape of Romance in Medieval France," 13.

2. Katharine Breen, *Imagining an English Reading Public, 1150–1400*, 11.

3. Rothwell, "The Role of French in Thirteenth-Century England."

as an icon of time-tested wisdom. A cosmopolitan writer like Chaucer might make fun of a character's reliance on such hoary utterances (as with Pandarus), but even his irony and humor depend upon the audience recognizing the proverb as a relic of the past.[4] This attachment to the past especially inheres in the use of an alliterative proverb with pre-Conquest roots, so I will begin by exploring the career of one such proverb through a number of romances. Afterward, I will examine what the introductions to proverbs in romance (e.g., "As is often said . . .") contribute to our understanding of their functions.

As we discovered in chapter 2, the proverb "After bale comes boot" is very common in Middle English. The proverb almost certainly has pre-Conquest origins, as the combination of *bealu* and *bot* appears numerous times in Old English texts. One Middle English narrative particularly stands out for its reliance on this proverb: *The Tale of Gamelyn*. *Gamelyn* is a difficult text to classify, and most scholars (including myself) somewhat uneasily group it with the romances for lack of a better place to put it in the context of fourteenth-century literature. W. R. J. Barron aptly describes the tale as one constructed from a collection of folktale motifs, but he notes that, at the same time, its realism "bears a resemblance to the world of contemporary English yeomen almost uncomfortably close for the romance mode," especially in its portrayal of fourteenth-century legal procedure.[5] Barron adds a third genre to the mix, observing that "*Gamelyn* is popular yet efficient and effective, resembling a series of six ballads, each introduced by a minstrel formula 'Liþeth and lestneþ and holdeþ your tonge.'"[6] The potential connection between *Gamelyn* and the popular ballad is reinforced by the presence in the former of a "king of the outlaws" in the forest—an unnamed Robin Hood or at least Robin Hood-type. The characters and events of the tale are decidedly nonaristocratic—in lieu of swords, the men fight with staves and cudgels; the violence is graphic and, to some readers, gratuitous; the anticlericalism is fierce; and there is no romance in this "romance."[7] *The Tale of Gamelyn* is a work of English popular literature, dependent on no French or even Celtic source. Had we more tales structured and peopled like *Gamelyn*, we would find it easier to assign

---

4. Marcelle Altieri argues that Chrétien de Troyes became dissatisfied with the lack of authorial authenticity inherent in the use of proverbs and continued to employ them only because his audience expected them: *Les Romans de Chrétien de Troyes: Leur perspective proverbiale et gnomique*, esp. ch. 5.

5. W. R. J. Barron, *English Medieval Romance*, 82–83. On the realism of *Gamelyn*, see also Richard W. Kaeuper, "An Historian's Reading of *The Tale of Gamelyn*."

6. Barron, *English Medieval Romance*, 84.

7. On the violence in *Gamelyn*, see Nancy Mason Bradbury, "Gamelyn."

them a generic classification. I have no doubt there were more such tales (the ballads did not arise out of nothing), but if *Gamelyn* reflects a popular mode of poetry, its companions are lost to us. (*Gamelyn* itself survives in around twenty-five manuscripts, but only because it got mixed up with the *Canterbury Tales* and circulated with them.)

The metrical structure of *Gamelyn* is another feature that situates the poem interestingly in the history of English literature. The lines of the poem are arrayed in rhymed couplets, but each line incorporates a caesura dividing it into half-lines. Walter W. Skeat's analysis finds significant variability in the poem's meter: the first half-line will contain three or four stresses, while the second half-line "is usually shorter, and less varied," mostly incorporating three stressed syllables.[8] As it is usually copied and printed, the poem's long lines visually recall Old English poetry. Presented differently on the page, *Gamelyn*'s meter would create four-line stanzas rhyming ABCB, which some scholars connect to the later ballad stanza, but even one such scholar must allow that "most manuscripts [of *Gamelyn*] use long lines with sporadic caesura markings."[9] Basing his analysis on the *Gamelyn* text from the Petworth manuscript, Stephen Knight perceives the base structure as a five-stress line that "is often amplified with weak or half stresses and can at times carry an extra stress in either or, exceptionally, both half lines." He rejects a connection with ballad meter, arguing instead that "it is in fact the line found in alliterative poetry of the period" and that "*Gamelyn*'s metric can be seen as an effective compromise between alliterative and rhymed techniques."[10]

Gamelyn may be a problematic text for the study of romance, but it is a promising one for discovering the survival of pre-Conquest features in later, popular literature. From our point of view, it does not disappoint, as the poet includes the proverb "After bale comes boot" not just once, but at two important junctures. The plot of *Gamelyn* proceeds episodically, but the episodes (and most of the characters) are arranged in binary structures; on the most general level, the poem describes the alternating and opposing triumphs and defeats of Gamelyn and his selfish, untrustworthy, eldest brother.[11] For both of these characters, boot repeatedly follows bale, and vice versa, although our sympathies lie with Gamelyn, of course. After Gamelyn has defeated his brother a second time, he and the brother's former butler—Adam

---

8. *The Tale of Gamelyn*, xxiii–xxv.
9. Bradbury, *Writing Aloud: Storytelling in Late Medieval England*, 210.
10. Stephen Knight, "'Harkeneth aright': Reading *Gamelyn* for Text Not Context," 17.
11. For a detailed study of dualities in *Gamelyn*, see Dean A. Hoffman, "'After Bale Comeþ Boote': Narrative Symmetry in *The Tale of Gamelyn*." Hoffman's only mention of the proverb is in the title of his article.

Spenser—find themselves needing to flee to the forest to escape the massed forces of the sheriff. It was Adam who devised the plan for their fight, and Adam who suggests they take to the woods, but as soon as they get there, Adam complains of the hardship of life in the wild. At this moment of crisis, the two characters exchange roles: Adam has served as (more or less) a helper figure up to this point, but outside of his comfort zone, he is at a loss, and Gamelyn steps up to take the lead. When they espy a group of outlaws sitting down to eat, Gamelyn interprets the encounter as likely to change their fortunes:

> "Adam," saide Gamelyn,   "now have we no doute;
> After bale cometh boote   thurgh grace of God Almight.
> Me thinketh of mete and drink   that I have a sight."[12]

The proverb serves multiple functions here: it prepares the audience for yet another turn in the plot, and it contributes significantly to the characterization of Gamelyn. As Cameron Louis points out, the utterance of a proverb "is implicitly performed from a position of superior power on the part of the speaker and lesser power on the part of the listener."[13] Gamelyn is revealed to possess the authoritative wisdom encapsulated in the proverb and by using that proverb in an appropriate, uncontested manner, he asserts his status over Adam, who was previously his adviser, now become his follower.

Were that the only appearance of this proverb in the tale, it would be interesting enough, as beyond its role in Gamelyn's character development, it introduces the popular figures of the greenwood outlaws and creates an expectation that they will turn out to be positive characters (in contrast to their real-life counterparts).[14] However, the poet refers to the same proverb much earlier in the tale, where questions of hierarchy, authority, and prediction are less straightforward. The first scene of the tale portrays the deathbed of Gamelyn's father, Sir John of Boundis. He calls together a collection of "wise knightes" (line 17) to help him settle his estate. When Sir John informs the assembled knights that he is dying, they are sorry for it and reply:

> Sir, for Goddes love,   ne dismay you nought.
> God may do bote of bale   that is now y-wrought.[15]

---

12. *Gamelyn*, lines 630–32, in *Middle English Verse Romances*, 173.

13. Louis, "Proverbs and the Politics of Language," 276. See also Roger D. Abrahams and Barbara A. Babcock, "The Literary Use of Proverbs."

14. See Kaeuper, "Historian's Reading," 54.

15. *Gamelyn*, lines 31–32, in *Middle English Verse Romances*, 157.

Sir John accepts the basic truth of the proverb, but rejects its use under these circumstances as a meaningless platitude:

> Boote of bale God may sende,   I wot it is no nay;
> But I beseke you, knightes,   for the love of me,
> Goth and dresseth my lond   among my sones three.[16]

These same knights who showed a lack of wisdom in their inapt use of a proverb directly contradict Sir John's specific request to divide his lands among all three of his sons (a request he supports with the proverb-like—perhaps proverbial—sentence "Selde ye see ony eir helpen his brother").[17] Sir John is furious with the knights' decision to cut Gamelyn out of his will; he rejects their plan and utters his own testament, in which each of his three sons gets a share of his property. Unfortunately, upon Sir John's death, the eldest son misappropriates Gamelyn's share (also proving the wisdom of the sententia just cited).

In Sir John's deathbed scene, the proverb "God may sende boot after bale" both possesses and lacks authority. It is true in and of itself, but it does not apply to the current situation. By understanding this, Sir John shows himself to be wiser than the knights he has called together to advise him. The unwisdom of the knights, shown by their misapplication of the proverb, extends to their failure to protect the property rights of young Gamelyn; had they done right by him, they would have forestalled the violent events of the rest of the tale.

One last issue remains regarding the use of this proverb in *Gamelyn*: the attribution of "bote" to the will of God. The foolish knights, Sir John, and Gamelyn himself all include references to God in their versions of the proverb, a connection that is made much more frequently in Old English than in Middle English variants of the proverb.[18] Granted, the Old English texts in which the proverb appears are somewhat more religious in nature than the Middle English, which may account for the difference to some degree, but the possibility remains that the earliest version of the proverb was something like the "God may turn bale into boot" we find in *Gamelyn*. This possibility seems more likely when we consider the other religious references in *Gamelyn*: they are legion, but usually blasphemous. Characters (both good and bad) incessantly swear and curse each other by God and various saints.[19] In a

---

16. Ibid., lines 34–36.
17. Ibid., line 40.
18. See pp. 32–35.
19. On the literary functions of such swearing, see Bradbury, *Writing Aloud*, 52–53.

spectacularly uncharitable misapplication of piety, Gamelyn's brother sees him off to a wrestling match

> And bisoughte Jesu Christ, that is Hevene king,
> He mighte breke his neck in that wrastling.[20]

The hope-filled faith expressed by the proverb fits uneasily with the religious (or antireligious) tone of this tale and may have been imported wholesale from the past.

In a strange coincidence, the turn from bale to boot involves the easing of hunger in *Sir Firumbras* just as it did when Gamelyn and Adam entered the forest. Of course, the subject matter of the two romances is entirely different: in contrast to the English gentry who stay close to home in *Gamelyn*, *Firumbras* tells a story of French knights fighting Saracens in far-off lands. The action of *Firumbras* is more remote from the audience in both time and place, but, as we shall see, the poet uses the narrative voice to connect his listeners to his foreign material.

The Fillingham version of *Firumbras*, in which our proverb occurs, is one of several Middle English redactions of a lost, twelfth-century, French *chanson*. Barron dates the Fillingham *Firumbras* to the last quarter of the fourteenth century.[21] The Fillingham version is acephalic and suffers several internal gaps, but none of these lacunae fall so close to our proverb as to affect our understanding of its use.[22] At the point in question, the flower of French chivalry has grown hungry from being trapped in a tower. Led by Roland, they sally out and defeat a Saracen army, but this victory, sweet as it is, fails to achieve their goal of acquiring provisions. However, what the knights' own efforts cannot produce may still be supplied by Providence, as the narrator explains:

> A gret anger thay hadden and that was al here care,
> ffor mete and drynke, ne fond thay none thare.
> But whenne god wyl helpe and hys grace sende,
> Whenne bale ys aldermest, bote ys ful hende.[23]

At first glance, the invocation of God in connection with the proverb might seem similar to the form the proverb takes in *Gamelyn*. However, close

---

20. *Gamelyn*, lines 193–94, in *Middle English Verse Romances*, 162.
21. Barron, *English Medieval Romance*, 102.
22. On the state of the text, see *Firumbras and Otuel and Roland*, xxiii.
23. Ibid., 15, lines 420–23.

examination shows that the poet of *Firumbras* has received the proverb without mention of God and has added it himself. The process has left a visible seam: the somewhat awkward repetition of the word "whenne." The grammar of the proverb has already limited and defined the circumstance under which "bote ys ful hende"—it is true "whenne bale ys aldermest." The poet wishes to expand the proverb into a couplet (a fairly common procedure), which he accomplishes by prefacing the proverb itself with a line stating yet another conditioning factor: "whenne god wyl helpe." Although the resulting couplet lacks syntactic elegance, the poet's additional line introducing the proverb is no mindless filler. Robert Warm argues that the Middle English Charlemagne romances provide support for the unity and authority of Christendom, in contrast to secular nation-states, by constructing "an idealised vision of the past, within which true Christian knights fought the infidel rather than one another."[24] Seen in that light, the failure of the martial efforts of the knights to achieve their goal, which is followed, immediately after the proverb, by the appearance of a Saracen driving twenty sumpters of foodstuffs, reinforces the theme that the divine plan supersedes secular efforts. The knights easily capture the sumpters, but in a rapid reversal of fortune—not introduced by a proverb—they are attacked by another Saracen army and lose both the bulk of the food and Guy of Burgundy. In *Firumbras*, then, the incorporation of the proverb may not seem as fluent as it is in *Gamelyn*, but, on the other hand, the poet's connection of God with a positive change of fortune provides a pause in the action wherein the audience can link the narrative events with the themes of the poem. The narrative voice encourages the English audience to identify with the French heroes by referring to them frequently as "our knights" and by asking the audience to pray for their success, as if they were contemporary crusaders.[25] The use of a decidedly English, alliterative proverb might also help to connect the audience with the Carolingian past by recalling proverbial and poetic forms of their own past.

One element that distinguishes Middle English romances as a group is the frequent focus on child or adolescent characters: "So marked is the presence of children in Middle English popular romances that it might even be thought of as a defining feature."[26] *Gamelyn*, like *Havelok the Dane*, illustrates the process

---

24. Robert Warm, "Identity, Narrative and Participation: Defining a Context for the Middle English Charlemagne Romances," 87.

25. Ibid., 96–99. Some further examples of the locution "our knights" can be found at lines 382, 402, and 408.

26. Phillipa Hardman, "Popular Romances and Young Readers," 153. Nicole Clifton offers a clear presentation of numerous issues associated with identifying and analyzing Middle English romances as children's literature: "'Of Arthour and of Merlin' as Medieval Children's Literature."

by which a young hero grows up and claims the inheritance that has been wrongly seized from him. Other romances, like *Guy of Warwick* or *Sir Percyvell of Gales,* show the chivalric education and growth of the hero. As Phillipa Hardman explains, "The narrative of self-making, embodied in stories of children and adolescents, is of obvious interest to young people," and the audience for such romances would likely have included children who had learned to read English but not yet French.[27] Of course, a child of any age could have the romance read to him or her. Hardman goes on to point out that the didactic element of such tales was directed not only toward children but also toward their parents, whose role in the education and moral shaping of their offspring constitutes another frequent theme in the Middle English popular romances.[28] The next romance that I wish to examine—*The Tale of Beryn*—fits easily into this context emphasizing the role of the family in education.

The Middle English *Tale of Beryn* survives in only one manuscript of c.1450–1470 and was probably composed a few decades earlier in the same century.[29] It forms part of an ambitious addition to Chaucer's *Canterbury Tales*: the so-called "Canterbury Interlude" describes the pilgrims' arrival and sojourn in Canterbury, and *The Tale of Beryn* is assigned to the Merchant as the first tale on the return journey. A Latin couplet at the end of the romance ascribes its translation (from a French original) to a "filius ecclesie Thome" [son of the church of Thomas], whom John Bowers suspects to be "a Christ Church [Canterbury] monk."[30] The Middle English romance begins with a wealthy Roman senator, Faunus, and his wife, Agea, who are blessed with a son after fifteen years of marriage. They cherish and pamper young Beryn, which, as the narrator explains using an alliterative proverb, will cause trouble later, "For after swete the soure cometh ful offte in many a place."[31] Beryn grows into a very spoiled child and youth who beats his playmates and servants, and eventually becomes addicted to gambling. The narrator blames Faunus for Beryn's bad behavior:

So was the fader cause the sone was so wild,
And so have many mo such of his own child
Because of his undoyng, as we mowe se al day.[32]

---

27. Hardman, "Popular Romances," 151–53 (quote on 153).
28. Ibid., 153–54.
29. John M. Bowers, "The Canterbury Interlude and Merchant's Tale of Beryn: Introduction."
30. Ibid.
31. Ibid., line 898; the sweet/sour pairing also appears in line 3686. See Whiting, *Proverbs . . . before 1500,* S942.
32. *The Canterbury Interlude and The Merchant's Tale of Beryn,* lines 935–37.

This part of the lesson is clearly directed toward parent rather than child. The narrator claims experiential authority for his statement of general censure—"as we mowe se al day"—but he goes on to use a proverbial image to explain further the unfortunate results of parental failure:

> As hors that ever trotted, trewlich I yew tell,
> It were hard to make hym after to ambill well.[33]

Such a cruel son is Beryn that he refuses to leave his dice game to visit his mother's deathbed and fails to attend any of the masses that the deeply grieving Faunus endows for a four-week period after Agea's death. Both the gambling and the heartlessness toward his mother will come back to afflict Beryn later in the tale; these are the narrative elements directed toward the moral development of children in the audience.

After his mother's death, Beryn continues his notorious profligacy for three more years, until conflict with his father's new wife causes him to trade his inheritance for five ships loaded with merchant wares. Beryn and his merchant fleet land in an unknown country where the inhabitants use various ruses (mostly judicial) to put him in danger of losing both his goods and his life. This being a romance, Beryn manages to mend his ways, turn the tables on his tormentors (with the help of Geoffrey, a father-figure), and eventually become ruler of this mystery land by marrying the lord's daughter. Our proverb describing the advent of boot after bale appears near the end of the tale, as Beryn and his crew celebrate their deliverance from "Fortune and myscheff" (line 3951):

> For after mysty cloudes, there cometh a clere sonne,
> So after bale cometh bote, whoso byde conne.[34]

Beryn's life story follows a simple trajectory from wasted love and prosperity to misery and despair, and thence back to happiness and success. Both the negative and positive movements are marked by proverbs: "Sour comes after sweet" and "Boot comes after bale." Romance is an episodic genre, which makes frequent change of one sort or another a regular feature. In this type of narrative, proverbs describing change serve two functions: they orient the reader to narrative shifts, and they teach the general lesson that no worldly condition—whether comfortable or dangerous—is permanent. Hence, the seemingly contradictory proverbs work together rather than in opposition.

---

33. Ibid., lines 938–39. See Whiting, *Proverbs . . . before 1500*, H513.
34. *Canterbury Interlude and The Merchant's Tale of Beryn*, lines 3953–54.

Despite its leanings toward moral education, the *Tale of Beryn* does not directly ascribe the advent of boot after bale to the hand of God; for this fifteenth-century author, cleric or not, the proverb has no overtly religious element.[35] The base form of the proverb with which the poet begins is simply "after bale cometh bote," which he expands into a full line not by reference to God, but with the alliterating tag "whoso byde conne." Just as we saw in the didactic texts examined in chapter 3, the poet of *Beryn* uses a concentration of alliteration to reinforce the sapiential authority of his pronouncement: not only does he extend the alliterative pattern of "after bale cometh bote," but he prefaces that proverb with another alliterative proverb: "For after mysty cloudes, there cometh a clere sonne."[36]

The ineffectiveness of parents in ordering the lives of their children also forms the basis for the plot of *Floris and Blauncheflour*, a romance composed in twelfth-century France that was subsequently retold not only in English but also in Middle High German, Middle Dutch, Old Norse, Italian, and Spanish.[37] The royal parents of the pagan Floris try to curtail his love for the Christian slave Blauncheflour, with whom he has been raised, by selling her off to Babylonian slavers and telling Floris that she is dead. Floris's extreme grief forces his parents to tell him the truth, whereupon he sets off to rescue Blauncheflour from the harem of the Emir of Babylon. Floris accomplishes the rescue, marries Blauncheflour, then returns to Spain to succeed his father as king. Of course, he converts to Christianity, as well. Like Beryn (but unlike Gamelyn), Floris finds success not by fighting but by persistence and enlisting the help of others. However, *Floris and Blauncheflour* is less legalistic than *The Tale of Beryn* and more sentimental: the Emir spares the lives of the two children (as they are consistently called) because he is moved by their self-sacrificing love for each other.

Despite its thematic similarities to *The Tale of Beryn* (and, to a lesser degree, to *Gamelyn*), *Floris and Blauncheflour* deploys the proverb of "boot after bale" in a manner more similar to *Firumbras*. The poet of *Firumbras* made two uses of the proverb: to introduce a turn of plot and to reinforce belief in the role of divine Providence. In *Floris and Blauncheflour*, the poet inserts the proverb at the very end of the tale, where it summarizes the plot and contributes to a religious link between narrator and audience:

---

35. There is one discernible supernatural influence on the vicissitudes of the narrative: the tale refers to Fortune no fewer than sixteen times, all but one of which describe a downward movement (lines 943, 1136, 1346, 1365, 1367, 1723, 1783, 1784, 1789, 1990, 1995, 2196, 2336, 2337, 2687, 3951).

36. Whiting, *Proverbs . . . before 1500*, C315.

37. *Floris and Blancheflour*, 7–8.

> Nou is þis tale browt to þende
> Of Florice and of his lemman hende,
> How after bale hem com bote;
> So wil oure Louerd þat ous mote,
> Amen siggeþ also,
> And ich schal helpe 3ou þerto.[38]

The non-Christian setting of *Floris and Blauncheflour*, like that of *Firumbras*, unites narrator, audience, and some characters on religious grounds. The theme of religious difference is less important—and certainly less violently developed—in *Floris and Blauncheflour* than in *Firumbras*, but it simmers beneath the surface of the sentimental romance, occasionally coming to the fore, just as with our proverb, which sometimes includes reference to God, sometimes not.

Floris and Blauncheflour uses the proverb to connect audience and characters in one further way: by manipulating its syntax. The poet inserts a personal pronoun into his version of the proverb—"How after bale <u>hem</u> com bote"—which shifts from the usual generality of a proverb to a specific instance of change. Of course, the underlying proverb remains clearly evident through the alliterating word pair "bale/bote" and the connecting "after." The specificity of this proverbial citation could have severed the connection with the audience, except that in the very next line the poet follows "them" with "us": "So wil <u>oure</u> Louerd þat <u>ous</u> mote." Two lines later, the poet adds the pronouns "I" and "you" to the mix. Ordinarily, English proverbs maintain a semantics of general applicability by avoiding personal pronouns, with the occasional exception of a generic "he" or "she." In *Floris and Blauncheflour*, the reworking of the proverb to apply specifically to the title characters concludes the romance by affording proverbial justification to its happy ending; having introduced a third-person pronoun to refer to the characters, the poet forthwith injects the first and second persons, thus inclusively reestablishing the connection between characters, audience, and even himself. I would not argue that this clustering of pronouns is particularly elegant, or even completely lucid, but like the alliterative clustering we have seen elsewhere, it demonstrates a stylistic choice in the service of thematics.

The fifth and final romance in which we find "after bale comes boot" is the fifteenth-century *Generydes*. The story of how Generydes becomes king of both Persia and India, winning his princess along the way, is told in two Middle English romances, one in couplets and one in rhyme-royal stanzas.

---

38. Ibid., lines 1306–11, 680. Taylor's base text is the Auchinleck version.

The couplet version (A) refers at its outset to a French original, but no such romance survives.[39] Our proverb appears only in A, but there it is used twice, with almost three thousand lines intervening.[40] Although *Generydes* is another of those romances in which the younger generation takes over from the elder, the proverb does not mark that transition. Instead, the poet uses the proverb for the flexible sort of narrative pointing for which it is well suited; in the first instance, it describes what will happen in the future, and in the second, what has already occurred.

Fairly early in this lengthy romance, King Aufreus of Ynde fortuitously meets Princess Sereyne of Surre; their union will produce the hero Generydes. Sereyne offers a prophecy to Aufreus, warning him of the impending treachery of his wife and his steward:

> Fiftene yere ye shal in pes
> Hold youre lond, but neuer-the-les
> Thenk of noo feith to you ward
> Of youre quene ne of youre steward.
> By than the fiftene yere be doon,
> Tithinges ye shal here soon,
> Sum what bitter, and noothing swete;
> But aftre bale there may come bote;—[41]

As prophesied, Aufreus is sent into exile by the treasonous pair, but he is subsequently avenged by his son, Generydes. Before that happens, however, Generydes travels to Persia, where he and the Sultan's daughter fall in love. The Sultan violently opposes this relationship until Generydes saves the kingdom; at this point the Sultan forgives his daughter:

> The Soudon rose vp to yeve hir grace,
> And in his armes he can hir brace,
> And kissed hir ther weping still,
> "Doghtre," he said, "I haue doon yll
> Ayeinst you, wel I wote;
> But aftre bale euer cometh bote;

---

39. Version A survives in one manuscript, edited by Furnivall, *A Royal History of the Excellent Knight Generides*.

40. Whiting notes that "none of the proverbs in *A* is in *B*": "Proverbs in Certain Middle English Romances in Relation to Their French Sources," 111.

41. *A Royal History of the Excellent Knight Generides*, lines 427–34, 14. Note that the later form "swete" replaces the better-rhyming "swote," but the proverb is unaffected.

Goo to youre chambre nov agayn,
Ye shal be at youre large certayn."⁴²

To some degree, the Sultan's pronouncement of the proverb seems to deflect responsibility for his ill treatment of his daughter, but for the most part, it simply marks a turn in the narrative. The same turn—from misfortune to success—is presented by Sereyne as a possibility, not a categorical given. Just as in *Floris and Blauncheflour*, the author of *Generydes* contextualizes the proverb by a subtle syntactic shift. The Sultan's direct version of the proverb provides closure to the narrative of discord between himself and his daughter. On the other hand, Sereyne's modification of the proverb with a modal verb appears much earlier in the romance, with many more plot twists to come; the proverb is used for foreshadowing rather than summation. The fact that Sereyne's statement *is* a proverb provides, by the authority inherent in the form, an extra measure of hope that things will ultimately work out for Aufreus. In both instances, the poet should be given credit for deploying the proverb to advance and explain the plot through dialogue rather than narration.

"After bale comes boot" is the only alliterative proverb appearing in more than two Middle English romances, which raises certain questions: why this proverb, and why these romances? This particular proverb is, as we have seen, very useful for narrative poets. It can orient readers or listeners to turns in the plot that have already occurred (as in *The Tale of Beryn* or *Floris and Blauncheflour*) or to those that will happen later (*Generydes*). In some instances (*Gamelyn, Firumbras*), the proverb points out the turn as it is in progress. The basic sense of the proverb—that bad times may be followed by good—fits the general medieval understanding of the transitoriness of the sublunary world. The positive turn of events described or predicted by the proverb is sometimes attributed to the will of God (*Gamelyn, Firumbras*) but not always. Whatever the twists and turns of a given story—and in the popular romances they are copious—this proverb can help to focus attention on them.

If this proverb is so apt for narrative use that two of the five romances include it twice, why is it only found in one particular type of romance: the end-rhymed popular romance? Why does it fit that context better than that of the courtly or alliterative romances, in which types it does not appear? Part of the answer must be that this is a popular proverb and hence appropriate for popular romances. A courtly poet would wish to distance himself (or herself) from a saying that was common among the non-elite population. "Bale" and "boot" are solidly Germanic lexemes whose combination in an alliterative

---

42. Ibid., 104, lines 3323–30.

pairing only reinforces the noncourtly nature of the sentence. The proverb has the wrong social and linguistic valence to help a poet who endeavors to compete, in English, with the prestige of French. On the other hand, a poet who works from the other direction—that is, who is attempting to naturalize foreign material—would find the familiarity of this proverb very useful. Four of the five romances we have examined derive (or claim to derive) from French originals. The adaptation of these (sometimes putative) French romances for a non-Francophone audience required an ongoing process of experimentation by English poets; hence the variety of verse forms in the popular romances.[43] "After bale comes boot" would be recognized by an English-speaking audience as an English proverb and would thereby mark the romance in which it appeared as an English romance. From the thirteenth century (*Floris and Blauncheflour*) to the fifteenth (*Generydes*), English popular romancers employed "after bale comes boot" as a token of Englishness helping to link an audience from one linguistic tradition with literary forms and content from another.

So recognizable was "After bale comes boot" that not one of the five romance poets feels the need to label it explicitly as a proverb. Other proverbs, in other romances, were tagged, either because they were assumed to be less familiar to the audience or because the author wished to strengthen some particular element associated with proverbiality. In chapter 3, we examined the explicit introduction of proverbs in sermons. The sermon writer might point to the antiquity of a sentence—"ffor men seyen in olde speche"—to its specific form of language—"men seit in old English"—its familiarity—"vulgariter dicitur" [it is commonly said]—or its truthfulness—"veraciter dicitur" [it is truly said].[44] Middle English romances predictably make no mention of a proverb's linguistic origin, but, like sermons, they may accentuate its authority, antiquity, truth, or familiarity. For example, the fifteenth-century versifier of *Guy of Warwick* somewhat diminishes the alliteration of the sentence "For the less men lose the more," which could have made it less recognizable as a proverb, but he takes advantage of the couplet form to introduce the saying as a well-known, hence authoritative, proverb:

In proverbs hyt ys seyde full yare:
Mony for þe lesse forgoyþ þe mare.[45]

---

43. Marianne Ailes and Phillipa Hardman, "How English are the English Charlemagne Romances," 46. Tail-rhyme romances are perhaps the most successful of these metrical experiments; see Rhiannon Purdie, *Anglicising Romance: Tail-Rhyme and Genre in Medieval English Literature*.

44. See pp. 94–96.

45. *Guy of Warwick*, lines 1493–94, 289.

The English prose translator of *Melusine,* unrestricted by the couplet form, expands the commentary on a proverb even further. Here, the speaker of the proverb, the King of the Bretons, possesses the authority of his office, but he nevertheless describes the methods by which the proverb acquires its authority: experience, familiarity, and truth—"I now perceyue wel & see that the prouerbe that is said commonly is trew that is 'that olde synne reneweth shame.'"⁴⁶ This author is very fond of proverbs, which he uses liberally to enhance the themes and characterizations of his lengthy narrative. In this instance, the proverb has a very literal application, as the King uses it to comment on Raymondin's accusation against Josselin for a forty-year-old act of treachery. In a twist from the more usual practice, the narrative here gives authority (or at least truth-value) to the proverb, rather than the other way around.

In his study of "Proverbs in Certain Middle English Romances in Relation to Their French Sources," B. J. Whiting comments that "there are few French romances which contain as many proverbs and sententious remarks" as the *Ipomedon* and *Protheselaus* of Hue of Rotelande.⁴⁷ Hue's *Ipomedon* enjoyed at least three translations into Middle English: two in verse and one in prose. The Middle English redactors sometimes omit a proverb found in the Anglo-Norman original (often because they are abridging or discarding an entire passage) and sometimes add a proverb of their own choosing; Middle English translations of proverbs found in the original may be close literal renderings or looser paraphrases.⁴⁸ Of the prose *Ipomedon*, Whiting says,

> We find much proverbial material of great interest. For the French:
>
> > Car hom dit, qe par eloingnance
> > Met l'en amur en obliance
>
> is substituted one of our best proverbs, "for the wiseman saith: 'Seldom seen, sone forgetyn.'"⁴⁹

I would not disagree with Whiting's assessment of this proverb, which is pithy and well balanced as well as alliterative. I suspect, though, that the Middle

---

46. *Melusine,* ch. 19, 79.
47. Whiting, "Proverbs in Certain Middle English Romances," 76.
48. See ibid., 78–79; and Brenda B. Hosington, "Proverb Translation as Linguistic and Cultural Transfer." On the types of changes that a "prosateur" might work on proverbs in his source, see Maria Columbo Timelli, "De l'*Erec* de Chrétien de Troyes à la prose du XVe siècle: le traitement des proverbes."
49. Whiting, "Proverbs in Certain Middle English Romances," 84.

English redactor may be not so much "substituting" the proverb as he is restoring it. Hue introduces his sentence as a proverb ("As one says") and expresses it as a rhymed couplet that fits his immediate purpose, but is not attested elsewhere. The Middle English prose redactor imbues the introduction of the sentence with somewhat greater authority—replacing "hom" [one/a man] with "wiseman"—but does not alter the basic structure of the passage. Little is known about Hue de Rotelande other than his probable Welsh origin and his residence around Hereford in the 1180s, but it is at least possible that he, like Gerald of Wales, was a little bit familiar with such English language icons as proverbs and that his *Ipomedon* contains an early, Anglo-Norman translation of "Seldom seen, soon forgotten." The English translator, freed of the exigencies of rhyme, may have unwittingly restored the form known to Hue. In this instance, the deliberate marking of a proverb preserved a locus of transition from one language to another, and back again. In twelfth-century Britain, the proverb was valued (by Hue) for its content, but obtained increased cultural status by undergoing translation into French; by the fifteenth century, both English and alliteration were deemed appropriate for proverbial expression, even in a romance.

The composition, transmission, and reception of Middle English popular romances all remain shrouded in a considerable amount of mystery, but the determined efforts of modern scholars have at least outlined some areas of probability. Because the popular romances were composed in the English vernacular, they were available for everyone (if orally delivered).[50] The thematic concerns of the popular romances differ from those of the courtly, chivalric romances, and seem to indicate an audience among the baronage, the gentry, and perhaps the mercantile class.[51] Alongside such specific concerns of the gentry as inheritance and legal process, the popular romances also present a certain cultural conservatism and communal ethos.[52] Alliterative proverbs contribute to both of these goals in that proverbs are, by their nature, culturally conservative, and, in the context of post-Conquest England, alliteration provides a token of shared cultural identity related to the past. Finally, the manuscript contexts of many popular romances indicate that they played an educational role for the entire family, with romances appearing alongside didactic

---

50. On orality and Middle English romances, see Karl Reichl, "Orality and Performance." On the role of minstrels, see Linda Marie Zaerr, *Performance and the Middle English Romance*.

51. See Crane, *Insular Romance: Politics, Faith, and Culture in Anglo-Norman and Middle English Literature*; Ad Putter, "A Historical Introduction," esp. 4–6.

52. Carol Fewster, *Traditionality and Genre in Middle English Romance*, 30; Pearsall, "The Pleasure of Popular Romance: A Prefatory Essay," 18.

materials such as religious primers and manuals of conduct.⁵³ We explored in chapter 3 the ways in which alliterative proverbs contributed to medieval English didactic literature; their firm establishment in that sphere would have rendered them useful for similar purposes in the romances. Proverbs in general are used in every type of medieval English romance, including courtly, in which they often produce some of the same literary effects we have seen here, including narrative pointing and character development. The proverbs found in romances directed toward a noble audience may be biblical, learned, native, or foreign in origin; the source of the proverb seems less important than its form. The courtly romances make hardly any use of the alliterative proverb, whereas the popular romances seem to embrace with enthusiasm its particular connections to the wisdom and identity of the past. In this contrast, we see two different approaches to the incorporation of romance literature into English vernacular culture.

LYRIC

In principle and practice, lyric poetry is less congenial than romance as a home for proverbs. The narrative functions served by proverbs in romances do not exist in a nonnarrative genre like the lyric. Furthermore, the role of the proverb as an expression of universal experience and wisdom fits poorly within a type of poetry that—however conventional—purports to express the subjective emotions of an individual. Thus, proverbs are extremely rare (indeed, almost nonexistent) in the most common types of Middle English lyric: the Marian and passion lyrics. The proverb has little to offer in the realm of affective piety. However, there are other types of lyric—moral, political, didactic, even courtly—in which the alliterative proverb does appear and through which we can continue to explore its contribution to medieval English verbal culture.

William of Shoreham was a Kentish cleric (vicar of the rectory of Chart) in the mid-fourteenth century. His poetic works survive in a single manuscript: BL Additional MS. 17376, also of the fourteenth century. William's seven extant poems, all in English, treat conventional Christian topics in fairly conventional ways. Based on his study of William's poems, Matthias Kornrath characterizes the vicar as "well read in the writings of the ecclesiastical

---

53. Hardman, "Popular Romances," 154–64; Ailes and Hardman, "How English," 54–55; Melissa Furrow, *Expectations of Romance: The Reception of a Genre in Medieval England*, 22–31, 41–42, 232–36.

authors most reputed in his day" but also a "practical Churchman, who had the cure of souls."[54] Kornrath notes that "four out of the seven poems . . . have a purely didactic aim" in pursuit of which William's "treatment of the subjects would sometimes seem to have a smack of scholasticism, yet, on the whole, is well calculated for the comprehension of lay folk."[55] In this combination of scholastic learning with lay instruction, William's poems resemble the sermon tradition explored in chapter 3. In fact, the specific poem I wish to examine—"De septem mortalibus peccatis"—resembles a sermon as much as it does a lyric. The first half of this lengthy poem teaches its readers a general lesson about the history, nature, attractiveness, and danger of sin before moving into a description of the Seven Deadly Sins themselves and concluding with a brief admonition to avoid them. Like many sermons, this is a lay catechism with practical applications.

William of Shoreham's poem on the Seven Deadly Sins comprises 106 quatrains, rhymed ABAB and employing fairly frequent ornamental alliteration.[56] The poem is not particularly proverbial or gnomic in its form of expression, but in stanza 5, William employs a version of the proverb "Old sin brings new shame":

Senne makeþ nywe schame,
    Þa3 hy for-3ete be;
And senne bryngeþ men in grame,
    Þar er was game and gle.[57]

The syntactic structure of this stanza is predetermined: the first six stanzas of the poem all begin with "Senne + V" (prefaced by "And" in stanza 6); in four of these six stanzas, the verb is "makeþ." The repetition of the structure in the second half of the stanza also occurs four times. In order to maintain this forceful pattern, William has had to drop the initial modifier "old" from the proverb, but he rescues the temporal contrast of the sentence by expanding the idea of "old" into the line "Þa3 hy for-3ete be." Despite this dislocation, the alliteration of "senne" and "schame" maintains the integrity of the proverb. Like some other writers we have seen, William is influenced by the alliteration of the proverb to continue in an alliterative mode, here executed with "grame, game, gle." It would be tempting to suppose that the structure of the proverb

---

54. William of Shoreham, *The Poems of William of Shoreham*, xiv–xv.
55. Ibid., xv.
56. For the text of the poem, see ibid., 98–114.
57. "De septem mortalibus peccatis," lines 17–20, in ibid., 98.

provided William with the syntactic template for the opening of this poem, but I doubt that is true, considering that William is not a great user of proverbs overall and that, in this instance, the proverb does not appear until stanza 5. Instead, I think it likely that William chose this particular repetitive structure for its rhetorical contribution to his didactic purpose, then chose the proverb because it fit the structure. The vernacular proverb would also strike a note of familiarity with William's lay audience, just like proverbs in sermons; the laicity or vernacularity of the passage is enhanced by its concentrated alliteration, inspired by the alliterative proverb. Kornrath calls William of Shoreham "a very mediocre poet,"[58] but here the good vicar shows a fine sensitivity to the rhetorical uses of structure and the pastoral effects of alliterative patterning.

Another, more controversial, cleric of the fourteenth century employed alliteration and alliterative proverbs with even greater emphasis on their appeal to an English-favoring audience. The priest John Ball was a longtime thorn in the side of the English ecclesiastical hierarchy: he was excommunicated several times and ultimately executed as one of the leaders of the Peasants' Revolt of 1381. None of Ball's apparently inflammatory and heterodox sermons survive, but his name is associated with half a dozen short, enigmatic, political texts that sometimes assume lyric form. Some of these "letters" are specifically attributed to Ball in the chronicles that record them; his authorship is less certain for the others.[59] The proverb "Be ware ere you be woe" appears in the letter attributed to John Ball by the chronicler Thomas Walsingham. The letter begins in prose, as "Iohan schep" (Pastor John) greets such allegorical representatives of the commons as John Nameless, John the Miller, and John Carter, bidding them to act together with Piers Plowman and John Trueman. The letter continues in verse:

> Iohan þe mullere haþ y-grounde smal, smal, smal.
> þe kynges sone of heuene schal paye for al.
> be war or þe be wo.
> knoweþ ȝour freend fro ȝour foo.
> haueth y-now & seith hoo!
> and do wel and bettre and fleth synne,
> and sekeþ pees and hold ȝow þer-inne.
> and so biddeþ Iohan trewaman and alle his felawes.[60]

---

58. Ibid., xvii.

59. Richard Firth Green supports Ball's authorship of all six texts: "John Ball's Letters: Literary History and Historical Literature."

60. "John Ball's Letters, II (1381)," in *Historical Poems of the XIVth and XVth Centuries*, 55.

In this short lyric, John Ball offers allusive (and sometimes elusive) guidance relating to both the spiritual and political realms. "Iohan þe mullere" and "Iohan trewaman" are, as in the prose preface, representatives of the commons, although the significance of the miller's grinding remains unclear.[61] Line 2 provides religious cover for the rebels as long as they behave as good Christians; such behavior is summarized in line 6 as "do wel and bettre and fleth synne," a possible, but not inevitable, reference to *Piers Plowman*. Richard Firth Green points out that the middle lines of the poem "are a variant on a well-known set of proverbs."[62] What Green calls a "set of proverbs" could also be characterized as a proverbial lyric: it survives in five versions, all comprising 3–5 monorhyming lines, and all beginning with a variant of "He is wise that can be ware ere him be woe."[63] Green considers the closest parallel to Ball's text to be the version preserved in BL Harley 2316:

> He is wys ʒat kan be war or him be wo;
> He is wys ʒat lovet his frend and ek his fo;
> He is wys ʒat havet i-now and kan seyn, "ho!"
> He is wys ʒat kan don wel, and doeth al so.[64]

Like much proverbial and lyric text, versions of this poem tended to be jotted down informally, on flyleaves or margins, and once in John Grimestone's sermon notebook. It is just the sort of text that a preacher like John Ball would be familiar with and find useful, and we are fortunate to be able to compare his version with the less contextualized others. First, we note the change of syntax: all five of the other versions use a declarative sentence structure, while Ball uses the more direct imperative. Our "Be ware ere you be woe" proverb is easily adapted to either structure, but Ball's use of the imperative better fits the context of one conspirator advising the others. Ball makes an even more meaningful alteration to the line "knoweþ ʒour freend fro ʒour foo." The other surviving versions of this line typically recommend a more forgiving attitude: "He is wise that loves his friend *and* his foe." Ball's version abandons that stance of Christian charity in favor of a continued tone of caution. Despite his (apparently deserved) reputation as a rabble-rouser, John Ball has, in this

---

61. Green proposes a parallel with the Latin proverb "Sera deum mola sed tenues molit undique partes" [God's mill grinds slow but small]: "John Ball's Letters," 198, note 52.
62. Ibid., 184.
63. See the Digital Index of Middle English Verse (DIMEV), No. 1834: http://www.dimev.net/record.php?recID=1834.
64. *Reliquiae Antiquae*, 2.120.

poem, reworked homiletic language to warn his fellow rebels to act with care and Christian justice.[65]

John Ball's deployment of alliterative proverbs is conditioned by attitudes toward the English language in the late fourteenth century. Although English was on the upswing in the realm of imaginative literature, its use created tension in both the religious and political spheres. As we saw in chapter 3, English-language texts for private devotions increased in availability following the Fourth Lateran Council of 1215, initially without apparent controversy. The laity could be trusted with English-language religious texts as long as they were under proper supervision. As lay literacy grew, so did the number and variety of these texts—William of Shoreham's poem on the Seven Deadly Sins may not have found a wide readership, but its limited circulation cannot be blamed on censorship. However, the particular time and place inhabited by John Ball and his fellow social reformers was also inhabited by a set of religious reformers who made an issue of the use of the vernacular: the Wycliffites. The rebellion of the commons that culminated in the events of 1381 was a different movement from the Wycliffite press for church reform, but it is not surprising that the two loomed as related threats in the minds of the secular and ecclesiastical hierarchs.[66] Russell Peck describes the fears of both church and state: "That the use of the vernacular was in itself a major act of rebellion against long established tradition . . . went not unnoticed in the fourteenth century as objections were raised against the translating of Holy Writ into English, whereby subjects might make decisions for themselves and thus rebel against sovereignty."[67] Jill Havens argues that the Lollards sought to elevate the status of the English language (by expanding its use in the religious domain) in order to raise the status of the English people relative to Continentals, and relative even to non-Anglophone people resident in England: "If you speak English as your native tongue, you are English, but if you live in England and speak some other tongue, you are not English."[68] John Ball's use of proverbs in his letter to the rebels derived from his training as a preacher, but in the context of religious and political upheaval to which he contributed and within which his letters were interpreted, his use of *alliterative* proverbs represents an assertive Englishness possessed by the vernacular of the commons. Alliterative proverbs—in English—were symbolic elements of their intellectual and verbal

---

65. Thomas Pettitt also links John Ball's use of proverbs to his training as a preacher: "'Folk Allegory' in the Idiom of John Ball."
66. See Steven Justice, *Writing and Rebellion: England in 1381*.
67. Russell A. Peck, "Social Conscience and the Poets," 119.
68. Havens, "'As Englishe is comoun longage to oure puple,'" 109.

heritage around which they could rally and by which they set themselves in opposition to the ruling class.

The placement of an alliterative proverb at the juncture of didactic, religious, and political discourse occurs in another fourteenth-century lyric, "The Death of Edward III." This poem eulogizes both Edward III and the Black Prince and enjoins loyal support for the young Richard II. The dominant image is that of the ship of state until Richard is introduced as a scion of the royal rootstock. The poem unfolds in fourteen end-rhymed stanzas, ten of which conclude with a version of "Seldom seen is soon forgotten."

Although "The Death of Edward III" is a political poem, it begins with a traditionally didactic admonition:

> A, dere God, what mai þis be,
>   Þat alle þing weres & wasteþ awai?
> ffrendschip is but a vanyte,
>   Vnneþe hit dures al a day.
> Þai beo so sliper at assai,
>   So leof to han, and loþ to lete,
> And so fikel in heore fai,
>   Þat selden I-sei3e is sone for3ete.[69]

This gnomic generalization—heavily alliterated—provides context for lamenting the loss of a particular "friend," the late King Edward. The proverb "Seldom seen is soon forgotten" is usually applied to friends or lovers, so it fits easily into this first stanza. The last lines of stanza 2 begin to focus on the loss of a specific individual, not yet named, and use the proverb as a synonym for "died":

> He þat was vr moste spede
>   Is selden I-seye and sone for3ete.[70]

The third stanza introduces the image of the ship, eventually interpreted as the English nobility, with Edward III as its rudder. From this point on, the relationship of the proverbial refrain to the topics of the stanzas is more complex, as King, Prince, and honorable chivalry are all characterized as "seldom seen and soon forgotten," which seems neither literal nor likely but does motivate

---

69. "The Death of Edward III," lines 1–8, in *Historical Poems of the XIVth and XVth Centuries*, 102–3.

70. Ibid., 103, lines 15–16.

the eulogizer's attempt to commemorate them. Nevertheless, the poet does not use the refrain mechanically, because when he comes to speak of the young King Richard, he hopes that the proverbial fate will be overturned:

Crist leeue we so fare him wiþ,
    Þat selden seȝe be neuer forȝete.⁷¹

At this point, a literal reading of the proverb is completely subordinated to its symbolic representation of a generally negative set of events.

"The Death of Edward III" is a little-read poem in a much-studied codex: the Vernon Manuscript (Oxford, Bodleian Library, MS. Eng. Poet. a.1). The Vernon Manuscript (like its sister volume, the Simeon Manuscript) is a massive compendium of religious and didactic texts.⁷² Alongside its other treasures, the Vernon Manuscript contains a set of twenty-seven lyric poems in English; "The Death of Edward III" sits among these primarily didactic and devotional lyrics. Our poem resembles the others in its formal features:

> All 27 Vernon Lyrics are written in either eight-line or twelve-line stanzas, with four-stress lines, and normally rhyming *abab (abab) bcbc*. . . . Most are also refrain poems. . . . Nearly all show signs of occasional decorative alliteration but this is often only apparent in the opening lines of individual poems. . . . There is a proverbial quality about much of this writing.⁷³

"The Death of Edward III" distinguishes itself from the other Vernon lyrics by its political theme and its heavier use of alliteration, but it resembles them in its moral tone and proverbiality. In fact, not just the lyric section but the entirety of the Vernon Manuscript is infused with proverbial discourse, including an Anglo-Norman version of the *Disticha Catonis* and other "bi- and trilingual sequences of proverbs derived from Scriptural, pagan and secular sources and retooled for the didactic purposes of Christian catechesis."⁷⁴

Although the orthodoxy of the Vernon Manuscript seems a far cry from John Ball's rebellious letters, it provides the same matrix of religious, didactic, and proverbial discourse that appealed to English readers of the late fourteenth

---

71. Ibid., 105, lines 95–96.

72. On the contents and compilation of the Vernon MS., see the essays in *Studies in the Vernon Manuscript*; and *The Vernon Manuscript: A Facsimile of Bodleian Library, Oxford, MS. Eng. Poet. a.1*, esp. the introduction by A. I. Doyle.

73. John J. Thompson, "The Textual Background and Reputation of the Vernon Lyrics," 201–2.

74. Vincent Gillespie, "Moral and Penitential Lyrics," 75.

century. Alliterative proverbs were important markers in that matrix, serving multiple functions. As in sermons, the alliterative proverb in the lyric denoted wisdom, often with a religious cast. A writer like William of Shoreham or the author of "The Death of Edward III" could use that proverbial authority to strengthen conventional ideas; John Ball used it to remind the commons of his religious authority but also to encourage them to find strength in their own traditional wisdom. The alliterative proverb also exuded a strong sense of Englishness, used to completely different political ends in the letters of John Ball and "The Death of Edward III." This flexibility in the use of one very specific sentence type—the alliterative proverb—illustrates the depth and complexity of the ecology of English by the late fourteenth century.

Julia Boffey points out that the massive bulk of the Vernon Manuscript indicates that it "might most effectively have been used for reading aloud" and that the vernacularity of its contents may point to a lay or female audience.[75] The same proverb deployed as the refrain of the Vernon lyric on "The Death of Edward III" appears in another poem, one representing our last lyric subgenre—the courtly love-lyric—and preserved in two manuscripts, one of which is closely associated with female readers. "Now wold I fayne some myrthis make" is a conventional courtly lyric preserved in two manuscripts of the fifteenth century: Oxford, Bodleian MS. Ashmole 191 and Cambridge University Library MS. Ff.1.6, also known as the Findern Manuscript.[76] The Findern Manuscript is a commonplace book compiled by many hands over a long period of time beginning in the mid-fifteenth century. The manuscript contains a number of longer texts like *The Parlement of Foules* and *Sir Degrevant* along with its lyrics. Scholars debate some details regarding the ownership and composition of the manuscript, but all agree that it was created by and for a gentry household in south Derbyshire and was "owned, read, and perhaps even partially compiled by women."[77] In late medieval England, French was still the preferred language for collections of love-lyrics,[78] but the time and place of the Findern Manuscript's creation were especially friendly to English. By the mid-fifteenth century, the influence of Chaucer's English works had spread beyond the circle of London nobility and begun to reach the

---

75. Julia Boffey, "Middle English Lyrics and Manuscripts," 11.

76. For the text from Ashmole 191, see *Secular Lyrics of the XIVth and XVth Centuries*, 159–60; for the Cambridge (Findern) text, see *A Literary Middle English Reader*, 416–17.

77. Kara A. Doyle, "Thisbe out of Context: Chaucer's Female Readers and the Findern Manuscript," 231. See also Kate Harris, "The Origins and Make-Up of Cambridge University Library MS Ff.1.6," and Ralph Hanna III, "The Production of Cambridge University Library Ms. Ff. i. 6."

78. Boffey, *Manuscripts of English Courtly Love Lyrics in the Later Middle Ages*, 138.

provinces. As we have seen, English romances were already popular among the gentry; the addition of works by Chaucer (and his peers) raised the cultural status of such texts when placed alongside them in manuscript collections. We have also seen (in chapter 3) how women formed an important audience for English-language (religious) texts as early as the thirteenth century. So, a gentry household of literary-minded women during the second half of the fifteenth century provided a natural home for the collection of secular, even courtly, literature in English.

"Now wold I fayne some myrthis make" comprises six stanzas (rhyming AABCB) in which a male speaker professes his undying devotion to his beloved, despite their physical separation. Our proverb appears in stanza 4:

> She sayth that she hath seen hit wreten
> That 'seldyn seen is soon foryeten';
>   Hit is nat so;
> For, in good feith, save oneli hir,
>   I love no moo.[79]

In this courtly lyric, the alliterative proverb does not carry resonances of Englishness, antiquity, or even wisdom. Such authority as the proverb may claim derives at several removes from the speaker: "She *says* that she *has seen* it *written*" (emphasis added). The proverb is more like a rumor, one that the speaker flatly rejects with "Hit is nat so." In this milieu of courtly literature, the proverb is written, rather than oral, and is falsifiable. The second manuscript containing the poem—Ashmole 191—provides it with musical notation;[80] in performance, the contrast between the orally expressed truth from the speaker and the report of a written, but false, sentence from his beloved would appear even starker. Ironically, a context that illustrates the rising status of English as a literary language at the same time devalues one of its long-standing icons, the alliterative proverb.

The Findern Manuscript illustrates how the acceptance of English as a language for courtly literature spread among the English provincial gentry during the fifteenth century; among the nobility, this expansion of linguistic prestige marched north, to Scotland. The last lyric poem I will examine is "The Lay of Sorrow," a long (185-line) love-lament in a female voice. The poem survives in Oxford, Bodleian MS. Arch. Selden B.24, a manuscript associated with Henry

---

79. "Now wold I fayne," lines 19–23, in *A Literary Middle English Reader*, 416.

80. Ashmole 191 "contains no particular details of [its] early owners," but as a collection of "alchemical and astrological material in English and Latin, with some English songs," it may be of clerical origin: Boffey, *Manuscripts of English Courtly Love Lyrics*, 128 and 195.

Sinclair (d. 1513), a Scottish lord. Henry "was the commissioner of Gavin Douglas's translation of the *Aeneid,* and his great-uncle King James I was the probable author of *The Kingis Quair,* which is included in MS Selden B.24."[81] Other contents of the manuscript include poems by Chaucer and Hoccleve, and a second anonymous courtly lyric, "The Lufaris Complaynt." Kenneth G. Wilson, who edited the two anonymous lyrics, concludes that the manuscript was produced by Scottish scribes around 1500; P. J. Frankis argues that the poems are Scottish in both their copying and their authorship.[82]

"The Lay of Sorrow" is in many ways a conventional courtly lyric, but the poet shows particular skill and innovation through his frequent introduction of new images. For example, the stanza in which we find an alliterative proverb continues a metaphor of falconry from the preceding stanza, moves easily from there to the equine image of the proverb, then concludes with reference to the game of chess:

> Is that a bird of gentill kind, think ȝowe,
> That quhare he most cherist is to eschew
> And for foramell forsakith his *rycht* pray?
> Allace, how suld I In ony suich trow?
> <u>Bot all to late to stek þe stable nowe;</u>
> <u>Begane I quhane þe stede Is stollin away.</u>
> Nocht In beloue of remed this I say,
> Bot to declare agane ȝo*ur* promise, how
> In courer thus ȝe matit haue my play.[83]

Unlike the Findern lyric, which sets the proverb apart from courtly language in both form and meaning, the Scottish poem incorporates it fully into the lover's speech. She uses the proverb to support the idea that she has acted foolishly and thus failed to achieve her goal. In a different context, the proverbial image of the stable could appear rustic, but surrounded by falconry and chess, it forms part of a very courtly world. In this case, it is a world where a courtly woman *can* speak truth with a proverb. For this poet, the alliterative proverb carries no connotations of religious didacticism or social solidarity; instead, it expresses a personal lesson couched in a metaphor that fits the setting of

---

81. Boffey, *Manuscripts of English Courtly Love Lyrics,* 118. For a summary and discussion of the contents of Selden B.24, see Boffey, "*The Kingis Quair* and the Other Poems of Bodleian Library MS Arch. Selden. B.24."

82. Kenneth G. Wilson, "*The Lay of Sorrow,*" 708; P. J. Frankis, "Notes on Two Fifteenth Century Scots Poems," 203–8.

83. "The Lay of Sorrow," lines 80–88, in Wilson, "*The Lay of Sorrow,*" 717 [emphasis added].

the poem. The fact that this courtly lyric is composed in English rather than French, and the incorporation of an alliterative proverb into this courtly milieu, combine to illustrate the expanded role of English and its proverbs toward the end of the Middle Ages.

DRAMA

With a sort of defiant perversity, Bartlett Jere Whiting begins his book on *Proverbs in the Earlier English Drama* by pointing out the near absence of proverbs in the earlier English drama, or at least a large segment of it: "The serious religious plays contain almost no proverbs, and, what is even more strange, few more sententious remarks than their immediate sources rendered inevitable."[84] Whiting finds that the biblical plays employ proverbs not for instruction, as one might expect, "but rather to enliven the dialogue in the comic scenes in an effort, perhaps, to give [them] realism."[85] My own collation of alliterative proverbs in the cycle plays supports Whiting's contention that their main purpose is not directly instructive. Of six uses of alliterative proverbs, only two are from characters of moral integrity: Abraham (York *Abraham and Isaac*) and Rex Salvatus (Chester *Judgment*); two are from characters showing evil intent or action: 1 Demon (Towneley *Judgment*) and 1 Miles (York *Dream of Pilate's Wife*); and two are from a character who will become a trustworthy witness but who is still in a prerevelatory state: 1 Pastor (Towneley *Prima Pastorum*). If, as Whiting argues, proverbs in the Middle English cycle plays mainly serve as tools of characterization,[86] the characters they help to create are, by and large, fairly flawed. However, when we recall the uses to which alliterative proverbs are put in other genres of late medieval English literature, their deployment in the cycle plays, sparse as it is, might become clearer.

In the Middle English popular romances and in a number of the lyric poems, alliterative proverbs serve as icons of Englishness. They may invoke Englishness in order to naturalize foreign *Stoff* or to link Latin religious concepts to traditional, vernacular wisdom, but very frequently alliterative proverbs serve to create a sense of social cohesiveness: the English audience is drawn to root for the French knights in a Charlemagne romance, the commons are urged to support each other in a conflict with the first estate, or the

---

84. Whiting, *Proverbs in the Earlier English Drama*, 4.
85. Ibid.
86. Ibid., x.

English people as a whole are exhorted to honor and obey their king. In all of these instances, the alliterative proverb helps to create shared identity for the audience and allows a bonding between that audience and the subject(s) of the literary text. This type of bonding, or identification, is an important mode of instruction in the late medieval cycle plays. In fact, because the observer of the cycle play sees characters directly before him or her, live and in the flesh, some degree of identification with these characters is inevitable; the accomplished playwright will manipulate that identification to his desired ends. The process is fairly straightforward with a character like Abraham: the audience empathizes with Abraham's parental grief at having to sacrifice his son, thereby learning how difficult it can be to obey God's commands even with the best of intentions. Early in the York *Abraham and Isaac*, Abraham's use of an alliterative proverb forges a link between his wisdom and that of the audience, but also helps his character to hide the truth from Isaac, at least temporarily, in realistic fashion:

> ISAAC: Fadir, I am euere at youre wille,
> As worthy is withowten trayne;
> Goddis comaundement to fulfille
> Awe all folke for to be fayne.
>
> ABRAHAM: Sone, þou sais me full gode skille,
> <u>Bott alle þe soth is noȝt to sayne.</u>
> Go we sen we sall þertille—
> I praye God send vs wele agayne.[87]

The generality and authority of the proverb deflect further questioning through a recognizably parental rhetoric.

Out of all the biblical pageants, it is perhaps the shepherds' plays that use identification between audience and characters to greatest effect. Whiting notes that the Towneley cycle contains the greatest amount of proverbial material, and that within the Towneley cycle, the *Prima Pastorum* and *Secunda Pastorum* are both well appointed with proverbs and sententiae.[88] The Towneley *Secunda Pastorum* includes none of our alliterative proverbs, but the *Prima Pastorum* has two. Both are spoken by the First Shepherd (Gyb) in the strange,

---

87. *The Parchemyners and Bokebynders [Abraham and Isaac]*, lines 101–8, in *The York Plays: A Critical Edition of the York Corpus Christi Play as Recorded in British Library Additional MS 35290*, I.58 [emphasis added].

88. Whiting, *Proverbs in the Earlier English Drama*, 11–22.

comic scene of the shepherds' imaginary feast. The First Shepherd calls for drink, which he is duly offered by his companion (Iohn Horne):

2 PASTOR: Haue good ayll of Hely!
Bewar now, I wynk,
For and thou drynk drely,
In thy poll wyll it synk.

1 PASTOR: A, so!
This is boyte of oure bayll,
Good holsom ayll.[89]

Just a little later in the same scene, the shepherds add a singing contest to their celebration; Gyb accepts the challenge with

1 PASTOR: Now prayse at the partyng;
I shall sett you on warke.[90]

The convivial act of feasting (including drinking and singing) is one in which the audience can take familiar pleasure. The colloquial register of the shepherds' speech is marked not only by the alliterative proverbs, but by such mild swearing as "Be my dam saull, Alyce" (line 374) and "By my thryft" (line 379). If the shepherds were actually enjoying a feast, members of the audience would share it vicariously. However, the feast on stage is a farce, a lavish banquet only imagined by the shepherds. Their lack of actual food and drink satirizes the socioeconomic structure that leaves them so poorly off compared to the lords and prelates. In addition, their physical emptiness may symbolize the spiritual emptiness that will soon be remedied by the birth of Jesus. As in the *Secunda Pastorum*, the self-recognition that the onlookers experience through the shepherds enhances their experience of the joy of revelation that comes at the end of the play.

Not every use of alliterative proverbs in the cycle plays promotes identification with the characters. Sometimes a proverb simply punctuates a doctrinal lesson, as when Rex Salvatus in the Chester *Last Judgment* thanks God with "After bale, boote thou bringes."[91] Or, similar to usage in the romances, a prov-

---

89. *First Shepherds' Play*, lines 352–58, in *The Towneley Plays*, I.116 [emphasis added].
90. Ibid., lines 385–86, I.117 [emphasis added].
91. *The Last Judgment*, line 113, in *The Chester Mystery Cycle*, I.442.

erb may mark a specific point in the action, as when 1 Demon in the Towneley *Judgment* tells the damned souls that they have reached the end of the line:

> 1 DEMON: No, bot prase at the partyng,
> For now mon ye fynde it.[92]

The Demon's ironic use of the verb "praise" reminds us of the comic role that Whiting noted for proverbs in the cycle plays. As we saw in the *Prima Pastorum*, characters who use proverbs in such scenes are not necessarily endowed with wisdom: Lois Roney aptly describes the shepherds as "men whose wills are good but whose intellects are deficient."[93] The alliterative proverbs mark such characters as possessing the simple wisdom of the people, but nothing more. In the York *Dream of Pilate's Wife*, the strongly colloquialized banter among two soldiers and a servant combines alliterative near-nonsense with alliterative proverbs:

> II MILES: We muste yappely wende in at þis yate,
> For he þat comes to courte, to curtesye muste vse hym.
> I MILES: Do rappe on the renkis, þat we may rayse with oure rolyng.
> Come for the, sir coward, why cowre ye behynde?
> BEDELLUS: O, what javellis are ye þat jappis with gollyng?
> I MILES: A, goode sir, be no3t wroth, <u>for wordis are as þe wynde</u>.
> BEDELLUS: I saye, gedlynges, gose bakke with youre gawdes.[94]

In this play, the act of speech (versus silence) and the forms into which speech is organized are often as important as the content of those speeches. For example, Cayphas and Anna frequently state that Jesus is worthy of execution, but they entreat Pilate to perform the actual speech act of condemning him. More immediately relevant to the scene at hand, Pilate has commanded silence in his vicinity so that he may sleep. Thus, the soldiers are nervous about approaching Pilate's chambers and ill at ease addressing his servant: they use proverbial speech to embolden and protect themselves. As the discomfited soldiers are neither admirable nor sympathetic, the audience is encouraged to laugh at, rather than with, them.

---

92. *Judgment*, lines 782–83, in *The Towneley Plays*, I.423.

93. Lois Roney, "The Wakefield *First* and *Second Shepherds' Plays* as Complements in Psychology and Parody," 720.

94. *The Tapiteres and Couchers [Christ before Pilate I: The Dream of Pilate's Wife]*, lines 231–37, in *The York Plays: A Critical Edition*, I.264–65 [emphasis added]. Line 232 has the form and feel of a proverb, but I have found no analogues to it.

For the most part, then, alliterative proverbs in the cycle plays serve to enhance a comic, folksy realism, rather than to add a sense of venerable wisdom to any character. They match, on a smaller scale, the uses that Whiting determined for all types of proverbs in these plays. The fact that proverbs tend not to connote wisdom in this genre sets it apart from other genres of religious didacticism like the sermons and treatises we examined in chapter 3. In the prose didactic texts, alliteration and proverbiality combine to create strongly marked sentences of authoritative wisdom. In the cycle plays, the alliteration of our proverbs does not typically stand out in context, as three of the five plays we have examined are heavily alliterated throughout (Chester *Last Judgment,* York *Abraham and Isaac,* and York *Dream of Pilate's Wife*). Garrett Epp argues that alliteration in the York plays is linked with a "high style" conveying emotion and dignity and that in the Passion sequence, especially, increased alliteration indicates a passage of enhanced significance.[95] However, alliteration does not automatically confer authority in the cycle plays, as both "good" and "bad" characters use alliterative speech. Moreover, the very concept of authority is a more complex issue in the plays than in such prose treatises as *Ancrene Wisse* or the *Benjamin Minor.* For example, Warren Edminster argues from a Bakhtinian perspective that the fake feast of the *Prima Pastorum* "parodies transubstantiation and the Eucharist" and "parallels much of the scepticism the populace felt towards the mystical treatment of the sacraments of the Church."[96] Tony Corbett's view is somewhat less oppositional, but he provides a substantial analysis of how the lower clergy and laity in late medieval England had various ways of expressing their spirituality that were not directly related to official liturgy or doctrine; the cycle plays often incorporate such heterodox spirituality.[97] In a study that contributes significantly to our understanding of language ecology in late medieval England, Richard Emmerson reveals that the use of Latin in the Towneley cycle is most frequently associated with a negative type of authority.[98] Cayphas, Anna, and especially Pilate make considerable use of Latin: "In fact, in these central plays Latin is so extensively associated with Pilate that it becomes his signature and a sign of his treachery."[99] In contrast, God (Deus), the angels, and Jesus use very little Latin. In the plays surrounding the Passion, the difference between

---

95. Garrett P. J. Epp, "Passion, Pomp, and Parody: Alliteration in the York Plays."

96. Warren Edminster, *The Preaching Fox: Festive Subversion in the Plays of the Wakefield Master,* 114.

97. Tony Corbett, *The Laity, the Church and the Mystery Plays: A Drama of Belonging.*

98. Richard K. Emmerson, "'Englysch Laten' and 'Franch': Language as Sign of Evil in Medieval English Drama."

99. Ibid., 318.

the Latin-spewing Pilate and the silent or English-speaking Jesus is especially noteworthy. Emmerson interprets Jesus' use of English in both religious and political terms:

> It is a linguistic analogue for the incarnation, in which the spiritual language of Jesus becomes flesh in the earthly language of his people. By putting English in the mouth of Jesus, the playwright elevates the everyday language of northern England spoken by the vast majority of the play's audience, while at the same time contrasting it to the privileged languages of the first and second estates, the aristocracy and clergy whose allegiances are to the authorities centered in the south.[100]

French is not as common as Latin in the Towneley cycle, but Emmerson finds that it has a negative valence similar to Latin.[101] As you will recall, Towneley is the most proverbial of the cycles. The proverbs in Towneley may not confer status or respectability on the characters who use them in the individual plays, but in light of Emmerson's analysis, the English-language proverbs—and alliterative proverbs always appear especially English—may contribute to the vernacular register that itself claims higher status in the cycle as a whole.

Finally, we arrive at the last genre to be considered: the morality play. As in the cycle plays, proverbs in the moralities serve a characterizing function more than a didactic one. In Whiting's analysis, "Proverbs were obviously not introduced in the moralities for educational purposes but rather because they were considered humorous and because a wealth of proverbial phrases was felt to increase the effect of low life realism which the Vices were expected to suggest."[102] With regard to its use of proverbs, *The Castle of Perseverance* stands out from the other Middle English morality plays on two counts. First, it distributes proverbs most equally between "good" and "bad" characters.[103] Second, it employs, or at least refers to, alliterative proverbs much more frequently than do the other morality plays, in which they can barely be found. The even-handed distribution of proverbs in *The Castle of Perseverance* makes them less informative as elements of characterization; the relative wealth of alliterative proverbialization in that play must point to some other purpose. That purpose likely is stylistic. *The Castle of Perseverance* is the most alliterative of the English moralities and distributes its alliteration, like its proverbs,

---

100. Ibid., 318.
101. Ibid., 318–20.
102. Whiting, *Proverbs in the Earlier English Drama*, 66. A similar point is made by Michael R. Kelley, "Fifteenth-Century Flamboyant Style and *The Castle of Perseverance*," 25.
103. Whiting, *Proverbs in the Earlier English Drama*, 65.

among all its characters. The alliterative proverbs in the play are not dropped in as independent sentences, but are stripped to their alliterative cores. For example, Whiting locates four instances of the collocation of *bale* and *bote*,[104] but none is in the form of an actual proverb; each has been reworked using the second person:

Þou schalt be my bote of bale	(Humanum Genus, line 443)
May any bote þi bale brewe	(Confessio, line 1302)
Al þi bale schal torne þe to bote	(Penitencia, line 1401)
Sum bote of bale þou me brewe.	(Humanum Genus, line 2863)[105]

Elsewhere in the play, *bale* is twice linked with *bete* and five times with *brewe* (not counting the two instances cited above).[106] Other alliterative proverbs receive the same treatment, though not with the degree of repetition and consistency enjoyed by *bale/bote/bete/brewe*. In the Banns, the First Standard-Bearer describes Mankind's character using a familiar proverbial collocation—"Haue he neuere so mykyl, 3yt he wold haue more" (Primus Vexillator, line 89)—while in Scene VI, Backbiter uses the same rhetorical technique to describe himself:

To speke fayre beforn and fowle behynde
    Amongys men at mete and mele
Trewly, lordys, þis is my kynde. (Detraccio, lines 664–66)[107]

Much of what gives a proverb its authority derives from its syntactic independence: a proverb is generalized in its reference, thus applying to many or all people, and it is recognized as a repeated saying. The allusions to alliterative proverbs in *The Castle of Perseverance* have dispensed with both of these sources of authority by rewriting the proverbial collocations into sentences of syntactic and grammatical specificity. These are not proverbs, but poetic idioms. Nevertheless, the mining of proverbs for alliterative language in *The Castle of Perseverance* might destroy their structural integrity, but it also evidences their cultural mainstreaming. The author of the play was sufficiently familiar with these proverbs to use them, or parts of them, as compositional units, incorporating them in such a way that they stand out not at all. At least

---

104. Ibid., 70.
105. *The Castle of Perseverance*, in *The Macro Plays*, 16, 41, 44, 87.
106. Whiting, *Proverbs in the Earlier English Drama*, 70.
107. *The Castle of Perseverance*, in *The Macro Plays*, 5, 23.

in *The Castle of Perseverance,* alliterative proverbiality has become part of the norm.

The creation of new literary forms in the twelfth through fifteenth centuries, and the introduction of those genres into English culture, often through the medium of a class-restricted language, proved a productive but also disruptive process. Over time, traditional Germanic genres such as the heroic lay and the elegy lost their cultural status to the romance and new forms of lyric. The biblical and morality plays had no precursors in Anglo-Saxon culture. Through this literary transition, the alliterative proverb persisted as an element of vernacular culture that both recalled the pre-Conquest past and adapted to new literary contexts. In this transformed literary world, the alliterative proverb appeared most often in genres directed toward a more general than courtly audience: popular romance, didactic and political lyric, religious drama. In these genres, alliterative proverbs contributed elements of instruction, characterization, and narrative structure, but their most comprehensive use was as a means of creating and manipulating a shared social identity based on the combination of proverbial wisdom, alliteration, and the English language. Romance authors could invoke this identity to create sympathy with certain characters; dramatists could do the same and then use the link between audience and characters to reinforce religious feelings. Of course, social cohesiveness has a political dimension as well: appeals to cultural unity could be employed to support existing political structures ("The Death of Edward III") or to subvert them (the letters of John Ball). Its consistency enhanced the role that the alliterative proverb played in helping to naturalize new literary genres in English despite the fact that each of these genres—whether associated with French like the romance or Latin like the drama—presented particular challenges of linguistic and literary ecology.

CHAPTER 5

Conclusion

Summary and Suggestions

IN ORDER TO understand the literary and linguistic environment that influenced medieval writers, it is important to examine their sources and the works of their contemporaries, as we often do. However, other, less literary, uses of language that contribute to the relevant language ecology should also be considered: these might include medium-length forms such as personal letters, business documents, legal writs, or, as here, a shorter form—the proverb. Because proverbs inhabited cultural domains running the gamut from rural orality to the Latin textuality of the urban universities, a medieval English author could not avoid their language whatever his or her educational level or preferred genre. In order to investigate some elements of that influence, this study of alliterative proverbs in medieval England has had two goals. The more general aim has been to explore the range of ways in which alliterative proverbs contributed to the language ecologies within which they functioned. The more specific goal has been to employ the study of alliterative proverbs as an index of continuity in the verbal culture of medieval England, particularly across the divide of the Norman Conquest. This process of discovery has, I think, found new evidence of such continuity, though untangling the co-occurring currents of change has proved equally informative. Without question, the political upheaval of the Norman Conquest introduced many forms of social, economic, linguistic, and literary change, but our knowledge of literary culture for the first 150 years following the Conquest is mostly restricted to that of the elite, Francophone minority. The Latinate domain of the church is fairly well documented, and, as we have seen, religious uses of English continued in interesting fashion, but in most areas of England, the secular verbal art of the majority possessed insufficient status to be recorded. Alliterative proverbs, with roots in Old English and continued life in Middle English, grant us a better understanding of the intellectual life and verbal expression of that segment of the population.

The most important fact with which to begin is that alliterative proverbs did survive the cultural disruption of the Norman Conquest, not by accident or coincidence, but as carriers of meaning. Indeed, our corpus of alliterative proverbs is richer in Middle English examples than in Old English. This disparity derives, first, from the sparse preservation of Old English texts, and second, from the development in Middle English of new genres in which contemporary, vernacular sayings were more at home: for example, both the romances and the cycle plays introduced colloquial registers of dialogue that had no real counterpart in Old English literature. In order to create these new literary forms, Middle English authors needed to incorporate different sorts of verbal art and utterance, one of which was the alliterative proverb. Nevertheless, I have shown (in chapter 2) that the roots of many alliterative proverbs lie in the Anglo-Saxon period, even if a full-blown version of the proverb is evidenced only later. Thus, the existence of the alliterative proverb remains consistent, but its textual uses change to meet the demands of new literary environments.

As a contribution to the linguistic history of England, I have demonstrated that alliteration remained a productive component of proverb formation long after the Norman Conquest. Of the myriad linguistic innovations occurring during the Middle English period, lexical change affected proverbs most directly. Such change could force the loss or alteration of a particular lexeme in the proverb as words became obsolete or shifted meaning. This process might then lead to the death of a proverb, but not necessarily—in some cases, proverbs preserved archaic words or meanings. Even more frequently, new alliterative proverbs were coined using new Romance vocabulary.[1] For the philologist, proverbs are like little language laboratories. On the sociolinguistic level, attention to the use of proverbs can help to track the ongoing adjustments among languages in various domains and among different socioeconomic classes. During the Anglo-Saxon period, a link was forged between

---

1. The same can be said for the creation of nonproverbial alliterative collocations: Manfred Markus, "Bed & Board: The Role of Alliteration in Twin Formulas of Middle English Prose."

proverbs, alliteration, authoritative wisdom, and the English language. Elements of that bond persisted through all the vicissitudes of sociolinguistic rebalancing in the course of the English Middle Ages.

In late Old English and early Middle English, alliterative proverbs negotiated the landscape where English met Latin. Early on, the territory in question was that of wisdom literature, where the vernacular tradition of proverbs and gnomic poetry competed successfully with such school-texts as the *Disticha Catonis*. The association of alliteration (and alliterative proverbs) with time-honored, native wisdom persisted in such post-Conquest works as the *Proverbs of Alfred* and the *Proverbs of Hendyng*; in the latter case, we see how the English alliterative tradition combined with the rhymes of French in the creation of an Anglo-Norman version of wisdom poetry that ultimately spanned both worlds. Standard literary histories of the Middle English period tend to overlook less exciting and imaginative genres like the wisdom poem and thus may also overlook such an instance when the movement of literary innovation flowed from England to France, rather than the reverse. It is important to recognize and quantify the "Anglo" element of Anglo-Norman culture, which is not simply a geographic or political construct.

In the realm of religious, didactic prose, alliterative proverbs helped to create a specifically English idiom that served the large Anglophone population. Texts like the *Ancrene Wisse* or the various redactions of the *Benjamin Minor* were clearly influenced by the Latin rhetoric in which their authors were schooled, and, like contemporary French texts, they were directed toward the laity, but ultimately, they drew from a distinctly English verbal past—one that included the alliterative proverb—and served a public who recognized and appreciated that tradition. The sermon—Latin, English, or macaronic—was another genre in which the alliterative proverb displayed its wealth of cultural connections. Highly educated, clerical rhetoricians were trained to use proverbs as structural markers in Latin, scholastic sermons, but they, and their pastoral brethren, also employed proverbs to appeal to lay audiences. The same dual background applies to alliteration: recommended as a feature of Latin style, but also effective in connecting with an Anglophone crowd. The established position of the alliterative proverb in both Latin and English discourse made it a useful tool for the vernacularization of religious culture. Matthew McCabe, following Alastair Minnis, defines "vernacularity" as "the diversification of textual cultures that occurs when writers intentionally accommodate their modes of writing to enhance accessibility for new kinds of readers."[2]

---

2. T. Matthew N. McCabe, *Gower's Vulgar Tongue*, 2; Minnis, *Translations of Authority in Medieval English Literature*.

Hence, sermons and religious treatises of the thirteenth century incorporate proverbs as they reach out to a broader pastoral audience of women in particular and the English-speaking laity in general. By the late fourteenth century, vernacularization in religious discourse became associated with the Wycliffites and subsequently lost favor with the official church. A comparison of the use of proverbs in pre-Lollard versus Lollard sermons would likely prove interesting, as would further exploration of the role of proverbs in the vernacularization of other religious genres.

The association of alliterative proverbs with a particularly English past helps to explain their appearance in the Middle English popular romances. During the fourteenth century, such urban, courtly poets as Chaucer and Gower leveraged their familiarity with the artistry of French poetry in the process of creating an English poesy of equivalent status.[3] Both authors were well familiar with proverbial discourse and handled proverbs with great sophistication and literary artistry.[4] However, their preferred literary models were courtly and French, so the alliterative proverb, product of a non-Francophone past and instead associated with the specifically English past that they sought to surmount, did not serve their purpose. On the other hand, another branch of English literature was also being created from French sources and models, though with a different strategy. The authors of the Middle English popular romances did not need to please an audience well versed in the aesthetics of French romance and lyric. Their audience—primarily the gentry rather than the nobility—savored the narrative materials and forms that could be borrowed from the French tradition, but their moral, political, and practical concerns were different from those of the court. For this audience, the alliterative proverb helped to create a recognizably English worldview giving local meaning to foreign stories. This same desire to create and promote a local literature is also reflected in the somewhat regionalized prominence of alliterative poetry in the later fourteenth century. Audiences for written literature were growing during this period, and were growing more diverse; just as different sociocultural domains called for the use of different languages, the tastes of different cultural subgroups within England were best met by a range of literary styles. The varieties of poetic forms circulating at the time were not necessarily in competition with each other, but were each developed to meet the demands of a particular readership during an exciting and creative period of English literary history. As it turns out, alliterative proverbs

---

3. For differing views on the nature of this achievement, see Christopher Cannon, *The Making of Chaucer's English,* and Jeremy Catto, "Written English."

4. Some of the earliest scholarship on proverbs in Middle English literature includes Whiting, *Chaucer's Use of Proverbs* (1934), and Gotthard Walz, *Das Sprichwort bei Gower* (1907).

were rarely used by Middle English alliterative poets. For some genres, like the short lyric, sentence-length proverbs would simply be a bad stylistic fit, but they would seem well suited to such long-line, morally infused works as *Sir Gawain and the Green Knight* and *Piers Plowman*. The lack of alliterative proverbs (or much of any proverbial material) in *Sir Gawain and the Green Knight* relates mostly to its courtly themes and settings: the alliterative proverb belongs to a different social sphere. Langland is less shy of proverbs in general and includes one or two alliterative variants, but overall he favors biblical (or other Latin) texts as icons of authority. He is concerned with issues of ethics and morality, as are proverbs, but he and his imitators also had political concerns; Langland's model for the link between alliteration and traditional authority may not be the alliterative proverb, but something different like the legal-homiletic tradition adduced by Stephen Yeager.[5] Because Langland's entire poem is alliterative (and English), the alliterative proverb would not stand out in a formal way as a marker of social wisdom. So, in a way, the near absence of the alliterative proverb in these exemplars of alliterative poetry and in the courtly works of Chaucer and Gower can be almost as telling as its presence elsewhere.

As the Middle Ages drew to a close, the association of alliterative proverbs with Englishness contracted to a representation of lower-class status, at least in the biblical and morality plays. In those plays, the alliterative proverb still connected the audience to the character who uttered it, but the proverb served to colloquialize rather than elevate the dialogue. The colloquialization helped the audience to identify with the characters, though they might need to reject that identification as the moral lesson of the play unfolded. In this context, the alliterative proverb could help to create a positive vernacularity, but the tone is far removed from the authoritative and regal wisdom of *The Proverbs of Alfred*. By the fifteenth century, English had become the language of choice in almost every domain; thus, writers no longer needed to signal their embrace of the vernacular through the alliterative proverb. Consequently, the alliterative proverb fell together with its nonalliterative mates and lost its association with the respected wisdom of the English past.

Like any other construct traced through a long expanse of history, the alliterative proverb in English has fulfilled various functions at different times; otherwise, it would have perished. By examining the evolution of both form and function, we can gain—have gained—a deeper understanding of the cultural milieux traversed by this peculiar icon of English verbal history. Alliteration and proverbiality tend to inhabit different domains in modern

---

5. Yeager, *From Lawmen to Plowmen*.

Anglophone culture, but together, they open a door to a wide variety of literary, linguistic, and social functions in the English Middle Ages. It is my hope that the present study will spur further research into the functions of proverbs in medieval literature. Despite the range of periods and genres I have addressed in this book, my self-imposed restriction to the alliterative proverb has left much ground to be covered in the future. The ubiquitousness of the proverb in medieval culture allows it to serve as a starting point for any number of scholarly approaches and to facilitate previously unexplored connections between periods, genres, and languages. Whether approached from the interests of linguistics, cultural history, literary history (including orality), or literary criticism, the proverb—alliterative or not—offers a powerful entry into the intellectual and social life of the Middle Ages.

BIBLIOGRAPHY

Note: Where I thought that there might be any confusion in locating an item, especially in the case of proverb collections, I have listed the item under both its title and the name of its editor.

Abrahams, Roger D., and Barbara A. Babcock. "The Literary Use of Proverbs." *Journal of American Folklore* 90 (1977): 414–29.
Ælfric. *Ælfric's Catholic Homilies: The First Series; Text.* Edited by Peter Clemoes. EETS, s.s. 17. Oxford: EETS, 1997.
———. *Ælfric's Catholic Homilies: The Second Series; Text.* Edited by Malcolm Godden. EETS, s.s. 5. London: EETS, 1979.
———. *Ælfric's Lives of Saints.* Edited by Walter W. Skeat. EETS, o.s. 76. London: EETS, 1881.
Aesop. *The Fables of Aesop as First Printed by William Caxton in 1484.* Edited by Joseph Jacobs. 2 vols. London: David Nutt, 1889.
Ailes, Marianne, and Phillipa Hardman. "How English Are the English Charlemagne Romances?" In *Boundaries in Medieval Romance,* edited by Neil Cartlidge, 43–55. Studies in Medieval Romance, 6. Cambridge: D. S. Brewer, 2008.
Alfred the Great. *King Alfred's Old English Version of Boethius De Consolatione Philosophiae.* Edited by Walter John Sedgefield. Oxford: Clarendon Press, 1899.
———. *King Alfred's West-Saxon Version of Gregory's Pastoral Care.* Edited by Henry Sweet. EETS, o.s. 45 and 50. London: EETS, 1871–72.
Altieri, Marcelle. *Les Romans de Chrétien de Troyes: Leur perspective proverbiale et gnomique.* Paris: Éditions A.-G. Nizet, 1976.
Amis and Amiloun. Edited by MacEdward Leach. EETS, 203. London: EETS, 1937.
Ancrene Wisse. Edited from Ms. Corpus Christi College Cambridge 402. Edited by J. R. R. Tolkien. EETS, o.s. 249. London: EETS, 1962.

Andrew of Wyntoun. *The Original Chronicle of Andrew of Wyntoun*. Edited by F. J. Amours. 6 vols. Scottish Text Society. Edinburgh: Scottish Text Society, 1903–14.

The Anglo-Saxon Minor Poems. Edited by Elliott Van Kirk Dobbie. ASPR, 6. New York: Columbia University Press; London: Routledge and Kegan Paul, 1942.

Apollonius of Tyre. See *The Old English Apollonius of Tyre*.

Apperson, G. L. *The Wordsworth Dictionary of Proverbs*. Ware, UK: Wordsworth Editions, 1993.

Aristotle. *Aristotelis Ars Rhetorica*. Translated by William of Moerbeke. Edited by Leonhard Spengel. 2 vols. Leipzig: Teubner, 1867.

———. *On Rhetoric: A Theory of Civic Discourse*. Translated by George A. Kennedy. 2nd ed. Oxford: Oxford University Press, 2007.

Arngart, Olof. "The Distichs of Cato and the Proverbs of Alfred." In *Kungl: Humanistika Vetenskapssamfundets i Lund Årberattelse 1951–52*, 95–118. Lund, Sweden: C. W. K. Gleerup, 1952.

Arora, Shirley L. "The Perception of Proverbiality." *Proverbium* 1 (1984): 1–38.

Ashe, Laura. *Fiction and History in England, 1066–1200*. Cambridge Studies in Medieval Literature, 68. Cambridge: Cambridge University Press, 2007.

The Asloan Manuscript: A Miscellany in Prose and Verse. Edited by W. A. Craigie. 2 vols. Edinburgh: Scottish Text Society, 1925.

Audelay, John. *The Poems of John Audelay*. Edited by Ella K. Whiting. EETS, o.s. 184. London: EETS, 1931.

———. *The Poems of John Audelay*. Edited by James Orchard Halliwell. London: Percy Society, 1844.

Augustine of Hippo. *Contra Julianum*. In *Patrologiae Cursus Completus, Series Latina*, edited by J.-P. Migne. 221 vols. Paris: Garnier, 1844–64, vol. 45.

———. *De musica*. In *Patrologiae Cursus Completus, Series Latina*, edited by J.-P. Migne. 221 vols. Paris: Garnier, 1844–64, vol. 32.

The Babees Book. Edited by F. J. Furnivall. EETS, 32. London: EETS, 1868.

Bacon, Roger. *Opus maius*. Edited by J. H. Bridges. 3 vols. Oxford: Clarendon Press, 1897–1900.

Barclay, Alexander. *The Ship of Fools*. Edited by T. H. Jamieson. 2 vols. Edinburgh: William Paterson, 1874.

Barratt, Alexandra. "English Translations of Didactic Literature for Women to 1550." In *What Nature Does Not Teach: Didactic Literature in the Medieval and Early Modern Periods*, edited by Juanita Feros Ruys, 287–301. Disputatio, 15. Turnhout, Belgium: Brepols, 2008.

Barron, W. R. J. *English Medieval Romance*. London and New York: Longman, 1987.

Basil. *The Anglo-Saxon Version of the Hexameron of St. Basil, or, Be Godes six daga weorcum. And the Anglo-Saxon Remains of St. Basil's Admonitio ad filium spiritualem*. Edited by Henry W. Norman. 2nd ed. London: J. R. Smith, 1849.

Bellis, Joanna, and Venetia Bridges. "'What shalt thou do when thou hast an english to make into Latin?': The Proverb Collection of Cambridge, St. John's College, MS F.26." *Studies in Philology* 112 (2015): 68–92.

Benham, W. Gurney. *A Book of Quotations, Proverbs, and Household Words*. Philadelphia: J. P. Leppincott Co.; London: Cassell & Co., 1907.

Beowulf. See *Klaeber's Beowulf and the Fight at Finnsburg*.

Beryn. See *The Canterbury Interlude and Merchant's Tale of Beryn*.

Bible, Middle English. See *The Holy Bible*; *The Psalter*.

Bible, Old English. See *Liber Psalmorum*; *The Old English Version of the Heptateuch*.

Bland, Dave L. "The Use of Proverbs in Two Medieval Genres of Discourse: 'The Art of Poetry' and 'The Art of Preaching.'" *Proverbium* 14 (1997): 1–21.

Böddeker, K., ed. *Altenglische Dichtungen des MS. Harl. 2253*. Berlin, 1878.

Boethius. See Alfred the Great.

Boffey, Julia. "*The Kingis Quair* and the Other Poems of Bodleian Library MS Arch. Selden. B.24." In *A Companion to Medieval Scottish Poetry*, edited by Priscilla Bawcutt and Janet Hadley Williams, 63–74. Cambridge: D. S. Brewer, 2006.

———. *Manuscripts of English Courtly Love Lyrics in the Later Middle Ages*. Woodbridge, Suffolk; and Dover, NH: D. S. Brewer, 1985.

———. "Middle English Lyrics and Manuscripts." In *A Companion to the Middle English Lyric*, edited by Thomas G. Duncan, 1–18. Cambridge: D. S. Brewer, 2005.

Bokenham, Osbern. *Mappula Angliae*. Edited by C. Horstmann. *Englische Studien* 10 (1887): 1–34.

Bowers, John M. "The Canterbury Interlude and Merchant's Tale of Beryn: Introduction." In *The Canterbury Tales: Fifteenth-Century Continuations and Additions*. TEAMS Middle English Texts Series. Kalamazoo, MI: Medieval Institute Publications, 1992. Accessed 14 October 2013 through the Robbins Library Digital Projects: d.lib.rochester.edu/teams/publication/bowers-canterbury-tales-fifteenth-century-interlude-and-merchants-tale-of-beryn-introduction.

Bowers, R. H. "Hichecoke's 'This Worlde is but a Vanyte' (HM 183)." *Modern Language Notes* 67 (1952): 331–33.

Boyle, Leonard E., O. P. "The Fourth Lateran Council and Manuals of Popular Theology." In *The Popular Literature of Medieval England*, edited by Thomas J. Heffernan, 30–43. Tennessee Studies in Literature, 28. Knoxville: University of Tennessee Press, 1985.

Bradbury, Nancy Mason. "Gamelyn." In *Heroes and Anti-Heroes in Medieval Romance*, edited by Neil Cartlidge, 129–44. Studies in Medieval Romance, 16. Cambridge: D. S. Brewer, 2012. Accessed 20 Sept 2013 on JSTOR: http://www.jstor.org/stable/10.7722/j.ctt81fr9.13.

———. *Writing Aloud: Storytelling in Late Medieval England*. Urbana and Chicago: University of Illinois Press, 1998.

Braunmüller, Kurt, and Gisella Ferraresi, eds. *Aspects of Multilingualism in European Language History*. Hamburg Studies on Multilingualism, 2. Amsterdam: John Benjamins, 2003.

Bredehoft, Thomas A. *Early English Metre*. Toronto: University of Toronto Press, 2005.

Breen, Katharine. *Imagining an English Reading Public, 1150–1400*. Cambridge Studies in Medieval Literature, 79. Cambridge: Cambridge University Press, 2010.

Bremmer, Rolf. "Continental Germanic Influences." In *A Companion to Anglo-Saxon Literature*, edited by Philip Pulsiano and Elaine Treharne, 375–87. Oxford: Blackwell, 2001.

Bríathra Flainn Fhína maic Ossu. See *Old Irish Wisdom Attributed to Aldfrith of Northumbria*.

Brooks, Nicholas. "Latin and Old English in Ninth-Century Canterbury." In *Spoken and Written Language: Relations Between Latin and the Vernacular in the Earlier Middle Ages*, edited by Mary Garrison, Arpad P. Orbán, and Marco Mostert, 113–31. Utrecht Studies in Medieval Literacy, 24. Turnhout, Belgium: Brepols, 2013.

Bruckner, Matilda Tomaryn. "The Shape of Romance in Medieval France." In *The Cambridge Companion to Medieval Romance*, edited by Roberta L. Krueger, 13–28. Cambridge: Cambridge University Press, 2000.

Brunner, Ingrid A. "On Some of the Vernacular Translations of Cato's Distichs." In *Helen Adolf Festschrift*, edited by Sheema Z. Buehne, James L. Hodge, and Lucille B. Pinto, 99–125. New York: Ungar, 1968.

Brunner, Karl. "Me. Disticha (aus Hs. Add. 37049)." *Archiv* 159 (1931): 86–92.

———. "Spätme. Lehrgedichte." *Archiv* 164 (1933): 178–99.

Buridant, Claude. "Les proverbes et la prédication au Moyen Age: De l'utilisation des proverbes vulgaires dans les sermons." In *Richesse du Proverbes*. Vol. 1: *Le proverbe au Moyen Age*, edited by François Suard and Claude Buridant, 23–54. Lille, France: Université de Lille, 1984.

Cable, Thomas. "Progress in Middle English Alliterative Metrics." *Yearbook of Langland Studies* 23 (2009): 243–64.

Cannon, Christopher. *The Making of Chaucer's English: A Study of Words*. Cambridge: Cambridge University Press, 1999.

———. "Proverbs and the Wisdom of Literature: The *Proverbs of Alfred* and Chaucer's *Tale of Melibee*." *Textual Practice* 24 (2010): 407–34.

The Canterbury Interlude and Merchant's Tale of Beryn. Edited by John M. Bowers. http://www.lib.rochester.edu/camelot/Teams/berynfrm.htm (accessed 6/17/2012). Originally published in *The Canterbury Tales: Fifteenth Century Continuations and Additions*. Kalamazoo, MI: Medieval Institute, 1992.

The Castle of Perseverance. See *The Macro Plays*.

Catto, Jeremy. "Written English: The Making of the Language 1370–1400." *Past & Present* 179 (2003): 24–59.

Caxton, William. *The Fables of Aesop as First Printed by William Caxton in 1484*. Edited by Joseph Jacobs. 2 vols. London: David Nutt, 1889.

———. *Ovyde, Hys Book of Methamorphose, Books X–XV*. Edited by Stephen Gaselee and H. F. B. Brett-Smith. Oxford: Basil Blackwell, 1924.

Chaucer, Geoffrey. *The Riverside Chaucer*. Edited by Larry D. Benson. 3rd ed. Boston: Houghton Mifflin, 1987.

The Chester Mystery Cycle. Edited by R. M. Lumiansky and David Mills. 2 vols. EETS, s.s. 3. Oxford: EETS, 1974–86.

Chism, Christine. *Alliterative Revivals*. Philadelphia: University of Pennsylvania Press, 2002.

Chrodegang. *The Old English Version of the Enlarged Rule of Chrodegang Together with the Latin Original*. Edited by Arthur S. Napier. EETS, o.s. 150. London: EETS, 1916.

Cicero. *De Finibus bonorum et malorum*. Edited and translated by H. Rackham. Loeb Classical Library. Cambridge, MA, and London: Harvard University Press, 1951.

Clanchy, Michael T. *From Memory to Written Record: England 1066–1307*. 2nd ed. Oxford: Oxford University Press, 1993.

Clark, Cecily. "The Myth of 'The Anglo-Norman Scribe.'" In *Words, Names and History: Selected Writings of Cecily Clark*, edited by Peter Jackson, 168–76. Cambridge: D. S. Brewer, 1995.

Clifton, Nicole. "'Of Arthour and of Merlin' as Medieval Children's Literature." *Arthuriana* 13.2 (2003): 9–22.

The Cloud of Unknowing and the Book of Privy Counselling. Edited by Phyllis Hodgson. EETS, o.s. 218. London: EETS, 1944; rpt. 1958.

Corbett, Tony. *The Laity, the Church and the Mystery Plays: A Drama of Belonging*. Dublin Studies in Medieval and Renaissance Literature. Vol. 1. Dublin: Four Courts Press, 2009.

Cornelius, Ian. "Alliterative Revival: Retrospect and Prospect." *Yearbook of Langland Studies* 26 (2012): 261–76.

———. "Classical Rhetoric and the Perception of Alliterative Verse." Paper delivered at the Annual Meeting of the Medieval Academy of America, St. Louis University, 23 March 2012.

———. *Cultural Promotion: Middle English Alliterative Writing and the "Ars Dictaminis."* PhD dissertation, University of Pennsylvania, 2009.

Cox, R. S. "The Old English Dicts of Cato." *Anglia* 90 (1972): 1–42.

Crane, Susan. "Anglo-Norman Cultures in England, 1066–1460." In *The Cambridge History of Medieval English Literature,* edited by David Wallace, 35–60. Cambridge: Cambridge University Press, 1999.

———. *Insular Romance: Politics, Faith, and Culture in Anglo-Norman and Middle English Literature*. Berkeley, Los Angeles, and London: University of California Press, 1986.

Crépin, André. "Mentalités anglaises au temps d'Henri II Plantagenêt d'après les *Proverbs of Alfred*." *Cahiers de civilisation médiévale, Xe–XIIe siècles* 37 (1994): 49–60.

Dalbiac, Philip Hugh. *Dictionary of Quotations*. London: Swan Sonnenschein & Co.; New York: Macmillan, 1897.

DaRold, Orietta, Takako Kato, Mary Swan, and Elaine Treharne. *The Production and Use of English Manuscripts 1060 to 1220*. Leicester: University of Leicester, 2010. http://www.le.ac.uk/ee/em1060to1220/.

Davidson, Mary Catherine. *Medievalism, Multilingualism, and Chaucer*. New York: Palgrave Macmillan, 2010.
Dean, Ruth J., with Maureen B. M. Boulton. *Anglo-Norman Literature: A Guide to Texts and Manuscripts*. Anglo-Norman Text Society Occasional Publications Series 3. London: Anglo-Norman Text Society, 1999.
de Caluwé-Dor, Juliette. "Les Proverbes de Hendyng: Héroïsme païen, charité chrétienne et réalisme bourgeois." In *Richesse du Proverbes*. Vol 1: *Le proverbe au Moyen Age*, edited by François Suard and Claude Buridant, 55–73. Lille, France: Université de Lille, 1984.
Defensor of Ligugé. *Defensor's Liber scintillarum: With an interlinear Anglo-Saxon Version*. Edited by E. W. Rhodes. EETS, o.s. 93. London: EETS, 1889.
Deonise Hid Diuinite and Other Treatises on Contemplative Prayer Related to "The Cloud of Unknowing." Edited by Phyllis Hodgson. EETS, o.s. 231. London: EETS, 1958.
Deschamps, Eustache. *Œuvres complètes des Eustache Deschamps*. Edited by Auguste-Henry-Edouard, Marquis de Queux de Saint-Hilaire. 11 vols. Paris: Firmin Didot, 1878–1903.
Deskis, Susan E. *"Beowulf" and the Medieval Proverb Tradition*. MRTS, 155. Tempe, AZ: MRTS, 1996.
———. "Exploring Text and Discourse in the Old English Gnomic Poems: The Problem of Narrative." *JEGP* 104 (2005): 326–44.
———. "Proverbs and Structure in *Maxims I. A.*" *Studies in Philology* 110 (2013): 667–89.
Dictionary of American Proverbs and Proverbial Phrases, 1820–1880. Edited by Archer Taylor and B. J. Whiting. Cambridge, MA: Belknap Press, 1958.
Dictionary of Old English Web Corpus. http://www.tapor.library.utoronto.ca/doecorpus/.
A Dictionary of the Proverbs in England in the Sixteenth and Seventeenth Centuries. Edited by Morris Palmer Tilley. Ann Arbor: University of Michigan Press, 1950.
Digital Index of Middle English Verse. http://www.dimev.net/record.php?recID=1834.
Disticha Catonis. Edited by Marcus Boas. Amsterdam: North-Holland Publ. Co., 1952.
Dor, Juliette. "Langues française et anglaise, et multilinguisme à l'époque d'Henri II Plantagenêt." *Cahiers de civilisation médiévale, Xe–XIIIe siècles* 37 (1994): 61–72.
Douglas, Gavin. *The Poetical Works of Gavin Douglas*. Edited by John Small. 4 vols. Edinburgh: W. Paterson, 1874.
Doyle, Kara A. "Thisbe out of Context: Chaucer's Female Readers and the Findern Manuscript." *Chaucer Review* 40 (2006): 231–61.
Drout, Michael D. C. "Possible Instructional Effects of the Exeter Book 'Wisdom Poems': A Benedictine Reform Context." In *Form and Content of Instruction in Anglo-Saxon England in the Light of Contemporary Manuscript Evidence*, edited by Patrizia Lendinara et al., 447–66. Turnhout, Belgium: Brepols, 2007.
"The Durham Proverbs." Edited by Olof Arngart. *Speculum* 56 (1981): 288–300.
The Durham Proverbs: An Eleventh Century Collection of Anglo-Saxon Proverbs Edited from Durham Cathedral MS. B.III.32. Edited by Olof Arngart. Lunds Universitets Årsskrift. N. F. Avd. 1, Bd 52, Nr 2. Lund, Sweden: C. W. K. Gleerup, 1956.
The Early English Carols. Edited by Richard Leighton Greene. Oxford: Clarendon Press, 1935.
The Early English Versions of the Gesta Romanorum. Edited by S. J. H. Herrtage. EETS, e.s. 33. London: EETS, 1879; rpt. 1962.
Edminster, Warren. *The Preaching Fox: Festive Subversion in the Plays of the Wakefield Master*. NY and London: Routledge, 2005.
Eger and Grime. Edited by James Ralston Caldwell. Harvard Studies in Comparative Literature, 9. Cambridge, MA: Harvard University Press, 1933.
Eleven Old English Rogationtide Homilies. Edited by Joyce Bazire and James E. Cross. Kings College London Medieval Studies, 4. Exeter: Kings College London, 1989.
Emmerson, Richard K. "'Englysch Laten' and 'Franch': Language as Sign of Evil in Medieval English Drama." In *The Devil, Heresy and Witchcraft in the Middle Ages: Essays in Honor*

of Jeffrey B. Russell, edited by Alberto Ferreiro, 305–26. Cultures, Beliefs and Traditions, 6. Leiden: Brill, 1998.

The English and Scottish Popular Ballads. Edited by Helen Child Sargent and George Lyman Kittredge. Boston and New York: Houghton Mifflin, 1904.

The English Conquest of Ireland. Edited by Frederick J. Furnivall. EETS, o.s. 107. London: EETS, 1896.

English Lyrics of the XIIIth Century. Edited by Carleton Brown. Oxford: Clarendon Press, 1932.

The English Text of the Ancrene Riwle: Edited from British Museum Cotton MS. Cleopatra C.vi. Edited by E. J. Dobson. EETS, 267. London: EETS, 1972.

Epp, Garrett P. J. "Passion, Pomp, and Parody: Alliteration in the York Plays." *Medieval English Theatre* 11 (1989): 150–61.

The Exeter Anthology of Old English Poetry: An Edition of Exeter Dean and Chapter MS 3501. Edited by Bernard J. Muir. 2 vols. 2nd ed. Exeter: Exeter University Press, 2000.

Facsimile of Oxford, Bodleian Library, MS Digby 86. Edited by Judith Tschann and M. B. Parkes. EETS, s.s. 16. Oxford: EETS, 1996.

Faulkner, Mark. "Archaism, Belatedness and Modernisation." *Review of English Studies* 63 (259) (2012): 179–203.

———. "Gerald of Wales and Standard Old English." *Notes & Queries* 58 (2011): 19–24.

Fewster, Carol. *Traditionality and Genre in Middle English Romance.* Cambridge: D. S. Brewer, 1987.

Firumbras and Otuel and Roland. Edited by Mary Isabelle O'Sullivan. EETS, o.s. 198. London: EETS, 1935.

Fletcher, Alan John. *Late Medieval Popular Preaching in Britain and Ireland: Texts, Studies, and Interpretations.* Sermo, 5. Turnhout, Belgium: Brepols, 2009.

Floris and Blancheflour: A Middle English Romance. Edited by A. B. Taylor. Oxford: Clarendon Press, 1927.

Förster, Max. "Frühmittelenglische Sprichwörter." *Englische Studien* 31 (1902): 1–20.

———. "Kleinere Mittelenglische Texte." *Anglia* 42 (1918): 145–224.

———. "Die mittelenglische Sprichwörtersammlung in Douce 52." In *Festschrift zum XII: Allgemeinen Deutschen Neuphilologentag in München, Pfingsten 1906,* edited by E. Stollreither, 40–60. Erlangen, Germany: Fr. Junge, 1906.

Frankis, P. J. "Notes on Two Fifteenth Century Scots Poems." *Neuphilologische Mitteilungen* 61 (1960): 203–13.

Franzen, Christine. *The Tremulous Hand of Worcester: A Study of Old English in the Thirteenth Century.* Oxford: Clarendon Press, 1991.

Froissart, Jean. *The Chronicle of Froissart.* Translated by Sir John Bourchier, Lord Berners. 6 vols. New York: AMS Press, 1967.

Fulk, Robert. "Old English Poetry and the Alliterative Revival: On Geoffrey Russom's 'The Evolution of Middle English Alliterative Meter.'" In *Studies in the History of the English Language II: Unfolding Conversations.* Edited by Anne Curzan and Kimberly Emmons, 305–12 (Russom's response, 313–14). Topics in English Linguistics, 45. Berlin and New York: Mouton de Gruyter, 2004.

Furrow, Melissa. *Expectations of Romance: The Reception of a Genre in Medieval England.* Cambridge: D. S. Brewer, 2009.

Gayk, Shannon. "'As Plouȝmen Han Preued': The Alliterative Work of a Set of Lollard Sermons." *Yearbook of Langland Studies* 20 (2007 for 2006): 43–65.

Genesis A: A New Edition, Revised. Edited by A. N. Doane. Medieval and Renaissance Texts and Studies, 435. Tempe, AZ: ACMRS, 2013.

Genesis B. See *The Saxon Genesis.*

The Gest Hystoriale of the Destruction of Troy. Edited by G. A. Panton and David Donaldson. EETS, 39. London: EETS, 1869.

Gillespie, Vincent. "Moral and Penitential Lyrics." In *A Companion to the Middle English Lyric,* edited by Thomas G. Duncan, 68–95. Cambridge: D. S. Brewer, 2005.

———. "Vernacular Books of Religion." In *Book Production and Publishing in Britain 1375–1475,* edited by Jeremy Griffiths and Derek Pearsall, 317–44. Cambridge: Cambridge University Press, 1989.

Giraldus Cambrensis. *Descriptio Kambriae.* Edited by James F. Dimock. Vol. 6 in *Giraldi Cambrensis Opera,* edited by J. S. Brewer et al. Rolls Series. 8 vols. London: Longmans, Green, Reader, and Dyer, 1861–91.

———. *The Journey through Wales and The Description of Wales.* Translated by Lewis Thorpe. New York: Penguin Books, 1978.

Goddu, A. A., and R. H. Rouse. "Gerald of Wales and the *Florilegium Angelicum.*" *Speculum* 52 (1977): 488–521.

The Good Wife Taught Her Daughter; The Good Wyfe Wold a Pylgremage; The Thewis of Gud Women. Edited by Tauno F. Mustanoja. Annales Academiae Scientiarum Fennicae, 61. Helsinki: Suomalaisen Kirjallisuuden Scuren, 1948.

Gower, John. *The Complete Works of John Gower.* Edited by G. C. Macaulay. 4 vols. Oxford: Clarendon Press, 1899–1902.

Green, Richard Firth. "John Ball's Letters: Literary History and Historical Literature." In *Chaucer's England: Literature in Historical Context,* edited by Barbara A. Hanawalt, 176–200. Medieval Studies at Minnesota, 4. Minneapolis: University of Minnesota Press, 1992.

Gregory the Great. See Alfred the Great.

Guy of Warwick. See *The Romance of Guy of Warwick.*

Halmari, Helena, and Timothy Regetz. "Syntactic Aspects of Code-Switching in Oxford, MS Bodley 649." In *Code-Switching in Early English,* edited by Herbert Schendl and Laura Wright, 115–53. Topics in English Linguistics, 76. Berlin: De Gruyter Mouton, 2011.

Hanna, Ralph. "Alliterative Poetry." In *The Cambridge History of Medieval English Literature,* 488–512. Cambridge: Cambridge University Press, 1999.

———. "The Production of Cambridge University Library Ms. Ff. i. 6." *Studies in Bibliography* 40 (1987): 62–70.

Hardman, Phillipa. "Popular Romances and Young Readers." In *A Companion to Medieval Popular Romance,* edited by Raluca L. Radulescu and Cory James Rushton, 150–64. Cambridge: D. S. Brewer, 2009.

Hardyng, John. *The Chronicle of Iohn Hardyng.* Edited by Henry Ellis. London: F. C. and J. Rivington, 1812.

Harris, A. Leslie. "Instructional Poetry for Medieval Children." *English Studies* 74 (1993): 124–32.

Harris, Kate. "The Origins and Make-Up of Cambridge University Library MS Ff.1.6." *Transactions of the Cambridge Bibliographical Society* 8 (1983): 299–333.

Harris, Richard L. *A Concordance to Proverbs and Proverbial Materials in the Old Icelandic Sagas.* http://www.usask.ca/english/icelanders/.

———. "'(opt) eru köld kvenna ráð'—a Critically Popular Old Icelandic Proverb and Its Uses in the Íslendingasögur and Elsewhere." Paper presented at a Meeting of the Association for the Advancement of Scandinavian Studies in Canada, 27 May 2007; http://www.usask.ca/english/icelanders/applic_kvennar%E1%Fo.html.

Hassell, James Woodrow, Jr. *Middle French Proverbs, Sentences, and Proverbial Phrases.* Subsidia Mediaevalia, 12. Toronto: Pontifical Institute of Mediaeval Studies, 1982.

Haugen, Einar. "The Ecology of Language." In *The Ecology of Language,* edited by Anwar S. Dil, 325–39. Stanford, CA: Stanford University Press, 1972.

Havelok. Edited by G. V. Smithers. Oxford: Clarendon Press, 1987.
Havens, Jill C. "'As Englishe is comoun longage to oure puple': The Lollards and Their Imagined 'English' Community." In *Imagining a Medieval English Nation*, edited by Kathy Lavezzo, 96–128. Medieval Cultures, 37. Minneapolis and London: University of Minnesota Press, 2004.
Hay, Sir Gilbert. *Gilbert of the Haye's Prose Manuscript (AD 1456)*. Edited by J. H. Stevenson. 2 vols. Scottish Text Society. Edinburgh: Scottish Text Society, 1901–14.
Hazelton, Richard. "The Christianization of 'Cato': The *Disticha Catonis* in the Light of Late Mediaeval Commentaries." *Mediaeval Studies* 19 (1957): 157–73.
Henryson, Robert. *The Poems of Robert Henryson*. Edited by Denton Fox. Oxford: Clarendon Press, 1981.
Heywood, John. *John Heywood's "A Dialogue of Proverbs."* Edited by Rudolph E. Habenicht. Berkeley and Los Angeles: University of California Press, 1963.
Higbee, Kenneth L., and Richard J. Millard. "Visual Imagery and Familiarity Ratings for 203 Sayings." *American Journal of Psychology* 96.2 (1983): 211–22.
Hill, Richard. *Songs, Carols, and Other Miscellaneous Poems from the Balliol Ms. 354, Richard Hill's Commonplace-Book*. Edited by Roman Dyboski. EETS, e.s. 101. London: EETS, 1908 for 1907.
Historical Poems of the XIVth and XVth Centuries. Edited by Rossell Hope Robbins. New York: Columbia University Press, 1959.
Hoffman, Dean A. "'After Bale Comeþ Boote': Narrative Symmetry in *The Tale of Gamelyn*." *Studia Neophilologica* 60 (1988): 159–66.
Hollis, Stephanie, and Michael Wright. *Old English Prose of Secular Learning*. Annotated Bibliographies of Old and Middle English Literature. Vol. 4. Cambridge: D. S. Brewer, 1992.
The Holy Bible . . . in the Earliest English Versions Made . . . by John Wycliffe and His Followers. Edited by Josiah Forshall and Frederic Madden. 4 vols. Oxford: Oxford University Press, 1850.
Horrall, Sarah M. "Christian Cato: A Middle English Translation of the *Disticha Catonis*." *Florilegium* 3 (1981): 158–97.
———. "Latin and Middle English Proverbs in a Manuscript at St. George's Chapel, Windsor Castle." *Mediaeval Studies* 45 (1983): 343–84.
———. "An Unknown Middle English Translation of the *Distichs* of Cato," *Anglia* 99 (1981): 25–37.
Hosington, Brenda B. "Proverb Translation as Linguistic and Cultural Transfer in Some Middle English Versions of Old French Romances." In *The Medieval Translator*, 5, edited by Roger Ellis and René Tixier, 170–86. Turnhout, Belgium: Brepols, 1996.
Hsy, Jonathan. *Trading Tongues: Merchants, Multilingualism, and Medieval Literature*. Columbus: The Ohio State University Press, 2013.
Hughes, Thomas. *The Misfortunes of Arthur: A Critical, Old-spelling Edition*. Edited by Brian Jay Corrigan. New York and London: Garland, 1992.
Ingham, Richard, ed. *The Anglo-Norman Language and Its Contexts*. York: York Medieval Press, 2010.
Introduction to Paremiology: A Comprehensive Guide to Proverb Studies. Edited by Hrisztalina Hrisztova-Gotthardt and Melita Aleksa Varga. Warsaw and Berlin: De Gruyter Open Ltd., 2014.
Ipomedon in drei englischen Bearbeitungen. Edited by Eugen Kölbing. Breslau, Germany: Wilhelm Koebner, 1889.
Irvine, Susan. "The Compilation and Use of Manuscripts Containing Old English in the Twelfth Century." In *Rewriting Old English in the Twelfth Century*, edited by Mary Swan and Elaine M. Treharne, 41–61. Cambridge Studies in Anglo-Saxon England, 30. Cambridge: Cambridge University Press, 2000.
Ives, D. V. "The Proverbs in the 'Ancren Riwle.'" *Modern Language Review* 29 (1934): 257–66.

John of Salisbury. *Ioannis Saresberiensis Policraticus I–IV.* Edited by K. S. B. Keats-Rohan. Corpus Christianorum Continuatio Mediaeualis, 118. Turnhout, Belgium: Brepols, 1993.

John of Trevisa. *Polychronicon Ranulphi Higden Monachi Cestrensis: Together with the English Translations of John Trevisa and of an Unknown Writer of the Fifteenth Century.* Edited by Joseph Rawson Lumby. 9 vols. Rerum Britannicarum Medii Ævi Scriptores. London: Stationery Office, 1869–86; rpt. Kraus, 1964.

Johnson, David F. "Who Read Gregory's *Dialogues* in Old English?" In *The Power of Words: Anglo-Saxon Studies Presented to Donald G. Scragg on His Seventieth Birthday,* edited by Hugh Magennis and Jonathan Wilcox, 171–204. Medieval European Studies, 8. Morgantown: West Virginia University Press, 2006.

Jones, Thomas. "Gerald the Welshman's 'Itinerary through Wales' and 'Description of Wales': An Appreciation and Analysis." *National Library of Wales Journal* 6 (1950): 197–222.

The Junius Manuscript. Edited by George Philip Krapp. ASPR, 1. New York: Columbia University Press; London: Routledge and Kegan Paul, 1931.

Justice, Steven. *Writing and Rebellion: England in 1381.* The New Historicism, 27. Berkeley and Los Angeles: University of California Press, 1994.

Kaeuper, Richard W. "An Historian's Reading of *The Tale of Gamelyn*." *Medium Ævum* 52 (1983): 51–62.

The Kalender of Shepherdes. Edited by H. Oskar Sommer. 3 vols. in 1. London: K. Paul, Trench, Trübner & Co., 1892.

Kelley, Michael R. "Fifteenth-Century Flamboyant Style and *The Castle of Perseverance*." *Comparative Drama* 6 (1972): 14–27.

Klaeber's Beowulf and the Fight at Finnsburg, edited by R. D. Fulk, Robert E. Bjork, and John D. Niles. 4th ed. Toronto: University of Toronto Press, 2008.

Kluge, Friedrich. "Zu altenglischen Dichtungen." *Englische Studien* 8 (1885): 472–79.

Knight, Stephen. "'Harkeneth aright': Reading *Gamelyn* for Text Not Context." In *Tradition and Transformation in Medieval Romance,* edited by Rosalind Field, 15–27. Cambridge: D. S. Brewer, 1999.

Kramer, Johanna. "The Study of Proverbs in Anglo-Saxon Literature: Recent Scholarship, Resources for Research, and the Future of the Field." *Literature Compass* 6.1 (2009): 71–96.

Krikmann, Arvo. "On Denotative Indefiniteness of Proverbs." *Proverbium* 1 (1984): 47–91.

Laȝamon. *Brut or Hystoria Brutonum.* Edited and translated by W. R. J. Barron and S. C. Weinberg. New York: Longman, 1995.

Lagan, F. Donald. *A History of the Church in the Middle Ages.* London and New York: Routledge, 2002.

Lateinische Sprichwörter und Sinnsprüche des Mittelalters aus Handschriften gesammelt. Edited by Jakob Werner. Darmstadt, Germany: Wissenschaftliche Buchgesellschaft, 1966.

Lawton, David A. "The Diversity of Middle English Alliterative Poetry." *Leeds Studies in English,* n.s. 20 (1989): 143–72.

Legends of the Holy Rood. Edited and translated by Richard Morris. EETS, 46. London: EETS, 1871.

Legends of the Saints in the Scottish Dialect of the Fourteenth Century. Edited by W. M. Metcalfe. 3 vols. Scottish Text Society. Edinburgh and London: STS, 1888–96.

Lendinara, Patrizia. "Instructional Manuscripts in England: The Tenth and Eleventh Century Codices and the Early Norman Ones." In *Form and Content of Instruction in Anglo-Saxon England in the Light of Contemporary Manuscript Evidence,* edited by Patrizia Lendinara, Loredana Lazzari, and Maria Amalia D'Aronco, 59–113. Textes et Études du Moyen Âge, 39. Turnhout, Belgium: Brepols, 2007.

Liber Psalmorum: The West-Saxon Psalms. Edited by James Wilson Bright and Robert Lee Ramsay. Boston: D. C. Heath, 1907.

Liebermann, Felix. *Die Gesetze der Angelsachsen*. 3 vols. Halle, Germany: M. Niemeyer, 1903–1916; rpt. Aalen, Germany: Scientia, 1960.

A Literary Middle English Reader. Edited by Albert Stanburrough Cook. Boston: Ginn & Co., 1915.

Lodge, R. A. "Language Attitudes and Linguistic Norms in France and England in the Thirteenth Century." In *Thirteenth Century England IV: Proceedings of the Newcastle upon Tyne Conference, 1991*, edited by P. R. Cross and S. D. Lloyd, 73–83. Woodbridge, UK: Boydell Press, 1992.

Louis, Cameron. "Authority in Middle English Proverb Literature." *Florilegium* 15 (1998): 85–123.

———. "The Concept of the Proverb in Middle English." *Proverbium* 14 (1997): 173–85.

———. "Manuscript Contexts of Middle English Proverb Literature." *Mediaeval Studies* 60 (1998): 219–38.

———. "Proverbs and the Politics of Language." *Proverbium* 17 (2000): 173–94.

———. "Proverbs, Precepts, and Monitory Pieces." In *A Manual of the Writings in Middle English 1050–1500*, ed. Albert E. Hartung, 9.2957–3001. New Haven, CT: Yale University Press, 1993.

Lyly, John. *Euphues: The Anatomy of Wit; Euphues & His England*. Edited by Morris William Croll and Harry Clemons. New York: Russell & Russell, 1964.

A Macaronic Sermon Collection from Late Medieval England, MS Bodley 649. Edited and translated by Patrick J. Horner. Studies and Texts, 153. Toronto: Pontifical Institute of Medieval Studies, 2006.

Machan, Tim William. *English in the Middle Ages*. Oxford: Oxford University Press, 2003.

———. "Language and Society in Twelfth-Century England." In *Placing Middle English in Context*, edited by Irma Taavitsainen, Terttu Nevalainen, Päivi Pahta, and Matti Rissanen, 43–65. Topics in English Linguistics, 35. Berlin and New York: Mouton de Gruyter, 2000.

The Macro Plays: The Castle of Perseverance, Wisdom, Mankind. Edited by Mark Eccles. EETS, 262. London: EETS, 1969.

Macrobius. *Saturnalia*. Edited and translated by Robert A. Kaster. 3 vols. Loeb Classical Library. Cambridge, MA, and London: Harvard University Press, 2011.

Mann, Jill. "'He Knew Nat Catoun': Medieval School-texts and Middle English Literature." In *The Text in the Community*, edited by Jill Mann and Maura Nolan, 41–74. Notre Dame: University of Notre Dame Press, 2006.

Mannyng, Robert. *Robert of Brunne's Handlyng Synne*. Edited by Frederick J. Furnivall. EETS, o.s. 119, 123. London: EETS, 1901; one-volume rpt., Kraus, 1973.

Markus, Manfred. "Bed & Board: The Role of Alliteration in Twin Formulas of Middle English Prose." *Folia Linguistica Historica* 26.1–2 (2005): 71–93.

McCabe, T. Matthew N. *Gower's Vulgar Tongue: Ovid, Lay Religion, and English Poetry in the "Confessio Amantis."* Publications of the John Gower Society, 6. Cambridge: D. S. Brewer, 2011.

Medwall, Henry. *Fulgens and Lucres*. Edited by Seymour de Ricci. Henry E. Huntington Facsimile Reprints, 1. New York: George D. Smith, 1920.

Meech, Sanford B. "A Collection of Proverbs in Rawlinson MS D 328." *Modern Philology* 38 (1940): 113–32.

Melusine, compiled (. . .) by Jean D'Arras, Englisht about 1500. Edited by A. K. Donald. EETS, e.s. 68. London: EETS, 1895.

Middle English Compendium. http://www.quod.lib.umich.edu/m/mec/.

Middle English Sermons Edited from British Museum MS. Royal 18 B. xxiii. Edited by Woodburn O. Ross. EETS, o.s. 209. London: EETS, 1940.

The Middle English Stanzaic Versions of the Life of Saint Anne. Edited by Roscoe E. Parker EETS, o.s. 174. London: EETS, 1928; rpt. 1971.

Middle English Verse Romances. Edited by Donald B. Sands. New York: Holt, Rinehart & Winston, 1966.

Milfull, Inge B. "Formen und Inhalte lateinisch-altenglischer Textensembles und Mischtexte: Durham Cathedral B. III. 32 und 'The Phoenix.'" In *Volkssprachig-lateinische Mischtexte und Textensembles in der althochdeutschen, altsächsischen und altenglischen Überlieferung*, edited by Rolf Bergmann, 467–91. Germanistische Bibliothek, 17 Heidelberg, Germany: Winter, 2003.
Millett, Bella. "The *Ancrene Wisse* Group." In *A Companion to Middle English Prose*, edited by A. S. G. Edwards, 1–17. Cambridge: D. S. Brewer, 2004.
Minkova, Donka. *Alliteration and Sound Change in Early English*. Cambridge Studies in Linguistics, 101. Cambridge: Cambridge University Press, 2003.
———. "The Credibility of Pseudo-Alfred: Prosodic Insights in Post-Conquest Mongrel Meter." *Modern Philology* 94 (1997): 427–54.
Minnis, Alastair. *Translations of Authority in Medieval English Literature: Valuing the Vernacular*. Cambridge: Cambridge University Press, 2009.
Modern Proverbs and Proverbial Sayings. Edited by Bartlett Jere Whiting. Cambridge, MA, and London: Harvard University Press, 1989.
Morawski, J. "Les recueils d'anciens proverbes français analysés et classés." *Romania* 48 (1922): 481–558.
Morenzoni, Franco. "Les proverbes dans la prédication du XIIIe siècle." In *Tradition des proverbes et des exempla dans l'Occident médiéval: Colloque fribourgeois 2007*, edited by Hugo O. Bizzarri and Martin Rohde, 131–49. Scrinium Friburgense, 24. Berlin and New York: Walter de Gruyter, 2009.
Mulcaster, Richard. *Positions*. Edited by Robert Hebert Quick. London: Longmans, Green, & Co., 1888.
Murphy, James J. *Rhetoric in the Middle Ages: A History of Rhetorical Theory from Saint Augustine to the Renaissance*. Berkeley, Los Angeles, and London: University of California Press, 1974.
Nafisi, Azar. *Reading Lolita in Tehran: A Memoir in Books*. New York: Random House, 2008.
Nevill, William. *The Castell of Pleasure*. Edited by Roberta D. Cornelius. EETS, o.s. 179. London: EETS, 1930.
Oakden, J. P. *Alliterative Poetry in Middle English: The Dialectal and Metrical Survey*. 2 vols. in 1. Manchester: Manchester University Press, 1930, 1935; rpt. Hamden, CT: Archon, 1968.
O'Brien, Bruce R. *Reversing Babel: Translation among the English during an Age of Conquests, c.800–c.1200*. Newark: University of Delaware Press, 2011.
O'Camb, Brian. "Bishop Æthelwold and the Shaping of the Old English *Exeter Maxims*." *English Studies* 90 (2009): 253–73.
Of Arthour and of Merlin. Edited by O. D. Macrae-Gibson. 2 vols. EETS, 268 and 279. London: EETS, 1973–79.
Ogle, Marbury B. "The Apple of the Eye." *Transactions and Proceedings of the American Philological Association* 73 (1942): 181–91.
The Old English Apollonius of Tyre. Edited by Peter Goolden. Oxford: Oxford University Press, 1958.
Old English Homilies and Homiletic Treatises of the Twelfth and Thirteenth Centuries. Edited and translated by Richard Morris. First Series. EETS, 29 and 34. London: EETS, 1868.
The Old English Version of the Heptateuch. Edited by S. J. Crawford. EETS, o.s. 160. London: EETS, 1922.
Old Irish Wisdom Attributed to Aldfrith of Northumbria: An Edition of Bríathra Flainn Fhína maic Ossu. Edited and translated by Colin A. Ireland. MRTS, 205. Tempe, AZ: ACMRS, 1999.
Otto, A. *Die Sprichwörter und sprichwörtlichen Redensarten der Römer*. Leipzig, 1890; rpt. Hildesheim, Germany: Georg Olms, 1962.
Ovid. *Ovyde, Hys Book of Methamorphose, Books X–XV,* translated by William Caxton. Edited by Stephen Gaselee and H. F. B. Brett-Smith. Oxford: Basil Blackwell, 1924.

The Owl and the Nightingale: Text and Translation. Edited and translated by Neil Cartlidge. Exeter: University of Exeter Press, 2001.
Owst, G. R. *Literature and Pulpit in Medieval England.* Oxford: Blackwell, 1961.
The Oxford Dictionary of English Proverbs. Edited by F. P. Wilson. 3rd ed. Oxford: Clarendon Press, 1970.
The Oxford English Dictionary. Edited by John A. Simpson, et al. 2nd ed. 20 vols. Oxford: Oxford University Press, 1989.
Pantin, W. A. "A Medieval Collection of Latin and English Proverbs and Riddles, from the Rylands Latin MS. 394." *Bulletin of the John Rylands Library* 14 (1930): 81–114.
The Paris Psalter and the Meters of Boethius. Edited by George Philip Krapp. ASPR, 5. New York: Columbia University Press; London: Routledge and Kegan Paul, 1932.
Paston Letters and Papers of the Fifteenth Century. Edited by Norman Davis, Richard Beadle, and Colin Richmond. 3 vols. EETS, s.s. 20, 21, 22. Oxford: EETS, 2004–5.
Patterson, Frank A. "A Sermon on the Lord's Prayer." *JEGP* 15 (1916): 406–18.
Pearsall, Derek. "The Alliterative Revival: Origins and Social Backgrounds." In *Middle English Alliterative Poetry and Its Literary Background: Seven Essays,* edited by David A. Lawton, 34–53. Woodbridge, Suff., and Totowa, NJ: D. S. Brewer, 1982.
———. "The Pleasure of Popular Romance: A Prefatory Essay." in *Medieval Romance, Medieval Contexts,* edited by Rhiannon Purdie and Michael Cichon, 9–18. Cambridge: D. S. Brewer, 2011.
Peck, Russell A. "Social Conscience and the Poets." In *Social Unrest in the Late Middle Ages,* edited by Francis X. Newman, 113–48. MRTS, 39. Binghamton, NY: MRTS, 1986.
Petrus Cellensis. *Commentaria in Ruth; Tractatus de tabernaculo.* Edited by G. de Martel. Corpus Christianorum Continuatio Mediaeualis, 54. Turnhout, Belgium: Brepols, 1983.
Pettitt, Thomas. "'Folk Allegory' in the Idiom of John Ball." In *'Divers toyes mengled': Essays on Medieval and Renaissance Culture in Honour of André Lascombes,* edited by Michel Bitot, 55–68. Tours, France: Université François Rabelais, 1996.
Piers Plowman: The B Version. Edited by George Kane and E. Talbot Donaldson. Rev. ed. London and Berkeley: The Athlone Press, 1988.
Porck, Thijs. "Treasures in a Sooty Bag? A Note on *Durham Proverb 7.*" *Notes & Queries* n.s. 62.2 (2015): 203–6.
Proverbes au vilain: Die Sprichwörter des gemeinen Mannes. Edited by Adolf Tobler. Leipzig, Germany: S. Herzel, 1895.
Proverbia Communia: A Fifteenth Century Collection of Dutch Proverbs Together with the Low German Version. Edited by Richard Jente. Indiana University Publications, Folklore Series No. 4. Bloomington: Indiana University, 1947.
Proverbia sententiaeque latinitatis medii aevi. Edited by Hans Walther; completed by Paul Gerhard Schmidt. Carmina Medii Aevi Posterioris Latina, part 2. Göttingen, Germany: Vandenhoeck & Ruprecht, 1963–69.
"The Proverbis of Wysdom." Edited by Julius Zupitza. *Archiv* 90 (1893): 241–68.
The Proverbs of Alfred. Edited by O. Arngart. 2 vols. Lund, Sweden: Gleerup, 1942–55.
The Proverbs of Alfred: An Emended Text. Edited and translated by O. Arngart. Scripta Minora, Kungl. Humanistika Vetenskapssamfundet i Lund. Lund, Sweden: C. W. K. Gleerup, 1978.
The Proverbs of Hendyng. See Singer, Samuel; Varnhagen, H.
The Psalter or Psalms of David and Certain Canticles. Translated by Richard Rolle. Edited by H. R. Bramley. Oxford: Clarendon Press, 1884.
Purdie, Rhiannon. *Anglicising Romance: Tail-Rhyme and Genre in Medieval English Literature.* Cambridge: D. S. Brewer, 2008.
Putter, Ad. "A Historical Introduction." In *The Spirit of Medieval English Popular Romance,* edited by Ad Putter and Jane Gilbert, 1–15. Harlow, Essex: Pearson Education Ltd., 2000.

———. "Multilingualism in England and Wales, c.1200: The Testimony of Gerald of Wales." In *Medieval Multilingualism: The Francophone World and Its Neighbours*, edited by Christopher Kleinhenz and Keith Busby, 83–105. Medieval Texts and Cultures of Northern Europe, 20. Turnhout, Belgium: Brepols, 2010.

Queene Elizabethes Achademy. Edited by F. J. Furnivall. EETS, e.s. 8. London: EETS, 1869.

Ratis Raving and Other Early Scots Poems on Morals. Edited by R. Girvan. Scottish Text Society, 11. Edinburgh: Scottish Text Society, 1939.

Reichl, Karl. "Orality and Performance." In *A Companion to Medieval Popular Romance*, edited by Raluca L. Radulescu and Cory James Rushton, 132–49. Cambridge: D. S. Brewer, 2009.

Religious Lyrics of the XIVth Century. Edited by Carleton Brown. 2nd ed. revised by G. V. Smithers. Oxford: Clarendon Press, 1957.

Reliquiae Antiquae. Edited by Thomas Wright and J. O. Halliwell. 2 vols. London: John Russell Smith, 1845.

Richard of St. Victor. *Richardi Sancti Victoris Operum Pars Prima Exegetica*. In *Patrologiae Cursus Completus, Series Latina*, edited by J.-P. Migne. 221 vols. Paris: Garnier, 1844–64, vol. 196.

Robbins, Rossell Hope. "Speculum Misericordie." *PMLA* 54 (1939): 935–66.

Robbins, Rossell Hope, and John L. Cutler, eds. *Supplement to the Index of Middle English Verse*. Lexington: University of Kentucky Press, 1965.

Rolle, Richard, trans. *The Psalter or Psalms of David and Certain Canticles*. Edited by H. R. Bramley. Oxford: Clarendon Press, 1884.

Romaine, Suzanne. *Bilingualism*. 2nd ed. Language in Society, 13. Oxford: Basil Blackwell, 1995.

The Romance of Guy of Warwick: The Second or 15th-century Version. Edited by Julius Zupitza. 2 vols. EETS, e.s. 25–26. London: EETS, 1875–76.

The Romance of Sir Beues of Hamtoun. Edited by Eugen Kölbing. EETS, e.s. 46, 48, 65. London: EETS, 1885, 1886, 1894.

Roney, Lois. "The Wakefield *First* and *Second Shepherds' Plays* as Complements in Psychology and Parody." *Speculum* 58 (1983): 696–723.

Roper, Jonathan, ed. *Alliteration in Culture*. New York: Palgrave Macmillan, 2011.

Rothwell, William. "English and French in England after 1362." *English Studies* 82 (2001): 539–59.

———. "Language and Government in Medieval England." *Zeitschrift für französische Sprache und Literatur* 93 (1983): 258–70.

———. "The Role of French in Thirteenth-Century England." *Bulletin of the John Rylands University Library* 58 (1976): 445–66.

Rouse, Robert Allen. *The Idea of Anglo-Saxon England in Middle English Romance*. Woodbridge and Rochester: Boydell & Brewer, 2005.

A Royal History of the Excellent Knight Generides. Edited by Frederick J. Furnivall. Roxburghe Club, 85. Hertford, UK: Roxburghe Club, 1865.

Russom, Geoffrey. "The Evolution of Middle English Alliterative Meter." In *Studies in the History of the English Language II: Unfolding Conversations*. Edited by Anne Curzan and Kimberly Emmons, 279–304. Topics in English Linguistics, 45. Berlin and New York: Mouton de Gruyter, 2004.

Salter, Elizabeth. *Fourteenth-Century English Poetry: Contexts and Readings*. Oxford: Clarendon Press, 1983.

Sauer, Hans. "Knowledge of Old English in the Middle English Period?" In *Language History and Linguistic Modelling: A Festschrift for Jacek Fisiak on His 60th Birthday*, edited by Raymond Hickey and Stanisław Puppel, 2 vols., I.791–814. Trends in Linguistics. Studies and Monographs, 101. Berlin and New York: Mouton de Gruyter, 1997.

The Saxon Genesis: An Edition of the West Saxon "Genesis B" and the Old Saxon Vatican "Genesis." Edited by A. N. Doane. Madison: University of Wisconsin Press, 1991.

Scahill, John. "Trilingualism in Early Middle English Miscellanies: Languages and Literature." *Yearbook of English Studies* 33 (2003): 18–32.
Schendl, Herbert, and Laura Wright. "Code-Switching in Early English: Historical Background and Methodological and Theoretical Issues." In *Code-Switching in Early English*, edited by Schendl and Wright, 15–45. Topics in English Linguistics, 76. Berlin: De Gruyter Mouton, 2011.
Schiff, Randy P. *Revivalist Fantasy: Alliterative Verse and Nationalist Literary History*. Columbus: The Ohio State University Press, 2011.
Schleich, G. "Die Sprichwörter Hendings und die Proverbis of Wysdom." *Anglia* 51 (1927): 220–77.
Schreiber, Carolin. *King Alfred's Old English Translation of Pope Gregory the Great's "Regula Pastoralis" and Its Cultural Context*. Frankfurt am Main: Peter Lang, 2003.
Schulze-Busacker, Elisabeth. "Au Carrefour des Genres: les 'Proverbes au vilain.'" In *Tradition des proverbes et des exempla dans l'Occident médiéval: Colloque fribourgeois 2007*, edited by Hugo Bizzari and Martin Rohde, 81–104. Scrinium Friburgense, 24. Berlin and New York: Walter de Gruyter, 2009.
———. "Proverbs and Maxims in Medieval French Literature." *Proverbium* 9 (1992): 205–20.
Scottish Alliterative Poems in Riming Stanzas. Edited by F. J. Amours. Scottish Text Society. Edinburgh and London: Scottish Text Society, 1897.
The Scottish Metrical Romance of Lancelot du Lak. Edited by Joseph Stevenson. Edinburgh: Maitland Club, 1839.
Secular Lyrics of the XIVth and XVth Centuries. Edited by Rossell Hope Robbins. Oxford: Clarendon Press, 1952.
Seinte Katerine. Edited by S. R. T. O. d'Ardenne and E. J. Dobson. EETS, s.s. 7. Oxford: EETS, 1981.
Shakespeare, William. *The Riverside Shakespeare*. Edited by G. Blakemore Evans et al. 2nd ed. Boston and New York: Houghton Mifflin, 1997.
Shaw, Judith. "The Influence of Canonical and Episcopal Reform on Popular Books of Instruction." In *The Popular Literature of Medieval England*, edited by Thomas J. Heffernan, 44–60. Tennessee Studies in Literature, 28. Knoxville: University of Tennessee Press, 1985.
Short, Ian. *Manual of Anglo-Norman*. 2nd ed. Anglo-Norman Text Society Occasional Publications Series 8. Oxford: Anglo-Norman Text Society, 2013.
———. "On Bilingualism in Anglo-Norman England." *Romance Philology* 33 (1980): 467–79.
———. "*Tam Angli quam Franci*: Self-Definition in Anglo-Norman England." *Anglo-Norman Studies* 18 (1995): 153–75.
The Siege of Jerusalem. Edited by Ralph Hanna and David Lawton. EETS, 320. Oxford: EETS, 2003.
Singer, Samuel. "Die Sprichwörter Hendings." *Studia Neophilologica* 14 (1941/42): 31–52.
Sir Gawain and the Green Knight. See *The Works of the Gawain-Poet*.
Skelton, John. *John Skelton: The Complete English Poems*. Edited by John Scattergood. New Haven, CT, and London: Yale University Press, 1983.
Somerset, Fiona. *Clerical Discourse and Lay Audience in Late Medieval England*. Cambridge Studies in Medieval Literature, 37. Cambridge: Cambridge University Press, 1998.
Spencer, H. Leith. *English Preaching in the Late Middle Ages*. Oxford: Clarendon Press, 1993.
Stenroos, Merja. "Identity and Intelligibility in Late Middle English Scribal Transmission: Local Dialect as an Active Choice in Fifteenth-Century Texts." In *Scribes as Agents of Language Change*, edited by Esther-Miriam Wagner, Ben Outhwaite, and Bettina Beinhoff, 159–81. Studies in Language Change, 10. Boston and Berlin: De Gruyter Mouton, 2013.
Studies in the Vernon Manuscript. Edited by Derek Pearsall. Cambridge: D. S. Brewer, 1990.
Swan, Mary. "Imagining a Readership for Post-Conquest Old English Manuscripts." In *Imagining the Book*, edited by Stephen Kelly and John J. Thompson, 145–57. Medieval Texts and Cultures of Northern Europe, 7. Turnhout, Belgium: Brepols, 2005.

———. "Old English Textual Activity in the Reign of Henry II." In *Writers of the Reign of Henry II*, edited by Ruth Kennedy and Simon Meecham-Jones, 151–68. New York: Palgrave Macmillan, 2006.

The Tale of Gamelyn. Edited by Walter W. Skeat. 2nd ed. Oxford: Clarendon Press, 1893.

A Talkyng of þe Loue of God. Edited by M. Salvina Westra, O. P. The Hague: Martinus Nijhoff, 1950.

Taylor, Archer, and B. J. Whiting. *Dictionary of American Proverbs and Proverbial Phrases, 1820–1880*. Cambridge, MA: Belknap Press, 1958.

Thesaurus proverbiorum medii aevi: Lexikon der Sprichwörter des romanisch-germanischen Mittelalters. Edited by Kuratorium Singer der Schweizerischen Akademie der Geistes- und Sozialwissenschaften. 14 vols. Berlin and New York: Walter de Gruyter, 1995–2002.

Thomas, Hugh M. *The English and the Normans: Ethnic Hostility, Assimilation, and Identity 1066–c.1220*. Oxford: Oxford University Press, 2003.

Thompson, John J. "The Textual Background and Reputation of the Vernon Lyrics." In *Studies in the Vernon Manuscript*, edited by Derek Pearsall, 201–24. Cambridge: D. S. Brewer, 1990.

Tilley, Morris Palmer. *A Dictionary of the Proverbs in England in the Sixteenth and Seventeenth Centuries*. Ann Arbor: University of Michigan Press, 1950.

———. *Elizabethan Proverb Lore in Lyly's "Euphues" and in Pettie's "Petite Pallace" with Parallels from Shakespeare*. New York: Macmillan, 1926.

Timelli, Maria Columbo. "De l'*Erec* de Chrétien de Troyes à la prose du XVe siècle: Le traitement des proverbes." *Le Moyen Français* 42 (1998): 87–113.

The Towneley Plays. Edited by Martin Stevens and A. C. Cawley. 2 vols. EETS, s.s. 13. Oxford: EETS, 1994.

Townend, Matthew. *Language and History in Viking Age England: Linguistic Relations between Speakers of Old Norse and Old English*. Studies in the Early Middle Ages, 6. Turnhout, Belgium: Brepols, 2002.

Tranter, Stephen N. "Significant Choices: The Interplay of Rhyme and Alliteration in Medieval English Poetry" *Literaturwissenschaftliches Jahrbuch* 39 (1998): 75–94.

Treharne, Elaine. "Form and Function of the Twelfth Century Old English Dicts of Cato." *JEGP* 102 (2003): 465–85.

———. *Living through Conquest: The Politics of Early English, 1020–1220*. Oxford: Oxford University Press, 2012.

———. "Reading from the Margins: The Uses of Old English Homiletic Manuscripts in the Post-Conquest Period." In *Beatus Vir: Studies in Early English and Norse Manuscripts in Memory of Philip Pulsiano*, edited by A. N. Doane and Kirsten Wolf, 329–58. Tempe, AZ: ACMRS, 2006.

The Tretyse of Loue. Edited by John H. Fisher. EETS, o.s. 223. London: EETS, 1951.

Trotter, David. "*Oceano vox*: You Never Know Where a Ship Comes From; On Multilingualism and Language-Mixing in Medieval Britain." In *Aspects of Multilingualism in European Language History*. Edited by Kurt Braunmüller and Gisella Ferraresi, 15–33. Hamburg Studies on Multilingualism, 2. Amsterdam: John Benjamins, 2003.

Turville-Petre, Thorlac. *The Alliterative Revival*. Cambridge: D. S. Brewer, 1977.

———. *England the Nation: Language, Literature, and National Identity, 1290–1340*. Oxford: Clarendon Press, 1996.

———. *Reading Middle English Literature*. Blackwell Introductions to Literature, 15. Maldon, MA, and Oxford: Blackwell, 2007.

Twenty-Six Political and Other Poems. Edited by J. Kail. EETS, o.s. 124. London: EETS, 1904.

Tyndale, William. *The Work of William Tyndale*. Edited by G. E. Duffield. Philadelphia: Fortress Press, 1965.

Usk, Thomas. *Testament of Love*. Edited by Gary W. Shawver. Toronto: University of Toronto Press, 2002.

Varnhagen, H. "Zu den Sprichwörtern Hending's (Cambridge und Oxford-Text)." *Anglia* 4 (1881): 182–91.
The Vercelli Book. Edited by George Philip Krapp. ASPR, 2. New York: Columbia University Press, 1932.
The Vercelli Homilies and Related Texts. Edited by D. G. Scragg. EETS, o.s. 300. Oxford: Oxford University Press, 1992.
The Vernon Manuscript: A Facsimile of Bodleian Library, Oxford, MS. Eng. Poet. a.1. Introduced by A. I. Doyle. Cambridge: Cambridge University Press, 1987.
W. "Proverbs [From MS. Harl. 3362, of the end of the fifteenth century.]." *Retrospective Review* 2 (1854): 309.
Wada, Yoko. "Gerald on Gerald: Self-Presentation by Giraldus Cambrensis." In *Anglo-Norman Studies XX. Proceedings of the Battle Conference 1997,* edited by Christopher Harper-Bill, 223–46. Woodbridge: Boydell Press, 1998.
Walter of Henley. *Walter of Henley's Husbandry, together with an anonymous Husbandry, Seneschaucie, and Robert Grosseteste's Rules.* Edited by Elizabeth Lamond. London: Longmans, Green, & Co., 1890.
Walther, Hans. *Proverbia sententiaeque latinitatis medii aevi.* Completed by Paul Gerhard Schmidt. Carmina Medii Aevi Posterioris Latina. Part 2. Göttingen: Vandenhoeck & Ruprecht, 1963–69.
Walz, Gotthard. *Das Sprichwort bei Gower: Mit besonderem Hinweis auf Quellen und Parallelen.* Nördlingen, Germany: C. H. Beck, 1907.
Warm, Robert. "Identity, Narrative and Participation: Defining a Context for the Middle English Charlemagne Romances." In *Tradition and Transformation in Medieval Romance,* edited by Rosalind Field, 87–100. Cambridge: D. S. Brewer, 1999.
The Wars of Alexander. Edited by Hoyt N. Duggan and Thorlac Turville-Petre. EETS, s.s. 10. Oxford: EETS, 1989.
Watson, Nicholas. "Censorship and Cultural Change in Late-Medieval England: Vernacular Theology, the Oxford Translation Debate, and Arundel's Constitutions of 1409." *Speculum* 70 (1995): 822–64.
Weiskott, Eric. "Phantom Syllables in the English Alliterative Tradition." *Modern Philology* 110 (2013): 444–58.
Wells, John Edwin. *A Manual of the Writings in Middle English, 1050–1400.* New Haven: Connecticut Academy of Arts and Sciences, 1926.
Wenzel, Siegfried. "French Proverbs from the Mouths of English Preachers?" In *"Contez me tout": Mèlanges de langue et de littérature médiévales offerts à Herman Braet,* edited by Catherine Bel et al., 543–55. Louvain, Belgium: Éditions Peeters, 2006.
———. *Macaronic Sermons: Bilingualism and Preaching in Late-Medieval England.* Ann Arbor: University of Michigan Press, 1994.
———. *Preachers, Poets, and the Early English Lyric.* Princeton, NJ: Princeton University Press, 1986.
———. *Verses in Sermons: "Fasciculus morum" and Its Middle English Poems.* Medieval Academy of America Publications, 87. Cambridge, MA: Medieval Academy of America, 1978.
Werner, Jakob. *Lateinische Sprichwörter und Sinnsprüche des Mittelalters aus Handschriften gesammelt.* Darmstadt, Germany: Wissenschaftliche Buchgesellschaft, 1966.
West, M. L. "Phocylides." *Journal of Hellenic Studies* 98 (1978): 164–67.
Whiting, Bartlett Jere. *Chaucer's Use of Proverbs.* Harvard Studies in Comparative Literature, 11. Cambridge, MA: Harvard University Press, 1934.
———. *Modern Proverbs and Proverbial Sayings.* Cambridge, MA, and London: Harvard University Press, 1989.
———. "Proverbial Material in the Popular Ballad." *Journal of American Folklore* 47 (1934): 22–44.

———. "Proverbs in Certain Middle English Romances in Relation to Their French Sources." *Harvard Studies and Notes in Philology and Literature* 15 (1933): 75–126.

———. *Proverbs in the Earlier English Drama*. Harvard Studies in Comparative Literature, 14. Cambridge, MA: Harvard University Press, 1938.

Whiting, Bartlett Jere with Helen Wescott Whiting. *Proverbs, Sentences, and Proverbial Phrases from English Writings Mainly before 1500*. Cambridge, MA: Belknap Press, 1968.

Whittinton, Robert. *The Vulgaria of John Stanbridge and the Vulgaria of Robert Whittinton*. Edited by Beatrice White. EETS, 187. London: EETS, 1932.

Wicker, Helen E. "Between Proverbs and Lyrics: Customization Practices in Late Medieval English Moral Verse." *English* 59.224 (2010): 3–24.

William of Moerbeke, trans. *Aristotelis Ars Rhetorica*. Edited by Leonhard Spengel. 2 vols. Leipzig: Teubner, 1867.

William of Shoreham. *The Poems of William of Shoreham*. Edited by M. Konrath. EETS, e.s. 86. London: EETS, 1902.

Wilson, F. P., ed. *The Oxford Dictionary of English Proverbs*. 3rd ed. Oxford: Clarendon Press, 1970.

Wilson, Kenneth G. "*The Lay of Sorrow* and *The Lufaris Complaynt*: An Edition." *Speculum* 29 (1954): 708–26.

Wogan-Browne, Jocelyn. "'Invisible Archives?' Late Medieval French in England." *Speculum* 90 (2015): 653–73.

———, ed. *Language and Culture in Medieval Britain: The French of England c.1100–c.1500*. York: York Medieval Press, 2009.

The Wordsworth Dictionary of Proverbs. Edited by G. L. Apperson. Ware, UK: Wordsworth Editions, 1993.

The Works of the Gawain-Poet. Edited by Charles Moorman. Jackson: University Press of Mississippi, 1977.

Wright, Laura. *Sources of London English: Medieval Thames Vocabulary*. Oxford: Clarendon Press, 1996.

Wulfstan. *The Homilies of Wulfstan*, edited by Dorothy Bethurum. Oxford: Clarendon Press, 1957.

———. *Die "Institutes of Polity, Civil and Ecclesiastical": Ein Werk Erzbischof Wulfstans von York*, edited by Karl Jost. Schweizer anglistische Arbeiten, 47. Bern: Francke, 1959.

———. *Wulfstan: Sammlung der ihm zugeschriebenen Homilien nebst Untersuchungen über ihre Echtheit*, edited by Arthur Napier. Berlin: Weidmannsche Buchhandlung, 1883.

Wyclif, John. *Select English Works of John Wyclif*. Edited by Thomas Arnold. 3 vols. Oxford: Clarendon Press, 1869–71.

Yeager, Stephen M. *From Lawmen to Plowmen: Anglo-Saxon Legal Tradition and the School of Langland*. Toronto Anglo-Saxon Series, 17. Toronto: University of Toronto Press, 2014.

Yonge, James. *The Governaunce of Pryncees*. In *Three Prose Versions of the Secreta Secretorum*, edited by Robert Steele, 121–248. EETS, e.s. 74. London: EETS, 1898.

The York Plays. Edited by Richard Beadle. London: Edward Arnold, 1982.

The York Plays: A Critical Edition of the York Corpus Christi Play as Recorded in British Library Additional MS 35290. Edited by Richard Beadle. 2 vols. EETS, s.s. 23. Oxford: EETS, 2009.

Yorkshire Writers: Richard Rolle of Hampole, an English Father and His Followers. Edited by Carl Horstman. 2 vols. London: Swan Sonnenschein; New York: Macmillan, 1895–96.

Ywain and Gawain. Edited by Albert B. Friedman and Norman T. Harrington. EETS, 254. London: EETS, 1964.

Zacher, Samantha. "Multilingualism at the Court of King Æthelstan: Latin Praise Poetry and *The Battle of Brunanburh*." In *Conceptualizing Multilingualism in Medieval England, c.800–c.1250*, edited by Elizabeth M. Tyler, 77–103. Studies in the Early Middle Ages, 27. Turnhout, Belgium: Brepols, 2011.

Zaerr, Linda Marie. *Performance and the Middle English Romance.* Studies in Medieval Romance, 17. Cambridge: D. S. Brewer, 2012.
Zimmerman, Harold C. "Continuity and Innovation: Scholarship on the Middle English Alliterative Revival." *Jahrbuch für Internationale Germanistik* 35.1 (2003): 107–23.
Zupitza, Julius. "The Proverbis of Wysdom." *Archiv* 90 (1893): 241–68.

INDEX TO PROVERBS

The alphanumeric figures in parentheses refer to Bartlett Jere Whiting, *Proverbs, Sentences, and Proverbial Phrases from English Writings Mainly before 1500*. Keywords are capitalized.

The Apple of one's eye (A156) 36–37

After Bale comes boot (B18) 32–35, 76, 100–105, 107–12, 127, 131
When Bale is highest boot is nighest (B22) 33–35

To buy a Cat in the sack (C102) 56
Lief Child behoves lore (C216) 25–29, 38, 76, 95
After misty Clouds a clear sun (C315) 107–8
When the Cup is fullest bear it fairest (C633) 20–21, 76
Custom is the second kind (C646) 57–59, 60

Ever at the End wrong will wend (E82) 47–48
Englishmen are envious (E107) 54–55

To curry Favel (F85) 95
Well Fights that well flees (F141) 40–42, 54

Game and wisdom are good together (G17) 87
God can provide for the lonely man 87
God's mill grinds slow but small 118n61
Guard thyself against evil desire 87

Hew not over your Head (H221) 12, 92, 95
Heart on the hoard and hands on the sore (H278) 31n70
In the Heart is the hoard of ilk man's word (H283) 31–32
From Heaven comes help (H308) 24–25
Shall never a cluck Hen be a well crowing cock 92
All Hights should be held (H378) 21
What you Hight see you hold (H379) 21
A Horse that ever trotted is hard to make amble (H513) 107
Full hard is Hunger in hale maw (H635) 29–31
There Hunger is hot, hearts are feeble (H645) 29–31

For the Less to lose the more (L207) 50–51, 112
Better is List than lither strength (L381) 43–44, 45, 54, 82–87

157

INDEX TO PROVERBS

First Look and afterward leap (L435) 53–54, 62

Mastery mows the meadow down (M413) 42, 54
Much will have more (M786) 22–24, 29, 131
Of Much they made more (M787) 22–24

As dark as Night (N103) 90

Praise at the Parting (P39) 60–61, 127–28
When the Pig is proffered open the poke (P192) 55–56

Oft Rape rues (R32) 59–60, 76
Better is Rede than rap (R65) 87
Cold Rede is quean rede (R66) 43, 54

Seldom Seen soon forgotten (S130) 51–53, 54, 96, 113–14, 120–23
Out of Sight out of mind (S307) 52
Old Sin makes new shame (S338) 45–47, 54, 94, 113, 116–17

All Sooth is not to be said (S485) 89n102, 126
Hold not all Sore said nor atwite all sorrow (S500) 87, 89
To Speak fair before but not behind (S580) 131
When the Steed is stolen make fast the stable door (S697) 48–50, 124–25
After Sweet the sour comes (S942) 106–7

In Trust is treason (T492) 96

Be Ware ere you be woe (W45) 44–45, 117–18
Weening is not wisdom 94
When Will oversties wit, then will and wit are lost (W268) 39–40
Wine and women make wise men go backwards (W358) 35–36, 66n20
Without Wisdom is weal well unworth (W390) 75
Words are but wind (W643) 38–39, 54, 128
A green Wound is but game (W695) 47, 94

GENERAL INDEX

Advent Lyrics, 24, 34
Ælfric of Eynsham, 3, 23, 25–27, 30, 38, 63
Alfred the Great, 21, 23, 37, 68–71, 75, 82
alliteration, as proverbial marker, 20–21, 38, 61, 64–65, 96, 108, 112, 114, 134; in Welsh and English, 86–90; significance of, 2, 5, 12, 14–15, 17–18, 67, 76–77, 83–86, 96, 108, 117, 129–30, 132, 135. *See also* proverbs, and alliteration
alliterative poetry, 2–5, 14, 18, 99, 101, 111, 137
alliterative proverbs, definition of, 14. *See also* proverbs
Alliterative Revival, 2–4, 14
Always Try to Say the Best, 40
Amis and Amiloun, 59
Ancrene Wisse, 9, 43, 82–83, 129, 135
Andreas, 35
Andrew of Wyntoun, 29, 42
Anglo-Norman, 8–9, 12–14, 41, 55, 63n1, 65n11, 66, 75, 78–79, 113–14, 121, 135. *See also* French
Apollonius of Tyre, 30
aristocracy, 9–10, 13, 55, 77, 79, 88, 115, 120, 123, 125, 127, 130, 134, 136

Aristotle, 57–58
Arundel, Thomas, 86
Ascension, 27
Audelay, John, 22, 45
audience, for gnomic poetry, 73–75, 77, 79, 97; for moral poems, 81; for plays, 126–28, 130, 132, 137; for religious prose, 81–82, 85–86, 97; for romances, 106–9, 112, 115, 132; for sermons, 90–93, 97. *See also* children; laity; men; women
Augustine of Hippo, 57–58
authority, 35–36, 60, 64–68, 70, 75, 77, 80, 83–85, 92, 94–95, 99, 102–3, 105, 107–8, 111–14, 122–23, 126, 129–31, 137

Bacon, Roger, 57–58
Ball, John, 45, 117–19, 121–22, 132
ballad, 61, 100–101
Ballad of Good Counsel, 21, 81
Barclay, Alexander, 49, 81
Basil of Caesarea, 24
Benedictine Reform, 74
Beniamyn, 44, 84–85
Beowulf, 2, 27, 34

Beryn. See Merchant's Tale of Beryn
Bible, 1, 13, 16, 25, 35–37, 69–70, 77–78, 82–86, 92, 96, 119, 137. *See also Paris Psalter*
bilingualism, 9–11, 92–93. *See also* multilingualism
Boethius. *See* Alfred the Great
Bokenham, Osbern, 59
Boner, Ulrich, 42
Bríathra Flainn Fhína maic Ossu, 70

Calisto and Melibœa, 39
Castle of Perseverance, 22, 130–32
Caxton, William, 36, 50, 66
characterization, 16n69, 102–3, 113, 115, 125–32
Chaucer, Geoffrey, 12n54, 16n69, 18, 43, 100–101, 106, 122–24, 136–37
Chester cycle, 32, 125, 127, 129
children, and moral poems, 81 (*see also* moral education); and romance literature, 105–8
Chrétien de Troyes, 100n4, 113n48
chria, 70
Christ I. *See Advent Lyrics*
Christ II. *See Ascension*
Christ III. *See Christ in Judgement*
Christ in Judgement, 31–32
Chrodegang, 36
Cicero, 57
clergy, 81–82, 85–86, 90–91, 93, 129–30, 135
Cloud of Unknowing, 44, 85
code-switching, 11–12, 92–93, 95
collocations, 20–35, 38–39, 40n126, 131, 134n1
colloquialism, 127–28, 134, 137
comedy, 125, 127–30
commons, 13, 117–20, 125, 134
Consail and Teiching at the Vys Man Gaif his Sone, 39
Contemplacioun of Synnaris, 59
continuity, cultural, 2–5, 14, 17, 19–20, 24, 28–29, 35, 37–38, 42, 44, 47–48, 54, 61, 68, 96, 101, 114, 132–35
courtly literature, 4, 53, 77, 111–12, 114–15, 122–24, 136–37

Death of Edward III, 51, 120–22, 132
Defensor of Ligugé, 23, 35
Deschamps, Eustache, 56
devotional prose, 8, 63, 81–86, 91, 96, 119, 123, 135–36
didactic literature, 26, 40, 46, 62–97, 106, 108, 114–17, 120–21, 129, 132, 135
Digby 86, 78–79

Disticha Catonis, 16, 36, 65–68, 70, 77–79, 121, 135
domains, sociocultural and linguistic, 9–10, 12–15, 37, 79, 86, 93, 119, 133–34, 136–37
Douce MS. 52, 22, 26, 42, 46, 50–53, 56, 80
Douglas, Gavin, 49
drama, 18, 48, 60–61, 98, 125–32, 134, 137. *See also* Chester cycle; Towneley plays; York cycle
Durham Proverbs, 20, 63–65, 77, 80, 89, 97
Dutch, 46n161

Early Modern English, 61, 66, 80
education. *See* moral education; pedagogy; school texts
Edward III, 120. *See also Death of Edward III*
Eger and Grime, 40
Elene, 34
English, status of, 6–9, 12–14, 37, 66, 68, 79–81, 83, 85–86, 89–90, 93–94, 112, 119, 123, 125, 130, 132, 135. *See also* Early Modern English; language choice; Middle English; Old English; vernacular
English Conquest of Ireland, 22
Englishness, 15, 47, 55, 76–77, 81, 83, 96, 112, 119, 122–23, 125, 130, 132, 135–37. *See also* identity and identification
Epistle of Othea to Hector, 40
Erasmus, 80
ethnography, 86–90, 96
Exeter Book, 73–74
Exhortation to Christian Living, 27
Exodus, 34–35

Findern MS., 122–23
Firumbras, 33, 104–5, 108–9, 111
Floris and Blauncheflour, 32, 108–9, 111–12
Fourth Lateran Council, 91, 119
French, 6–10, 12–14, 20, 36, 41–42, 46n161, 47, 50, 54–56, 66, 76, 78–79, 81–82, 86, 88–92, 93n118, 94, 99, 106, 112–14, 122, 125, 130, 132, 135–36. *See also* Anglo-Norman
Froissart, Jean, 55
Fyrst þou sal luf god and drede, 40, 46, 48

Gamelyn, 32, 100–105, 111
Generides, 32, 109–12
Genesis A, 28–29
Genesis B, 24
genre, 17–18, 62–64, 75, 96, 98, 100–101, 129, 132, 134–35

gentry, 104, 114, 122–23, 136
geography, and language use, 8–10, 130. See also Midlands
Gest Hystoriale of the Destruction of Troy, 30
Gesta Romanorum, 41, 60
Giraldus Cambrensis, 44, 86–90, 114
gnomic poetry, 63, 66, 69–79, 89, 96, 135
God, in gnomic poems, 72–73; in proverbs, 87, 102–5, 108–9, 111, 117–18
God of hefne, þat sittest in trone, 47
Good Wife Taught Her Daughter, 26, 81
Good Wyfe Wold a Pylgremage, 26
government, and language use, 7–8, 10
Gower, John, 38, 46, 49, 51, 56, 58, 60, 136–37
Greek, 57, 70, 73n46
Gregory the Great. See Alfred the Great
Guy of Warwick, 51, 106, 112

Hardyng, John, 47
Harley MS. 3362, 52
Hávamál, 70, 73n46, 75
Havelok the Dane, 46, 105
Hay, Sir Gilbert, 59
Henryson, Robert, 21
Hermann von Fritzlar, 41
Heywood, John, 49, 52, 56, 80n70
Hichecoke, W., 48
Hill, Richard, 49, 52, 56
Homiletic Fragment I, 31
homilies. See Rogationtide Homilies; sermons; Vercelli Homilies
Hue de Rotelande, 41, 113–14. See also *Ipomedon*
Hugh Spencer's Feats in France, 61
Hughes, Thomas, 40

identity and identification, 13–14, 18, 105, 108–9, 112, 114–15, 125–27, 132, 137. See also Englishness
Instructions of Šuruppak, 70
Ipomedon, 52, 113–14. See also Hue de Rotelande

Jacobus Minor, 29
John of Salisbury, 58
John of Trevisa, 58
Juliana, 25, 27

Kalender of Shepherdes, 45
Katherine Group, 85
kingship, 69–70, 74, 120–22

Lagamon, 9, 43
laity, 116–17, 122, 129, 136; and religious texts, 82, 85–86, 96, 119, 135–36; and sermons, 90–91, 93, 96
Langland, William, 3, 4n14, 12n54, 26, 85, 118, 137
language choice, 10–11, 13–15, 17, 79, 85–86, 93–94, 99, 117, 119, 122, 125, 130, 136–37. See also domains; geography
language ecology, 5–6, 8–9, 11–15, 17, 20, 63, 80, 92, 97–98, 122, 129, 132–33
Latin, 1, 6–9, 12–14, 35–37, 42, 44n150, 46, 50, 57–59, 63–67, 71, 75, 77–83, 86–93, 95–96, 99, 106, 118n61, 125, 129–30, 132, 135, 137
law, 8, 40n126, 70, 79, 100, 114
Lay of Sorrow, 49, 123–24
Legends of the Holy Rood, 30
Leis Willelme, 8
Life of Saint Anne, 24
literacy, 1–2, 5, 7, 15–16, 19, 62–63, 66, 69–71, 79–82, 91–93, 106, 119, 123, 136. See also pedagogy
Lollards, 13, 36, 85, 119, 136
Lord's Prayer II, 46
Lydgate, John, 36, 38
Lyly, John, 61
lyric poetry, 77, 94, 98, 115–25, 132, 136–37

Macrobius, 57
Man, be warre er the be woo, 45
Mannyng, Robert, 54
manuscripts, as context, 63, 78–79, 114–15, 121–24. See also Digby 86; Douce MS. 52; Exeter Book; Findern MS.; Harley MS. 3362; Peniarth MS. 356; Rawlinson MS. D 328; Rylands Latin MS. 394; Selden B.24; Vernon MS.
Marcolf, 77
Maxims I, 71–75, 77
Medwall, Henry, 60
Melusine, 47, 113
men, as audience, 73–74
Merchant's Tale of Beryn, 32, 106–8, 111
metaphor, 16, 30, 54, 62, 95, 120, 124
meter, 3–4, 46, 64, 67–68, 70, 74, 76, 81, 101, 112. See also alliteration; rhyme
Middle English, 2–5, 12, 14, 16–18, 20, 22–33, 35–56, 58–61, 63–86, 94, 96, 98–132, 134–37. See also English
Middle High German, 41–42
Middle Scots, 21, 29, 39, 49, 60, 123–24

162 · GENERAL INDEX

Midlands, 4, 9, 69, 76, 83
monasticism, 36, 63, 66, 69–70, 73–75
moral education, 79, 81, 106–8, 125, 137
moral poems, 81. *See also* gnomic poetry
Mulcaster, Richard, 61
multilingualism, 5–7, 10–13, 63, 78, 92. *See also* bilingualism

Nafisi, Azar, 53
narrative, 75, 99, 105, 107, 110–11, 113, 115, 132, 136
Nevill, William, 39
nobility. *See* aristocracy
Norman Conquest, 2, 5, 7–8, 54, 61, 68, 86, 96, 133–34
Now wold I fayne some myrthis make, 52, 122–24

Of Arthour and of Merlin, 48
Of the Manners to Bring One to Honour and Welfare, 40
Old English, 2–7, 9, 13–17, 19–38, 40n126, 46, 50, 56, 61, 63–66, 68–77, 80–82, 90, 94, 96, 98, 100–101, 103, 132, 134–35. *See also* English
Old Irish, 70
Old Norse, 6, 43, 70, 75
orality, 1, 5, 15–16, 19, 69–71, 75, 77, 79–80, 91–93, 99, 114, 123
Owl and the Nightingale, 16n69, 33, 41, 69

parents, 71, 106–8, 126
Paris Psalter, 30, 37
Paston letters, 52, 60
Pearl, 51
Peasants' Revolt, 117, 119
pedagogy, 26–28, 63–66, 71, 77, 79–81, 88, 106. *See also* moral education; school texts
Peniarth MS. 356, 53
performance, 53, 92–93, 114, 123
periodization, 61
Petrus Cellensis, 58
Phocylides, 70
Phoenix, 30
Pistle of Preier, 44, 85
politics, 7, 10, 117–22, 130, 132, 137
popular culture, 53, 61, 69, 100–101. *See also* romance, popular
Precepts, 70
Proverbes au vilain, 50, 76, 78–79
Proverbis of Wysdom, 33, 39, 48, 52, 60, 80n69, 95

proverbs, and alliteration, 14–15, 17–18, 67, 90, 94, 116; and lexical change, 43–45, 54–56, 59–60, 134; as object of study, 1, 5–6, 8–9, 14–20, 28–29, 136–38; collections of, 15–16, 46, 63, 65–67, 78–81, 89–90; definition of, 15–16; evoking the past, 65, 75–76, 94, 97, 100, 105, 114–15, 136; syntax of, 16, 31, 38–40, 48, 54, 75, 105, 109, 111, 118, 131
Proverbs of Alfred, 43, 68–79, 135, 137
Proverbs of Good Counsel, 40
Proverbs of Hendyng, 20–21, 26, 33, 41, 50, 55, 59, 68, 76–79, 81, 135
Proverbs of Salamon, 22, 45

Rauf Coilȝear, 60
Rawlinson MS. D 328, 33, 46, 80
realism, 125–26, 129–30
Renaissance, 80
Resignation A, 34
rhetoric, 70, 80, 84–85, 88, 91, 93–94, 96, 99, 117, 135
rhyme, 29, 31, 35, 41–43, 47–48, 51–53, 66–68, 74–76, 80–81, 94, 99, 101, 111, 114, 116, 118, 120–21, 123, 135
Richard II, 120–21
Richard of St. Victor, 43, 83–85, 129
Rogationtide Homilies, 28, 30
Rolle, Richard, 37
romance, 18, 46, 77, 79, 98–115, 123, 127–28, 132, 134, 136; courtly, 111–12, 114–15; popular, 100–101, 105–6, 111–12, 114–15, 125, 132, 136
Rylands Latin MS. 394, 42, 80

Sanson de Nanteuil, 78
scholasticism, 116. *See also* sermons, scholastic
school texts, 65–66, 77, 79–80, 88, 90, 135. *See also* pedagogy
Selden B.24, 123–24
sententiousness, 64–65
Serlo of Wilton, 78
sermons, 7, 12, 15n66, 28, 52, 63, 79, 90–97, 99, 112, 116–17, 122, 135–36; macaronic, 11, 92–93, 95–97, 135; scholastic, 90–91, 93, 116, 135. *See also* Rogationtide Homilies; Vercelli Homilies
Shakespeare, William, 61
Siege of Jerusalem, 30
Sir Gawain and the Green Knight, 137
Skelton, John, 49

Solomon, 69–70, 75, 77
Soul and Body I, 29
Soul and Body II, 29
Speculum Misericordie, 33
Statute of Pleading, 8
Symon's Lesson of Wysedome, 26, 81
syntax. *See* proverbs, syntax of

Talkyng of þe Loue of God, 33
Titus and Vespasian, 39
Tom Tyler and His Wife, 61
Towneley plays, 60, 125–30
translation, 16, 21, 37, 42–43, 54, 64–67, 78–79, 82–83, 86, 94–95, 99n1, 106, 108, 112–14, 119
Tremulous Hand of Worcester, 7n27
Tretyse of Loue, 37
Tyndale, William, 53–54

universities, 90–91, 93
Usk, Thomas, 33

Vercelli Homilies, 28
vernacular, 6, 13, 36, 42, 59, 64–68, 70–71, 77–81, 83, 86, 88–91, 97–99, 114–15, 117, 119, 122, 125, 130, 132, 134–37. *See also* colloquialism

Vernon MS., 121–22
Virgil, 88

Wakefield cycle. *See* Towneley plays
Walter of Henley, 47
Wanderer, 27
Wars of Alexander, 22
Welsh, 86–90
Whittinton, Robert, 56, 60
Will and Wit, 39
William of Moerbeke, 58n235
William of Shoreham, 46, 115–17, 119, 122
wisdom, 26, 64, 67, 69–71, 73, 75–77, 79, 84–85, 91, 96–97, 100, 102–3, 115, 122–23, 125–26, 128–29, 132, 135, 137
Wohunge of Ure Laverd, 33
women, as readers, 7–8, 82, 96, 122–23, 136
Wulfstan of York, 21, 27–28
Wyclif, John, 56. *See also* Lollards
Wycliffites. *See* Lollards

Yonge, James, 59
York cycle, 39, 125–26, 128–29
Ywain and Gawain, 31, 38

www.ingramcontent.com/pod-product-compliance
Lightning Source LLC
Chambersburg PA
CBHW020949230426
43666CB00005B/242